The Just Shall Live by Fai

Faith Therapy

The Ultimate Program For Salvation-based Counseling in the Church

The Just Shall Live by Faith Series

Faith Therapy

**The Ultimate Program For Salvation-based
Counseling in the Church**

Dr. Troy Reiner

Pleasant Word

Pleasant Word (a division of WinePress Publishing, PO Box 428, Enumclaw, WA 98022) functions only as book publisher. As such, the ultimate design, content, editorial accuracy, and views expressed or implied in this work are those of the author.

Unless otherwise noted, Scripture quotations in this book are taken from the King James Version of the Bible.

Scripture references marked AMP are taken from The "Amplified" trademark is registered in the United States Patent and Trademark Office by The Lockman Foundation. Use of this trademark requires the permission of The Lockman Foundation.

Scripture references marked NLT are taken from Holy Bible. New Living Translation copyright © 1996 by Tyndale Charitable Trust. Used by permission of Tyndale House Publishers.

Scripture references marked NIV are taken from the Holy Bible, New International Version, Copyright © 1973, 1978, 1984 by the International Bible Society. Used by permission of Zondervan Publishing House. The "NIV" and "New International Version" trademarks are registered in the United States Patent and Trademark Office by International Bible Society.

Scripture references marked WEY are taken from Weymouth: The Modern Speech New Testament by Richard F. Weymouth, 3rd Edition (1912), Revised & edited by E. Hampden-Cooke.

ISBN 1-4141-0542-8
Library of Congress Catalog Card Number: 2005905977

Table of Contents

Introduction

From the time I was a young child, I have always had a strong desire to understand how things worked. Possibly, it was because when I was a boy, my father, who was a watchmaker, challenged my brother and me to take apart pocket watches in order to learn how they worked. Maybe it was because I served in the United States Air Force working with various air traffic control, computer and space systems. It could be because my first Master's Degree was in Cybernetic (man-machine feedback) Systems. Consequently, when I fully dedicated my life to Christ in 1974, and later, as I studied the Word of God and ministered as a pastor, I began to wonder how the process of salvation worked. I understood that verse after verse of Bible text clearly states that salvation is by faith, but I had no understanding of how faith could or would somehow save us, change us, or make us whole. As the Lord directed my ministry more clearly in the direction of counseling, I realized that if I truly was to help my clients, it was essential that I understand how God had designed us and what His plan was to make us whole. As I began my studies in psychology and counseling, somehow none of the secular theories seemed to satisfy me. I realized that only God, our "design engineer," could really have a full and complete understanding of mankind, His very complex and wonderful creation.

This was the beginning of my quest to understand the process of salvation by faith and to use what I learned to develop a new method of Christian counseling based on this process of salvation by faith. I have called this specific application of faith to resolve deeply rooted psychological problems "Faith Therapy." In this book, I will explain in detail, using numerous Bible references, how the process of salvation or complete wholeness is brought about in our lives, as we learn to trust God to meet our needs. Since this overall process of salvation is based on faith, it is clear that one of the counselor's jobs is to build the faith of the client, so that he can trust God to meet all his needs. In order to do this, the counselor must help the client know God and His Word in a personal and intimate way. Problems in the client's life should be seen as symptoms of the dysfunctional ways the client has attempted to meet his own needs in his own strength, "through the flesh." The very existence of these symptoms demonstrates a lack of faith that God will meet and continue to meet all of his needs. To alleviate these symptoms, the client must learn the basic principles of how we, as people, function most effectively. Then he must apply these basic principles as God intended. As he does his part—by faith—he will see God meet his needs. It is my experience that as the root issue of trusting God is resolved, the problem symptoms begin to disappear.

Faith Therapy was designed to provide a means of integrating counseling as a whole within the overall process of salvation by faith and for dealing with the core, root issues that underlie all psychological problems. Unfortunately, much of what is called Christian counseling today is focused on commanding others to "do what is right," or attempting to "fix what is wrong," without integrating what is done within the overall context of God's plan of salvation. Consequently, when only the surface actions or symptoms of the problem are dealt with, the solutions are short-lived, and the root cause resurfaces as another type of problem. This book has been designed to provide a basic understanding of the overall process of salvation by faith and to provide the tools required for using faith in therapy. These tools include methods for finding the root problem, assessing the faith of the client, identifying specific roadblocks to the development of faith and helping the client grow in his faith.

This book is part of a complete system for implementing salvation-based therapy within the church. The remaining three books in the series – *Transformation!, Principles for Life, and Revelations That Will Set You Free* – provide a detailed plan for the conduct of counseling, biblical models for addressing the most complex and difficult problems, a comprehensive method for building counseling plans from biblical principles, and a step-by-step process for spiritual growth.

I want specifically to thank all of my clients and students, my wife, Nancy, my mother, Hildegard, my daughter, Sarah, and our assistant administrator, Loretta Goetting for their contributions in preparing this manuscript for publication. My gratitude also goes to Athena Dean and all the other wonderful people at Pleasant Word Publishing for their patience and assistance in publishing this book.

All Bible references are from the Authorized Version (AV) of the King James Bible, The New Living Translation (NLT), New International Version (NIV), The Amplified Bible (AMP) or the Weymouth New Testament (WEY). These versions of the Bible are quoted as originally written and therefore spelling, grammar and capitalization may not agree with modern usage. For example, in my writing I have chosen to capitalize all references to God. This is not done in the King James Version of the Bible. Greek, Hebrew, most Bible translations and biblical dictionary references are obtained and quoted directly from The Online Bible Millennium Edition (2000) by Larry Pierce. I have chosen to use the Standard College Dictionary (1963) because it provides more precise definitions for some of the English words discussed in this book.

It is my hope that this book will provide the methodology for integrating therapy within the process of salvation by faith. I believe that, with it, we can provide more effective help for the emotionally and psychologically hurting people in our churches. Our Lord promised that He came to "heal the broken hearted and set the captive free." (Luke 4:18)

PART I

Faith Therapy

Chapter 1

The Need for a Salvation-Based Therapy in the Church

The numbers of dysfunctional and emotionally hurting people in our society and churches are rapidly increasing. Some churches seem to be in denial of these facts and have even challenged the need for counseling within the church at all. Many other churches have taken the approach that if preaching, repentance and spiritual warfare are not enough, it is the person's fault because the person lacks faith or is not willing to be helped. We, as pastors, have to admit that many times we have given shallow and simplistic advice for complex problems that we did not fully understand, with meager results.

The Growing Number of Hurting People in Our Society

The statistics of tragedy, dysfunction and emotional trauma within our society began to increase significantly around 1950 and reached epidemic proportions in the 1980's. The trend has continued since that time. Currently, over one-half of our marriages are ending in divorce (Kreider, 2002, p. 18). One-half of those who are married are reported to have had at least one affair (Wright, 1996, p. 281). One-third of the women in America have been sexually abused and one-sixth have suffered incest (Martin, 1987, p. 147). Domestic violence occurs repeatedly in at least 25% of our homes (Paymar, 1993, p. ix) and at least once in two-thirds of marriages (Lindsey, McBride, Platt, 1996, p. 7). Approximately 20% of men abuse alcohol, 10% are dependent on it and 6% use illicit drugs (Grant, 1994, SAMHSA, 2001).

Even though most of us would like to believe that these statistics do not apply in our churches, studies have indicated that there is little difference concerning psychological and abuse problems within Christian churches in comparison to the United States' society as a whole. A national survey of pastors conducted by the Task Force on the Family for the National Association of Evangelicals in 1984 concluded by saying that the "problems of today's Christian families compared to those of non-Christian families are more similar than different" (Martin, 1987, p. 15). The Barna Research Group in Ventura, California reported that the number of persons divorced among evangelical Christians, especially Baptists and non-denominationals, exceeded those of agnostics and atheists, and of our society as a whole. (The Barna Report, October 1999). Six to seven percent of Christians are problem drinkers or alcoholics (Minirth, Meier, Fink, Byrd, and Hawkins, 1988, p. 19). Battered spouses and children seemed to be more prevalent inside than outside the church (Martin, 1987, p. 15, 21, 130). Sexual abuse was estimated to be at least as high in Christian as non-Christian homes (Martin, 1987, p. 148). In fact, both incest and physical abuse have been more highly associated with those holding religious values than those who do not (Hoorwitz, 1983 and Wetzel, Ross, 1983). Archibald Hart, in his book, *The Sexual Man,* reported that approximately 12% to 30% of ministers have had some inappropriate sexual contact while in the ministry (1994, p. 185).

We Have Been Burying Our Heads in the Sand

For many Christians the statistics that I have cited concerning the problems within the church seem almost unbelievable. This is because the modern church has a long history of attempting to deny, hide, or refer rather than admit these problems and effectively deal with them. We have attempted superficial solutions by giving shallow advice and commanding repentance. Although most pastors have a good general understanding of Bible principles, they lack a deeper understanding of how to address most of the more difficult psychological, addiction, and abuse problems. The survey of pastors cited above went on to say that pastors as a whole lack sufficient training to meet these challenges effectively (Martin, p. 15). As an example, pastors in most fundamental churches have a notoriously bad record of sending battered women back into abusive relationships without help (Alsdurf, 1989, p. 20-24). With the lack of comprehensive biblical answers, it is not surprising that the most usual response of a pastor facing problems like abuse or addictions is to refer them to an "expert" outside of the church.

The Large Disparity of What is Considered Christian Counseling

In spite of the great numbers of people who are in desperate need of help, the Christian counseling community itself is embroiled in an ongoing controversy concerning what Christian counseling should be, and to what extent it should be based on the Bible. Biblical counseling has been limited to a few basic approaches that are many times ineffective when applied to complicated psychological problems. In fact, it is almost impossible to even define what Christian counseling is, since it spans the range from Christians who call themselves counselors to counselors who call themselves Christians (in order to attract clients.)

Many Christians, especially those who come from the fundamentalist and evangelical denominations, would rather seek help from a "Christian counselor." Unfortunately, even when seeking a Christian counselor, many times they become frustrated or disillusioned because of the large disparity in what is considered "Christian counseling" today. In actual application, Christian counselors may include

1. Christians, without any counseling training who try to help by applying biblical concepts.
2. Christian 12-Step Programs and other types of support and self-help groups.
3. Pastors, who give their best advice, based on their experience and seminary education.
4. Christians who have a "deliverance ministry."
5. Christian Marriage and Family Therapists.
6. Christian Social Workers.
7. Ph.D. Clinical Psychologists (who attempt to integrate Christian principles and secular counseling knowledge).
8. Christian professional counselors.
9. Secular counselors who call themselves Christians.

It is even more difficult to determine which of those who advertise themselves as "Christian counselors" are actually using counseling theory based on the Bible rather than secular theory and techniques. Let me demonstrate this from my own experience.

After I received my Master's Degree in Psychology, Guidance and Counseling from the University of Northern Colorado, I was looking for some part-time employment or volunteer work to put into practice what I had learned. For many years, I had believed that God had called me to be a Christian counselor. The first counseling center I contacted sounded somewhat interested in what I could offer, so I went for an interview. What I discovered was that the psychologist who advertised as a Christian counselor, attended a Christian church, and this was his sole qualification to be called a Christian counselor. His entire theory and practice were no different from any other secular psychologist. To him, a Christian counselor was a secular counselor who was not adverse to Christians or a Christian worldview.

My second contact was slightly better. It was a Christian counseling center that even provided seminars for Christians who wanted to learn how to counsel. But when I asked them several questions about how they treated particular problems that I was familiar with, I was again disappointed. They lacked any in-depth understanding of these specific problems and what they were doing, at least in these areas, was destined to produce little or no results.

My third experience was the most revealing of all. At that time, I was pursuing a Specialist in Education Degree in counseling, with an emphasis in Marriage and Family Therapy, from Wichita State University in Wichita, Kansas. I was taking a course in ethics and the instructor wanted us to realize how different counselors applied in actual practice what they had been taught. He had given us an assignment to interview a counselor of our choice to determine what theory and methods the counselor was actually applying in his therapy. I had been working with a number of clients with mental disorders who had told me of the opposition they had encountered to their Christianity in secular counseling and day hospitals. They said that there was one center that did not object to them talking about Jesus, which they thought was probably Christian. Because I realized that some Christian counselors and psychologists do not necessarily advertise as such, in order to attract a wider range of clients, I decided to interview the Licensed Ph.D. Clinical Psychologist, who ran the center. In the interview, I asked him what theory and type of therapy he practiced, to assist his mentally ill patients. He said that he used a combination of the Alcoholic Anonymous' 12-Step Program and Eastern mysticism! He had found out that almost nothing else worked. As an example, he would have one of the clients sit in the middle of the group and have all the other clients "throw" their power at him to help him recover!

Churches today are caught between the growing epidemic of difficult psychological problems for which they do not have clear biblical answers, a secular psychological community that cannot assist from a biblical point of view, and a confusing array of what is called "Christian counseling." Most pastors have attempted to resolve this situation by referring their members to counselors that others have recommended or with whom they have personally developed a relationship, or, at least, to a counseling center associated with a church of a similar doctrine. Unfortunately, not even this approach is without its problems. In many cases, even Christian counselors, working out of church counseling centers, have been primarily educated in secular training programs in order to be licensed by the state. Some churches only recruit counselors based on their secular accreditation. Because these counselors usually have had little or no actual Christian counseling training, they continue to use primarily secular theories and techniques. In fact, most of the Christian counselors I know have been trained as Marriage and Family Therapists and primarily use secular Marriage and Family Therapy techniques.

The Church Has "Admitted" it Does Not Have the Answers

In spite of the mixed results, the church of our day continues to refer its more difficult problems outside the church and, in doing so, to a large degree has abdicated the psychological battlefield to the secular community. In a world filled with more and more hurting people, we have chosen to "admit" that we do not have the answers to these more difficult problems. It is as if we have forgotten that part of Jesus' commission was to "heal the brokenhearted and to set the captive free." The mission of the church is not only to bring sinners to Christ, but also to assist those who have been saved to become completely whole and to be conformed to the image of Christ.

In addition, we have missed one of the greatest possibilities in our society to demonstrate that Jesus is indeed the answer for the world in which we live. What greater opportunity could we ask for than that hurting people come to us, looking for the answers to the problems in their lives? The Bible puts it this way:

When [men] are cast down, then thou shalt say, [There is] lifting up; and he shall save the humble person. (Job 22:29)

Few Agree on What Christian Counseling Should Be

Because we have not had a clear biblical picture of what Christian counseling should be or detailed biblical answers for many of the harder psychological problems, the entire area of Christian counseling has been caught up in controversy for many years. The basic underlying question is how much should

Christian counseling be based directly on the Bible and how much should it be based on secular research and counseling methods.

In the Spring, 1996, issue of *Christian Counseling Today,* Dr. Worthington addressed this ongoing controversy,

> Christian psychology, including marital therapy, has been under attack for years by critics such as Jay Adams and the Bobgans. Attacks have centered around whether the assumptions of psychology are compatible with Christianity, whether psychology is scripturally correct (since it uses concepts, such as self-esteem, not found in scriptures), and whether science as a way of knowing is incompatible with revelation as a way of knowing. (pp 9-10)

The 1997 spring issue of *Christian Counseling Today,* entitled "The Heat of Controversy," featured a number of articles concerning this question. Dr. Ed Bulkley suggested that Christian counseling has sold its birthright by trying to integrate psychology with the Bible, to produce a Christian system of counseling. He was backed by Dr. Douglas Groolmis in "The Hidden Dangers of Carl Jung," who warned of the dangers of adopting secular counseling theory into Christian counseling. In contrast, Dr. David E. Dillon explained in his article, the new technique of Eye Movement Desensitization and Reprocessing (EMDR). He concluded that although EMDR is not biblically based, since it does not contradict the Bible, it should be judged as a Christian counseling technique solely based on its effectiveness. Secular theorist, Dr. Albert Ellis, known for his anti-Christian views and statements, suggested in "Can Rational Counseling Be Christian?" that his theories of Rational Emotive Behavioral Therapy (REBT) can be effectively used by Christians "using terms that most Christians would understand, and concepts that the Scriptures endorse." The most extreme article was authored by Dr. John H. Court who stated in "Unraveling the Mystery of Hypnosis" that the state of hypnosis is similar to spiritual experiences like "being slain in the spirit" or the "Toronto blessing" (p. 35) and therefore should be acceptable as a tool by Christian counselors.

Churches Do Not Agree on the Role and Content of Christian Counseling

There are numerous schools of thought on the subject of Christian counseling in our churches. Positions are as varied as the many flavors of Christian churches and denominations. Based on my experience, I recognize five distinct general categories or positions on these issues.

The first position is associated with churches that believe counseling does not have a place in the church at all. Among some of the most strict, fundamental churches, the feeling seems to be that when a person is saved and becomes a "new creature," (according to 2nd Corinthians 5:17), all his problems should rapidly be resolved. They admit that in actual experience, they see quicker results for some than others. In any case, the solution is to simply repent, stop sinning and rededicate your life. Any suggestion that these problems might have roots in the past is looked upon as trying to excuse wrong behavior or avoid responsibility for sin. The advice given by a pastor or elder should be enough to resolve any and every situation. "Spiritual warfare" is seen as the answer for the more difficult problems. If repenting, praying, laying on of hands, basic biblical principles, and deliverance sessions are not enough, then the problem must lie in the individual's unwillingness or lack of faith. Problems are usually seen as simplistic, short term, isolated, and individualistic. Psychology is seen as something to be avoided at all costs, since its basis is in humanism, many of its theories are anti-biblical and some of its techniques are reminiscent of the new age movement. A strong fear, not unjustified, is that "counseling" could provide an inroad for humanism into the church.

The second position is also taken by fundamentalist and evangelical churches and is many times referred to as "biblical" counseling. These churches would agree with many of the viewpoints already discussed, but they see counseling as the application of the Bible to life's situations. Sometimes counseling training seminars, which try to apply Bible principles to the lives of people, are given for pastors and laymen. Lay counseling programs are many times established in larger churches. The most important principle is that everything must be derived from the Bible. Usually secular psychology is not acceptable in any form. They would generally quote Colossians 2:8: "See to it that no one takes you captive through hollow and deceptive philosophy, which depends on human tradition and the basic principles of this world rather than on Christ." (NIV) Frequently, problems are seen as individual and simplistic. Unfortunately, this has often resulted in a shallow understanding of many of life's more difficult problems.

The third position is that the basic theories of Christian counseling are yet to be developed, based on a combination of biblical knowledge and a psychological (though not secular) understanding of the human soul. They are attempting to go beyond a secular understanding of psychology to develop a more uniquely Christian approach to counseling. Secular psychological theories are only accepted to the extent that they are perceived to agree with the Bible. Many of these theories are general in nature or problem specific, and fail to give quality answers to long-standing psychological problems. They are usually based out of a particular Bible college, school, or counseling center and, up to this point, have had a somewhat limited following.

The fourth category attempts to integrate secular counseling theory and techniques with Christian principles. It usually takes the form of Christian counseling within explicitly Christian counseling centers, Christian clinics or hospitals. In these settings, Christian counseling is based on the Bible as much as possible, but also uses experientially developed research and psychological knowledge, which does not contradict the Bible. Many of these counselors have degrees from secular universities and are licensed or registered in their states. Especially in Christian clinics or hospitals, Christian counseling is merged with secular medical and psychological practices. The emphasis is on providing effective help through a thorough understanding of the problem and applying whatever techniques are most effective. The justification is that all real truth is "God's truth," so that whatever is true and does not contradict the Bible is using God's revealed truth no matter which way it was revealed. They believe that psychology has discovered many relevant facts about the soul that can be used to help people.

The fifth category is the position taken by many of the more main line and liberal denominations. Christian and psychological principles are liberally mixed and biblical authority is not necessarily seen as the primary source of truth. Many of these denominations teach courses on psychology and pastoral counseling as part of their required seminary education for pastors. Much of what has been termed pastoral counseling also suffers from a shallow understanding of the more difficult problems, and in many cases is limited to the giving of advice based on the pastor's experience.

We Need More Effective Biblically Based Therapy to Resolve this Controversy

At the core of this controversy is a dilemma. We are caught between two alternatives. At one end is a shallow level of biblical counseling which attempts to apply basic biblical principles to difficult life-dominating problems. This is the reductionistic approach. The other alternative is to lean more to secular theories or at least to research methods in order to more adequately address these problems. At the very heart of this issue is the lack of solid biblical theory and deeper biblical answers for these intricate problems.

The real question here is a doctrinal one: How much are we to rely on the Bible for the direction and the healing of our lives? This is the real issue between fundamentalist and liberal churches. To the extent that a person believes that the Bible is God's totally inspired, complete, and infallible revelation, the more he will usually want to have Christian counseling based on the Bible. Broger (1994) states the most conservative point of view when he suggests that, "These man-made solutions to problems of mind, heart, and spirit are as unacceptable to God as are man's futile speculations and substitutes for salvation and the unalterable truths of God's Word." (Lesson 1, page 7) He backs this position with several verses:

1 Co 3:19 For the wisdom of this world is foolishness with God. For it is written, He taketh the wise in their own craftiness.

20 And again, The Lord knoweth the thoughts of the wise, that they are vain.

The opposite point of view agrees that God <u>does</u> reject man's wisdom and considers it vain or useless, but that does not necessarily mean He rejects knowledge, part of which, in reality, is God's knowledge or truth. Peter states that everything we need is available through "the knowledge of Him,"

2 Pe 1:3 According as his divine power hath given unto us all things that [pertain] unto life and godliness, <u>through the knowledge of him</u> that hath called us to glory and virtue:

The Apostle Paul suggests that one of the ways we learn this "knowledge of Him" is through our observation of His creation:

Ro 1:20 For the <u>invisible things of him</u> from the creation of the world are clearly seen, <u>being understood by the things that are made,</u> [even] his eternal power and Godhead; so that they are without excuse:

According to this point of view, Christian counseling should be based as much as possible on the Bible, but God does not reject knowledge discovered through research (the study of the things that were made). In addition, spiritual revelation is clearly supported by the Bible. However, we must be careful to determine, in each circumstance, what is really God's truth. This can be a difficult challenge.

Let me clarify the use of these three types of knowledge by an analogy: Your car is having a problem and needs to be fixed. You have three sources of help available:

1. <u>A friend who is a backyard mechanic</u>. He has no contact with the manufacturer and has never gone to a factory-authorized school to learn to work on cars, but has been working on them for some time. He has not necessarily even read the shop manual. Some of his ideas about cars may be misguided, but through trial and error and his own experience, he has had some success at fixing cars.

2. <u>A mechanic with training from a technical school</u>. He thoroughly knows the maintenance manual. He may not have as much experience fixing cars as the backyard mechanic; but by following the steps in the manual, he is successful most of the time.

3. <u>A factory trained mechanic</u>. He knows the engineer who designed the car. He understands the maintenance manual, but many times relies more on the engineer, who designed the car, when he cannot figure out a problem.

All three have some idea of what to do and all have their particular strengths, but not one of them can handle all automobile problems better than the others can. Which mechanic would you choose?

Of course, the analogy is simple. The backyard mechanic is the psychologist who has learned much of what he knows through research and experience, but you cannot trust his theories. We should remember that psychology is simply:

1. The science of the human mind in any of its aspects, operations, powers, or functions.
2. The systematic investigation of mental phenomena, especially those associated with consciousness, behavior, and the problems of adjustment to the environment.
3. The aggregate of the emotions, traits, and behavior patterns regarded as characteristics of the individual… or group….(Funk & Wagnalls, 1963)

If the psychologist does not agree with the maintenance manual—the Bible—you better not let him work on your car. Some of his methods work extremely well and agree with the Bible, such as the use of systematic desensitization to overcome irrational fears, and others do not. Some backyard mechanics are absolutely dangerous, like a counselor who introduced a person who I knew was struggling with homosexuality, to homosexual friends. The backyard mechanic's strong points are his many years of experience fixing cars, his knowledge concerning specific problems, and a number of proven techniques. His weaknesses are some of his "off the wall" theories, his tendency to be influenced by political correctness, his unbiblical worldview and goals and his lack of spiritual insight. "Truth," in this context must be very closely examined, and only relied on when it clearly agrees with the Bible.

The technical school trained mechanic is the counselor who not only knows the Bible, but also has had some experience applying it effectively to people's lives. He understands the principles of the Bible, what the Bible says about most problems, and how to apply it in many cases. His strong point is a comprehensive knowledge of the Bible. His weak point is usually a lack of full understanding of multifaceted psychological problems. We can strongly rely on his biblical knowledge as far as it goes, but we must be careful to remember that he is limited by his depth of understanding the Bible, his correctness in interpreting the Scripture, his knowledge of the problem, and his ability to apply these correctly to a particular problem. I remember "biblical" advice that I gave as a new pastor, which was inappropriate because I lacked an in-depth understanding of the presenting problem.

The factory-trained mechanic is the spiritually sensitive pastor, who can hear from the Holy Spirit and knows how to get help from the design engineer (God). His strong points are his spiritual application of the power of the Holy Spirit, the Chief Counselor, through spiritual gifts and prayer. His weak points are usually a lack of in-depth understanding of psychological problems, the lack of absolute reliability in knowing for sure which insights are from God or himself, and not having the time to provide long-term therapy to deal with the more difficult cases. Here again, he must be careful not to think that every insight he has is unequivocally "God's complete truth."

We Need to Rely Primarily on the Bible for Our Answers

Even if we accept that we need a combination of all three—practical experience and research, Bible knowledge and spiritual revelation—the real question still remains concerning how much our Christian counseling should rely on each type of knowledge. The answer, I believe, is that we need to rely on each to the extent that it is reliable. I believe that for most Christians, the Bible is clearly seen to be the most reliable of the three. Therefore, Christian counseling should rely as much as possible on the Bible, secondly on spiritual revelation, and, thirdly, on secular research, theories and techniques (that agree with the Bible) as is necessary to bring complete psychological healing to the client.

We Need a Therapy that is Based on the Biblical Process of Salvation by Faith

Ideally, if the Bible is God's most complete and reliable revelation, then it should provide the foundation for all that is done within the church. If God's process of making people whole in the Bible is salvation by faith, then it should provide the basis for the counseling process in the church. I believe that if deeper biblical answers, based on the process of salvation by faith, were readily available for the tough psychological problems in the church, what has been called biblical or pastoral counseling and what has been called Christian counseling would become more congruent. In addition, I believe that if Christian counseling was primarily based on the process of salvation by faith, it would be more readily accepted into the church, and more churches would be willing to incorporate it within their church programs.

Chapter 2

The Principles of Faith Therapy

As I will develop in detail later in this book, the biblical process of salvation or wholeness is based on faith in God and His promises to meet our needs. We start out in life motivated totally by our own self-interests and getting our needs met. When we believe in Christ, we begin a process of learning to trust God to meet all our needs. Only as we believe that our needs have been, are, and shall always be met by God, are we set free from the bondage of trying to meet selfishly our basic needs for love, security, worth and significance. As our faith grows and we experience the love of God, our self-bias or selfishness is replaced by love for others. Finally, it is this love that replaces self-interest as the primary motivation of our lives. This is the ultimate sign of both spiritual and psychological wholeness.

Because salvation by faith is God's chosen method to bring healing and wholeness to people, then it only makes sense that whatever is done in the realm of Christian counseling must fit within God's plan of salvation. As we will see, all other Christian counseling modalities can be integrated into this process, as a means for removing the blockages to what God is attempting to do in our lives. In addition, we must learn how to identify and discover the root causes that underlie the hindrances to the process of salvation by faith and resolve them through the application of faith. Underlying each blockage is always an unmet need, which the client has attempted to meet in some fashion through the flesh. When these problems are primarily the result of need deficits, I refer to them as deeply rooted problems since the root of the problem resides in the core psychological needs of the person himself. Therefore, the primary component of a deeply rooted problem is a lack of faith that God will meet that need.

What is Faith Therapy?

Faith Therapy is a biblically derived and integrated method for psychological healing and spiritual *Paper* growth based on the process of salvation by faith. Biblical models, principles and methods are used to identify the root cause of a problem, remove any hindrance to spiritual growth and develop the faith necessary to overcome the problem. The tenants of Faith Therapy were derived directly from the Bible, as God provided greater insights over a period of years. It began with an attempt to understand how the process of salvation or wholeness was achieved by faith in God. As this revelation began to unfold through the story of Abraham, the father of faith, it led to a widening understanding of additional models, principles and methods that effectively dealt with more and more of these deeply rooted psychological problems.

Faith Therapy is biblically integrated, because it has been derived directly from the Bible and embraces all aspects and doctrines of the Bible as a whole. It attempts to integrate all the principles of the Bible into a coherent, holistic approach for healing the entire person, including mind, will, emotions and spirit. In dealing with complex problems, it uses a narrative approach because it relies heavily on a biblical world-view and a study of numerous biblical narrative stories, using a types and shadows interpretation of the Bible. These narratives provide the advanced biblical principles and psychological truth that serve as strategies for therapy or healing. Faith Therapy focuses on dealing with the root cause, which is a lack of faith, not just the symptoms of the problem. It also addresses the overall growth of psychological and spiritual wholeness over the life span of the client. It suggests that the overall orchestration of the process of healing is the job of the Holy Spirit and that the counselor is enlisted for a limited time to address specific blockages in the process of salvation.

What Makes Faith Therapy Unique?

Faith Therapy is unique in that it is based solely on the process of biblical salvation by faith. After determining the root problem and helping the client to realize that he cannot resolve it without God, the most fundamental step in the healing process is leading the client to accept Christ as his Lord and Savior. Once Christ has been accepted, the Holy Spirit orchestrates the process of salvation or wholeness. The Christian counselor's job is to help the client remove any roadblocks to this process and assist him to grow in Christian maturity once the roadblocks are removed. In addition to bringing relief to the presenting problem, faith therapy views all problems as symptoms of deeper life issues, which are rooted in a lack of faith in God to meet the client's most basic needs. Bible principles and models are used for the overall direction of therapy to overcome the original presenting problem, since relying on God's Word builds faith in God—the ultimate answer. These models focus directly on areas where faith is needed to overcome a particular psychological or spiritual vulnerability. In this process, numerous methods, ministries and counseling modalities are applied: preaching, teaching, intercession, prayer, worship, discipleship, confrontation, deliverance, compassion, insight therapy, faith healing, the gifts of the Spirit, prophetic ministry, Theophostic healing of emotions, mentoring, support groups, supportive relationships and many others. Faith Therapy is best applied within a dynamic body of believers in a local Church, where faith is taught and put into practice on a daily basis.

On What Psychological Model is Faith Therapy Based?

As I have already stated a number of times, Faith Therapy has been derived directly from the Bible. Therefore, this question really becomes, "What is the basic psychological model on which the Bible is based?" As I will discuss in more detail later in this book, according to the Bible the basis of most psychological problems is sin or "missing the mark." In fact, it was the sin of Adam and Eve that is responsible for all sickness and pain in the world. If we accept the fact that, as a minimum, sin is the basis of at least all psychological problems that result from our free choices, then what is the basis of sin? It is based on our free choice to try to direct our own lives in order to meet our needs without God. Each of us is driven to meet our most fundamental psychological needs of the self: for love, security, worth and significance. Attempting to meet these needs of the self, in our own strength, is called self-centeredness or selfishness, and it lies at the core of our sin nature. These needs provide the motivation for everything that we do or attempt to do in the flesh. The flesh wars against the Spirit for the control of the soul in order to fulfill the lust of the flesh, the lust of the eyes, and the pride of life (1 John 2:16). What I have just described constitutes what I call the "basic need model" and it provides the psychological basis for Faith Therapy.

How are Psychological Symptoms Related to Root Problems?

Just as a doctor tries to determine a medical problem from the symptoms of his patient, the Faith Therapist begins with the symptoms of the presenting problem, which many times are some of the manifestations of the flesh.

Ga 5:19 Now the works of the flesh are manifest, which are these; Adultery, fornication, uncleanness, lasciviousness,
20 Idolatry, witchcraft, hatred, variance, emulations, wrath, strife, seditions, heresies,
21 Envyings, murders, drunkenness, revellings, and such like: of the which I tell you before, as I have also told you in time past, that they which do such things shall not inherit the kingdom of God.

From these, the counselor determines the function of these manifestations and the lies and misperceptions that underlie them. These lies and misperceptions are indications of the root problem, which is an attempt to meet one or more basic needs through the flesh. Underneath these is the true cause—a lack of faith in God to meet the client's needs.

Once a hypothesis concerning the root problem is determined and verified, biblical principles are applied to replace the lies with the truth of the Word of God and to change the way the client perceives the problem. In complex problems, applicable biblical models are identified and used to guide the course of the therapy. The goal is to remove the blockage to the process of salvation or wholeness, and to build the faith of the client in order to overcome the root cause of the problem.

What Are the Primary Areas of Application?

Faith Therapy provides for the integration of Christian counseling within the framework of the process of salvation by faith and for the direct application of faith to resolve deeply rooted psychological and spiritual problems. This direct application of faith is especially effective in treating fears, anxiety, insecurity and stress. It specifically leads the client to accept Christ as Savior and Lord, and addresses problems that arise out of selfish attempts to meet the core psychological needs of love, security, worth, and significance through the flesh. However, through the application of counseling models and the development of counseling plans based on biblical principles, it is effective in addressing all spiritual and psychological problems.

How is Faith Therapy Integrated with Other Counseling Modalities?

Faith Therapy plays a pivotal role in integrating all Christian counseling modalities within a single overall framework, through an understanding of the process of salvation by faith. It fills the gap with faith, between the unmet needs of the person and the person's unsuccessful attempts to meet those needs in their own strength.

Chapter 3

Faith Therapy in the Church

As I have already discussed, there is a wide diversity of opinions as to the role of counseling in the church. Therefore, before proceeding with further discussion, let me first establish from the Bible that counseling belongs and is needed in today's church.

Christian Counseling Belongs in the Church

The Bible is clear that counseling was to be an important part of Jesus' earthly ministry and anointing,

Isa 9:6 For unto us a child is born, unto us a son is given: and the government shall be upon his shoulder: and his name shall be called <u>Wonderful, Counselor,</u> The mighty God, The everlasting Father, The Prince of Peace.

11:2 And the spirit of the LORD shall rest upon him, the spirit of wisdom and understanding, the <u>spirit of counsel</u> and might, the spirit of knowledge and of the fear of the LORD;

The biblical basis for establishing Christian counseling in the church is found, in part, in Jesus' declaration of His own mission on earth.

Lu 4:18 The Spirit of the Lord [is] upon me, because he hath anointed me to preach the gospel to the poor; <u>he hath sent me to heal the brokenhearted, to preach deliverance to the captives,</u> and recovering of sight to the blind, <u>to set at liberty them that are bruised,</u>

19 To preach the acceptable year of the Lord.

Unfortunately, in most churches there are many people who have accepted Christ, but just do not seem to be able to receive an emotional healing by faith, overcome their past or acquire God's abundant life. They seem to have invisible obstacles that they just cannot overcome. They are stuck in the process of salvation; or at least, they need assistance in knowing what to do to become whole. Since the Greek word for salvation, *sozo*, also means to be made completely whole, this should not be the case. Although not all of these obstacles are psychological, the majority are, and in order to carry out the mission that Christ has now passed on to His church, we are going to have to learn how to deal effectively with these problems.

If counseling was to be part of Jesus' ministry and He is the head of the church, then where does counseling fit into the New Testament church? Since the goal of counseling is to assist in bringing individuals into complete wholeness, I believe that counseling must be accomplished by those within the leadership and ministry of the church. Ephesians Chapter 4 makes it clear that the leadership of the local church is God's means of bringing Christians into "the measure of the stature of the fullness of Christ."

Eph 4:11 And he gave some, apostles; and some, prophets; and some, evangelists; and some, pastors and teachers;

12 For the perfecting of the saints, for the work of the ministry, for the edifying of the body of Christ:

13 Till we all come in the unity of the faith, and of the knowledge of the Son of God, unto a perfect man, unto the measure of the stature of the fullness of Christ:

I see counseling as a specialized and specifically anointed ministry within these callings, filling the role of a shepherd who helps very sick sheep or of a spiritual "veterinarian." Ideally, counseling should be a fully integrated function of the leadership of each church, possibly through pastor-counselors or elders who specialize in counseling. In smaller churches, if elders or trained counselors are not available, this ministry may have to take the form of a pastor who has learned to counsel, or a lay counselor who helps with long-term problems through individual counseling or support groups.

A second biblical reason for including Christian counseling within the church is that Christ directed His church to go into all the world with the gospel (Mark 16:15) and "make disciples of all nations" (Matthew 28:19 NLT). Since counseling will draw significant numbers of people to the church in order to get their needs met, it can become a very effective method of evangelism in our society. People with problems naturally seek the answers for those problems by turning to support groups and counselors. When those support groups and counseling methods are salvation-based, the counseling process naturally leads to addressing the subject of the client's salvation. Although it is never appropriate to attempt to coerce the client into accepting Christ, the majority of those who are not already saved will accept Him once they understand that Jesus is indeed the answer to their problems. When the counseling is conducted within the church setting, it is natural for those who are not already established in churches to want to attend where they have found the answers that have improved their lives. Consequently, both reaching out to our society in an appropriate way and making disciples is facilitated through the integration of Christian counseling within the church.

At Word of Life Counseling Center, we draw clients from all parts of our community. In fact, less than 25 percent of our clients and support group members are members of Word of Life Church. The large majority come through referrals from the courts, from the pastors of other churches, or by responding to ads in the yellow pages. Although the vast majority are Christians, at least several clients accept Christ through our counseling program each month. Although Word of Life is not an exceptionally large church, we minister to over a hundred clients and support group members weekly through our counseling programs.

The Structure of Christian Counseling in the Church

When we attempt to determine how Christian counseling should be structured in the church, I believe that under the direction of the Holy Spirit, it must provide the most effective structure or means that helps the largest number of hurting people within the resources of the church. For most churches, this means a combination of approaches: Pastoral counseling, some professional or lay counseling and a support group or care ministry.

I believe that almost any attempt to begin a counseling ministry in the church will eventually result in this same basic structure. This structure will be shaped by the needs of the hurting people coming and the limited resources of the church. Counselors attempting to practice in a church will eventually realize that they can only help a small number of people on an individual basis. Support groups effectively minister to large numbers of people at little or no cost. Certain types of problems, such as addictions and codependency, are most effectively dealt with in groups. In addition, support groups provide the unconditional acceptance, nurturing and long-term care that is required by many clients after therapy has been completed.

I do not believe that because Christian counseling and especially Faith Therapy primarily belong in the church that this excludes a role for the Christian counselor who practices outside the church in private practice, a separate counseling center, or Christian clinic or hospital. Most churches cannot afford to have a professional counselor, counseling center, clinic, day hospital or hospital to deal with the more specialized or extreme problems. Most of these centers include comprehensive programs that cannot be easily supported in a church environment. Just as the general practitioner medical doctor refers to a specialist for difficult cases, I believe this is one of the functions of the Christian counselor in the church: to refer clients beyond his general expertise to specialized Christian counseling centers, clinics, or hospitals. Reciprocally, these Christian centers, clinics, and hospitals need to provide as much technical support to church counselors, support groups, and local churches as possible, since a coordinated healing process is essential.

In reality, there is a natural dividing line between Christian counselors in the church and Christian counselors who have also had secularly approved training. Most states do not license, register or regulate Christian, biblical, or pastoral counseling. They usually do license, register and regulate Psychiatrists, Psychologists, Marriage and Family Therapists, Professional Counselors, Social Workers, and Drug and Alcohol Counselors. In almost all cases, Christian counseling training programs, especially if they are faith based and not regionally accredited, are not accepted for licensure in any of these secular specialties. Some Christian counselors have chosen to obtain a secular degree in order to be licensed. Others are not willing to spend the time or money to learn secular counseling theory and methods that do not agree with the Bible in order to obtain licensure. Unlicensed counselors are not usually accepted as insurance providers and, therefore, find it hard to establish a financially successful independent practice. This natural dividing line between those with and without licensure usually separates the few stand-alone Christian counseling centers, clinics, and hospitals which are capable of becoming financially successful outside of the church because they are insurance providers, from Christian counselors associated or integrated into the church.

Consequently, I suggest two practical roles for Christian counselors. First, each church should have at least one full or part-time trained pastor-counselor, Christian counselor, or elder who is part of the church staff who can provide individual counseling in the church or at least lead a support group ministry. He would probably not be licensed, would not accept insurance, and serves as a "general Christian counseling practitioner." He would usually charge fees determined by an income-based sliding scale, or he may be a lay counselor who provides his services for free. Because he would not be licensed, he would be less restricted by state regulations and secular ethical codes. He would still be required to maintain professional counseling insurance if he charges fees. Otherwise, he could be covered by the church's pastoral counseling insurance. The second role is that of the licensed professional Christian counselor who practices in a private practice, explicitly Christian counseling center, clinic or hospital. This counselor is able to take insurance and develop specific expertise beyond that of the church counselor. His role is that of the specialist. He deals with the most difficult cases and provides capabilities like inpatient care which are beyond the capabilities of almost all churches. This role does not preclude the use of Faith Therapy theory or methods that may integrate other Christian counseling modalities.

Counselors and Support Group Leaders Should Meet Certain Qualifications

Just as the counselor should be a part of the leadership of the church, I believe he must also meet the basic qualifications of the elders (or leaders) of the church, such as the requirements for the apostle, prophet, evangelist, pastor and teacher.

1 Ti 3:2 A bishop then must be blameless, the husband of one wife, vigilant, sober, of good behaviour, given to hospitality, apt to teach;

3 Not given to wine, no striker, not greedy of filthy lucre; but patient, not a brawler, not covetous;

4 One that ruleth well his own house, having his children in subjection with all gravity;

6 Not a novice, lest being lifted up with pride he fall into the condemnation of the devil.

7 Moreover he must have a good report of them which are without; lest he fall into reproach and the snare of the devil.

These qualifications are not enough in themselves. The Christian counselor must have a passion and empathy for helping people. Just like the other ministries, counseling requires a specific calling and anointing, as well as training. If lay counseling or support group ministries are also established in the church, these leaders, who are supervised by the church counselor or ministry leader, should meet the qualifications of a deacon.

> 1 Ti 3:8 Likewise must the deacons be grave, not doubletongued, not given to much wine, not greedy of filthy lucre;
>
> 9 Holding the mystery of the faith in a pure conscience.
>
> 10 And let these also first be proved; then let them use the office of a deacon, being found blameless.
>
> 11 Even so must their wives be grave, not slanderers, sober, faithful in all things.
>
> 12 Let the deacons be the husbands of one wife, ruling their children and their own houses well.

The Role of the Church Counselor

Just as the apostle, prophet, teacher, and evangelist must be submitted to the senior pastor, so the church counselor should be submitted to the local church pastor, so that the church and the "perfecting of the saints" can be conducted as an integrated, unified whole. It is common for a person to seek advice from several ministers and get different opinions based on the different ministers' backgrounds and approaches to counseling. Because of this, it is important that the role of the church counselor be clearly defined. He should deal only with the support group ministry and counsel long-term critical problems. Short-term problems and the giving of advice, direction, pastoral care and discipline should remain another pastor's job.

This position of counseling in the church presents some unique challenges for the counselor. He must be integrated thoroughly into the church, but avoid dual relationships with the members of the church where he counsels. This means that he cannot counsel personal friends or make church decisions that personally impact his clients. Consequently, it is important that the church counselor avoid disciplinary or executive roles in the church. The counselor must be able to flow with the amateur, volunteer atmosphere of most churches. Professional counseling offices require well-trained staff, excellent maintenance, top-notch facilities, soundproofing and the exclusive use of offices. This ideal situation will probably not be available in most churches. Flexibility is an important trait for anyone hoping to provide counseling and work with support groups within the church setting.

The church counselor must be involved in all aspects of the church, but not take sides in conflicts. To be effective, the counselor must be seen as impartial. His job must be structured in such a way that he can support and bring healing to the church, without becoming embroiled in conflicts in the church. He must be the solid supporting rock that weathers even the most severe divisional storms. Pastoral staffs, in most churches, have a notoriously high turnover rate. He must not see his job as a stepping-stone to another position. He must be convinced that, ultimately, he has been called by God to fill the position of a church counselor. His position in the church should have the title of an associate pastor or elder to reflect the authority necessary to be effective in helping to resolve church conflicts and the problems of his clients in the church. These restrictions should not be taken to mean that the counselor should be isolated from the other functions of the church. He should be closely involved in staff meetings, boards, and other decisions in the church, especially those that affect the well-being of the members of the church.

As is the case with other staff, the counselor must loyally support the Senior Pastor in every way. This does not mean that he is a "yes" man, but that when a final decision has been made that he comes under spiritual authority and supports it (unless it violates clear legal, moral, or scriptural principles). If clients criticize a pastor or question decisions made by leaders, he should direct them to the offending person, according to Matthew Chapter 18.

The church counselor should be expected to raise up, teach, and supervise additional counselors and support group facilitators in order to meet the needs of the congregation better. As the counseling ministry grows, he will also need to disciple additional leaders to become involved in various aspects of the counseling ministry. Although he might also provide counseling for those outside of the congregation, members of the congregation should be given priority. Counselors working with members of other congregations need to obtain a specific written release of confidentiality in order to discuss issues that may relate to the client's church and to coordinate efforts with the client's pastor.

Licensed Counseling in the Church

In some cases, larger churches will find it desirable to have support groups, church counselors, and licensed professionals operating within the church. I believe that all of these ministries can and should employ the methods of Faith Therapy, since it will be more easily accepted and integrated within the church structure and doctrine. When handled in a coordinated manner, this combination of groups, church counselors and licensed professionals provides more credibility and increased potential to reach unsaved people in the community. Licensed or court approved programs, such as drug and alcohol counseling, domestic violence programs and sexual abuse support groups draw hurting people to the church. However, additional specific counseling programs should be carefully evaluated before inclusion in the church setting. Whatever is done must be integrated with and not contradict biblical principles and models appropriate to the church situation.

Liability Issues with Christian Counseling in the Church

One of the biggest hindrances to the growth of Christian counseling in our churches is the fear that it could lead to malpractice litigation. In actuality, if a counseling program is carefully constructed, the increased risk of litigation is small. This additional risk can be easily overcome through the use of counseling malpractice insurance at a minimal cost. I suggest the following guidelines:

1. <u>Advertise and conduct group therapy as self-help or support groups</u>. Self-help or support groups claim only that they attempt to support members in their recovery from a particular problem, facilitate exchange of common experiences and attempt to help each of the members grow in the recovery process. In fact, many self-help leaders are simply those that have recovered or are in the process of recovery and have a burden for others still suffering from the identified problem. Because self-help groups do not claim to provide expert advice and counseling, there is almost no potential for filing a malpractice lawsuit.

2. <u>Cover any support group leaders, lay counselors and pastors under the church's pastoral counseling rider, on the church insurance</u>. As long as no money is received for counseling services, most church insurance will add any "ministers" to the policy for a very nominal cost.

3. <u>Add any professional Christian counselor or counselors, who charge for their services, as contractors and require them to carry their own counseling insurance covering the church as an "additional insured."</u> Contractors are normally self-employed and hired to provide a complete service to the church, meet their own ethical and legal obligations to their profession, and provide their own supervision if required. The normal obligations that a church has to its employees like workman's compensation, income tax withholding, employee evaluations, being totally responsible for the employees conduct and providing detailed oversight are not required to the same extent for contractors, as long as the contractors fulfill the obligations of their contract. If they fail to provide these services, the contract can simply be terminated. Consequently, claims of negligence due to a lack of detailed oversight are difficult to prove. One million dollars of mental health practitioners insurance for a self-employed counselor currently costs less than $200 per year when purchased through professional organizations such as the American Association of Christian Counselors. The additional charge for covering a church as an "other insured" usually costs less than fifty dollars. Unfortunately, most mental health insurance agencies require that counselors have at least a Bachelor's degree in a mental health field.

An exception is NAADAC, which serves Drug and Alcohol counselors. Consequently, lay counselors that have not obtained at least a Bachelor's degree will not usually be able to obtain professional counseling insurance and, therefore, should not charge for their services, so that they can be covered by the church's insurance policy.

4. <u>Require that all counselors attend counseling supervision on a periodic basis and discuss all of their cases with a licensed or degreed therapist</u>. Supervision is required by most states for all licensed therapists for at least the first few years after they obtain their license. Although this is not normally required of Christian counselors, this practice is one of the best methods of insulating the church from litigation. Supervision can be provided by any licensed or degreed therapist on staff or by a contract counselor. Charges for supervision, which is normally done in groups, are usually not expensive.

Using the guidelines that I have just discussed, we have not even had one threat of litigation in more than ten years. We provide support groups, lay counseling, drug and alcohol counseling, Christian counseling, and licensed professional therapy involving over twenty group leaders and counselors. Of course, we thank the Lord for His protection because we live in a litigious society.

Counseling Outside the Church

Although it is my opinion that Christian counseling will be more effective and do more to advance the Kingdom of God when integrated within church programs, I still believe that there is a place for Christian counseling outside of the church setting. As I have already stated, licensed Christian counselors practicing outside of the church should develop full-time counseling practices at Christian counseling centers, clinics or hospitals that specialize in meeting the unfulfilled needs of the church. Their goal should be to serve as a specialist for a number of churches or the entire community. They must be careful to walk the fine line between the obligations of their Christian counseling calling, state regulations and the secular ethical codes of their licensed profession. This is especially problematic when it comes to avoiding dual relationship with members of their own church, and the temptation to suggest strongly that Christian truth is the only answer. In most states and licensed counseling professions, it is considered unethical for a licensed therapist to tell a client what is or is not absolutely right or wrong for him. Instead, the counselor is expected to help the client understand his own values and explore the alternatives. Licensed professionals are clearly at more risk for complaints to regulatory boards and malpractice litigation.

Training of the Faith Therapist in the Church

Faith Therapy was developed within a church setting and has been designed primarily for use within the church or explicitly Christian counseling centers. Because all of the methods and principles are derived directly from the Bible, much of the information used in therapy will already be familiar to the dedicated Bible student. Consequently, required training is kept to a minimum.

The training of Christian counselors in the church seems to have a natural flow as it progresses from one level to another. My suggestion is that a church, wishing to become involved in Christian counseling, assist one of its members or staff to get a basic level of training and experience or that the church sponsor a series of seminars to prepare church members as Faith Therapists.

Once group leaders or lay counselors experience the satisfaction of being used by God to meet the needs of hurting people, they will naturally desire more advanced training. Those who feel that they are called by God to a full time counseling ministry will want to pursue a degree in counseling. This in turn, will lead to an increased need for training and the development of, or connections with, a Christian counseling training ministry.

Pre-requisites for beginning training as a Faith Therapist include: a heart for helping people, acceptable communication skills, a good knowledge of the Bible, and a reasonable level of Christian maturity. The only

Set This

required books are those in *The Just Shall Live by Faith* series of books. Video courses on DVD disks leading to certification as a Faith Therapist are also available. In addition, a large number of additional references are listed in this series of books, which provide additional detailed information or assist in counseling specific problems.

Supervision is especially important when developing a lay counseling program. It can be provided either by an experienced staff counselor or through a contract with a professional therapist. In extreme circumstances, supervision can be conducted via the Internet or by secure long distance communication. New counselors usually learn more when they are actually counseling with supervision than through their initial coursework. Supervision is actually a form of discipleship.

With only the basic background described above and training as a Faith Therapy counselor, members of the congregation will be qualified to counsel as lay counselors within the church setting. Once an individual or a group of individuals become established as counselors, they can then begin an ongoing training program within the church using a large number of additional courses that are available for this purpose. The American Association of Christian Counselors offers a number of video tape series in lay counseling, advanced lay counseling, marriage ministry, healthy sexuality and women's ministry that can be used to augment any training program. Through LOGOS Christian College and Graduate School, and a number of other Christian Colleges, degrees in Christian Counseling and a large number of other areas can be obtained through residence, extension campus, and extended learning methods.

Even though, in these sections, I have discussed Christian counseling in the church and Faith Therapy interchangeably, I want to reiterate that I believe that Faith Therapy and the process of salvation by faith should provide the basis for the integration of all counseling within the church. All other counseling modalities, specific problem related research, and methods need to be understood in the context of the process of salvation by faith. Without this integration, the counseling program and what is taught concerning faith and salvation from the pulpit will not be a coordinated whole.

PART II

A Biblical Foundation

Chapter 4

Salvation by Faith
How it changes us

If Faith Therapy is to be based on the process of salvation by faith then it is essential that we clearly understand this process as it is described and explained in the Bible. We understand from numerous verses in the Bible that God's method of salvation or wholeness is somehow accomplished through faith, but how?

Sling Shot Faith

One of the best analogies that I can use to introduce the topic of faith as it relates to the process of salvation and spiritual growth is the story of David's encounter with Goliath. David was a young man of limited strength, with a few small stones, and a sling shot. But when he took one of those small stones (of truth) and swung it around again and again, it gained in momentum, revolution by revolution, until, with the help of God, it had such force that when it was released, it killed one of the largest giants of that time. In the same way, God has chosen such a simple thing as faith, as it increases through use, to bring salvation or wholeness first to each individual and finally to the entire world. In this Old Testament story, the Philistines are a type of the forces of Satan that attempt to psychologically and spiritually dominate us, and David is a type of Christ.

1 Sa 17: 4 And there went out a champion out of the camp of the Philistines, named Goliath, of Gath, whose height was six cubits and a span.

5 And he had an helmet of brass upon his head, and he was armed with a coat of mail; and the weight of the coat was five thousand shekels of brass.

6 And he had greaves of brass upon his legs, and a target of brass between his shoulders.

7 And the staff of his spear was like a weaver's beam; and his spear's head weighed six hundred shekels of iron: and one bearing a shield went before him.

8 And he stood and cried unto the armies of Israel, and said unto them, Why are ye come out to set your battle in array? am not I a Philistine, and ye servants to Saul? choose you a man for you, and let him come down to me.

48 And it came to pass, when the Philistine arose, and came and drew nigh to meet David, that David hasted, and ran toward the army to meet the Philistine.

49 And David put his hand in his bag, and took thence a stone, and slang it, and smote the Philistine in his forehead, that the stone sunk into his forehead; and he fell upon his face to the earth.

50 So David prevailed over the Philistine with a sling and with a stone, and smote the Philistine, and slew him; but there was no sword in the hand of David.

51 Therefore David ran, and stood upon the Philistine, and took his sword, and drew it out of the sheath thereof, and slew him, and cut off his head therewith. And when the Philistines saw their champion was dead, they fled.

The Process of Salvation by Faith

One of the clearest detailed descriptions of salvation by faith is found in 2nd Peter Chapter 1, which includes a step-by-step explanation of the developmental stages of this process. Here we see that God has given us all things necessary to meet our needs for "life and godliness," and that the entire process begins with faith and ends with unconditional love. Finally, these verses promise that if we do these things, we will be fruitful, never fall, fulfill our calling and find an abundant entrance into heaven itself.

2 Pe 1:3 According as his divine power hath given unto us all things that pertain unto life and godliness, through the knowledge of him that hath called us to glory and virtue:

4 Whereby are given unto us exceeding great and precious promises: that by these ye might be partakers of the divine nature, having escaped the corruption that is in the world through lust.

5 And beside this, giving all diligence, add to your faith virtue; and to virtue, knowledge;

6 And to knowledge temperance; and to temperance patience; and to patience godliness;

7 And to godliness, brotherly kindness; and to brotherly kindness charity.

8 For if these things be in you, and abound, they make [you that ye shall] neither [be] barren nor unfruitful in the knowledge of our Lord Jesus Christ.

10 Wherefore the rather, brethren, give diligence to make your calling and election sure: for if ye do these things, ye shall never fall:

11 For so an entrance shall be ministered unto you abundantly into the everlasting kingdom of our Lord and Saviour Jesus Christ.

Salvation by Faith in the Life of Abraham

Perhaps the best illustration of this entire process is found in the life of Abraham, the "father of faith." As we examine his life, we can trace the steps just identified in 2nd Peter 1:5-7. Abraham progressed through these steps of salvation from being an idol worshipper, as his faith was developed and tried by the circumstances of his life, until he became a hero of faith.

1. <u>We must step out in faith if we want to inherit the promises of God</u>. In Genesis 12, we find that Abram (his original name before God changed his name to Abraham) chose to leave his country and family to go to the land of Canaan, which is later called the "Promised Land." God promised to make him a great nation and to bless him. In the same way, the Holy Spirit calls each of us to leave the world of selfishness and sin, and to trust God to meet our needs through Him. Abram began his process of salvation through faith by leaving his own country even though he was unsure of where God was leading him.

    Ge 12:1 Now the LORD had said unto Abram, Get thee out of thy country, and from thy kindred, and from thy father's house, unto a land that I will shew thee:

    2 And I will make of thee a great nation, and I will bless thee, and make thy name great; and thou shalt be a blessing:

    3 And I will bless them that bless thee, and curse him that curseth thee: and in thee shall all families of the earth be blessed.

    4 So Abram departed, as the LORD had spoken unto him; and Lot went with him: and Abram was seventy and five years old when he departed out of Haran.

2. <u>Our faith will be tried and even though we may suffer failures as we continue to develop our relationship with God, we must learn that He will even use our failures for our good</u>. Although

Abram's faith was enough to get him to move to the land of God's promises, when he arrived he was tested by a famine. He decided to meet his own needs by moving to Egypt, which is a type of the world. He yielded to fear and asked his wife, Sarai, to say that she was his sister. The fact that he disowned his own wife is definitely not virtuous. Whatever is not of faith leads to sin. God Himself had to rescue Sarai from Pharaoh's harem. As we grow in faith through our trials, we learn that God is able to use even our failures for our good. Through this failure they became rich and were required to leave Egypt.

Ge 12:11 And it came to pass, when he was come near to enter into Egypt, that he said unto Sarai his wife, Behold now, I know that thou art a fair woman to look upon:

12 Therefore it shall come to pass, when the Egyptians shall see thee, that they shall say, This is his wife: and they will kill me, but they will save thee alive.

13 Say, I pray thee, thou art my sister: that it may be well with me for thy sake; and my soul shall live because of thee.

15 The princes also of Pharaoh saw her, and commended her before Pharaoh: and the woman was taken into Pharaoh's house.

16 And he entreated Abram well for her sake: and he had sheep, and oxen, and he asses, and menservants, and maidservants, and she asses, and camels.

17 And the LORD plagued Pharaoh and his house with great plagues because of Sarai Abram's wife.

18 And Pharaoh called Abram, and said, What is this that thou hast done unto me? why didst thou not tell me that she was thy wife?

19 Why saidst thou, She is my sister? so I might have taken her to me to wife: now therefore behold thy wife, take her, and go thy way.

Ge 13:1 And Abram went up out of Egypt, he, and his wife, and all that he had, and Lot with him, into the south.

2 And Abram was very rich in cattle, in silver, and in gold.

3. <u>We must trust God to meet all our needs and give up attempting to direct our own lives</u>. When Lot and Abram had to separate because of the size of their flocks, Abram trusted God and allowed Lot first choice in selecting the land he wanted. This showed that Abram believed that God would meet his needs, no matter where he lived. In this, we see Abram's selfishness beginning to lose ground and his virtue increasing. God again promised to bless him and make his posterity as numerous as the stars. Abram believed God's promise. As a result, we see the reward and goal of faith, "and he (God) counted it to him for righteousness." (Genesis 15:6)

Ge 13:8 And Abram said unto Lot, Let there be no strife, I pray thee, between me and thee, and between my herdmen and thy herdmen; for we be brethren.

9 Is not the whole land before thee? separate thyself, I pray thee, from me: if thou wilt take the left hand, then I will go to the right; or if thou depart to the right hand, then I will go to the left.

10 And Lot lifted up his eyes, and beheld all the plain of Jordan, that it was well watered every where, before the LORD destroyed Sodom and Gomorrah, even as the garden of the LORD, like the land of Egypt, as thou comest unto Zoar.

11 Then Lot chose him all the plain of Jordan; and Lot journeyed east: and they separated themselves the one from the other.

4. <u>We must learn to persevere in our faith, until we actually see the answer manifested in our lives,</u> <u>no matter how long it takes.</u> Although Abram's faith had grown, his self-control failed when a child was not born to them for many years. He sought to meet his own need and sinned by taking Hagar as a concubine. Through that union, he conceived Ishmael. Abram had not yet achieved patience or perseverance. He was still learning the knowledge of what is good and evil. The consequences of this failure of faith are still being experienced in the conflict in the Middle East between the Arabs (the descendants of Ishmael) and the nation of Israel (the descendants of Isaac). Through his choices and his consequences, he learned self-control.

Ge 14:4 And, behold, the word of the LORD came unto him, saying, This shall not be thine heir; but he that shall come forth out of thine own bowels shall be thine heir.

5 And he brought him forth abroad, and said, Look now toward heaven, and tell the stars, if thou be able to number them: and he said unto him, So shall thy seed be.

6 And he believed in the LORD; and he counted it to him for righteousness.

15:2 And Sarai said unto Abram, Behold now, the LORD hath restrained me from bearing: I pray thee, go in unto my maid; it may be that I may obtain children by her. And Abram hearkened to the voice of Sarai.

3 And Sarai Abram's wife took Hagar her maid the Egyptian, after Abram had dwelt ten years in the land of Canaan, and gave her to her husband Abram to be his wife.

4 And he went in unto Hagar, and she conceived: and when she saw that she had conceived, her mistress was despised in her eyes.

5. <u>Even after we have begun to experience transformation through faith and begin to care for oth-</u><u>ers, we must be careful not to repeat our fleshly old ways.</u> Even after the covenant, where God changed Abram's name to Abraham (father of multitudes), he repeated his sin of asking Sarah to say she was his sister. Although Abraham had achieved some measure of self-control, his faith still lacked the perseverance to do what is right under the most difficult circumstances. This time, Sarah was taken to Abimelech's harem and God had to intervene. Again, even after the failure God blessed Abraham with more sheep, oxen, and servants, and a choice of dwelling wherever he chose. The unmerited favor of God was still on Abraham, in spite of his failures.

Ge 17: 1 And when Abram was ninety years old and nine, the LORD appeared to Abram, and said unto him, I am the Almighty God; walk before me, and be thou perfect.

2 And I will make my covenant between me and thee, and will multiply thee exceedingly.

5 Neither shall thy name any more be called Abram, but thy name shall be Abraham; for a father of many nations have I made thee.

20:2 And Abraham said of Sarah his wife, She is my sister: and Abimelech king of Gerar sent, and took Sarah.

3 But God came to Abimelech in a dream by night, and said to him, Behold, thou art but a dead man, for the woman which thou hast taken; for she is a man's wife.

14 And Abimelech took sheep, and oxen, and menservants, and womenservants, and gave them unto Abraham, and restored him Sarah his wife.

15 And Abimelech said, Behold, my land is before thee: dwell where it pleaseth thee.

6. <u>God is so merciful and forgiving, that He will carry out what He has promised us, in spite of our</u> <u>failures, if we will rely on Him.</u> Even though Abraham had taken Hagar for his wife in unbelief and

Sarah had laughed when God said she would have a son, God was still faithful to His promise and Sarah conceived. They had finally persevered in their faith and received the reward of God's promise. In response to God's faithfulness, Abraham fulfilled his part of the covenant by circumcising Isaac. In fulfilling his covenant with God through circumcision (dying to the flesh), He was now beginning to take on the character of God, or Godliness.

Ge 21:1 And the LORD visited Sarah as he had said, and the LORD did unto Sarah as he had spoken.

2 For Sarah conceived, and bare Abraham a son in his old age, at the set time of which God had spoken to him.

3 And Abraham called the name of his son that was born unto him, whom Sarah bare to him, Isaac.

4 And Abraham circumcised his son Isaac being eight days old, as God had commanded him.

7. Our faith must be worked out in our actions toward others. Faith without works is dead. We see the development of brotherly kindness in Abraham's life through his concern for Hagar, even though she was only a slave. He would not send her away at Sarah's prodding until her future was assured by God.

Ge 21:12 And God said unto Abraham, Let it not be grievous in thy sight because of the lad, and because of thy bondwoman; in all that Sarah hath said unto thee, hearken unto her voice; for in Isaac shall thy seed be called.

13 And also of the son of the bondwoman will I make a nation, because he is thy seed.

14 And Abraham rose up early in the morning, and took bread, and a bottle of water, and gave it unto Hagar, putting it on her shoulder, and the child, and sent her away: and she departed, and wandered in the wilderness of Beersheba.

8. Our faith is perfected when we love and trust God unconditionally, even when we are called to do things that do not seem reasonable to us. Abraham's greatest test of faith came when God challenged him to sacrifice his long awaited son on Mount Moriah. The fact that Abraham was willing to sacrifice Isaac, who was the key to all the previous promises of God, demonstrated that he now relied on God to meet all of his needs, more than anything in this physical world. In response to his faith, when he was about to slay his son, God provided a ram for the sacrifice. This event previewed the sacrifice of Jesus on the cross. Abraham now loved unconditionally, as God loved. Both were willing to sacrifice their sons for someone else. In Genesis Chapter 22, we find the conclusion of this process of salvation by faith.

Ge 22:1 And it came to pass after these things, that God did tempt Abraham, and said unto him, Abraham: and he said, Behold, here I am.

2 And he said, Take now thy son, thine only son Isaac, whom thou lovest, and get thee into the land of Moriah; and offer him there for a burnt offering upon one of the mountains which I will tell thee of.

9 And they came to the place which God had told him of; and Abraham built an altar there, and laid the wood in order, and bound Isaac his son, and laid him on the altar upon the wood.

10 And Abraham stretched forth his hand, and took the knife to slay his son.

11 And the angel of the LORD called unto him out of heaven, and said, Abraham, Abraham: and he said, Here am I.

12 And he said, Lay not thine hand upon the lad, neither do thou any thing unto him: for now I know that thou fearest God, seeing thou hast not withheld thy son, thine only son from me.

13 And Abraham lifted up his eyes, and looked, and behold behind [him] a ram caught in a thicket by his horns: and Abraham went and took the ram, and offered him up for a burnt offering in the stead of his son.

14 And Abraham called the name of that place Jehovahjireh: as it is said [to] this day, In the mount of the LORD it shall be seen.

Jehovah Jireh means, "the Lord, my provider." What was it that was seen on the mount of the Lord? It was that God will meet all our needs through Jesus Christ, even in the most difficult trials of our faith, if we will only believe. Abraham came from a land of idol worship, learned how to trust God by faith, and as his faith increased through his relationship with God, he was transformed into a righteous hero of faith. This is the destiny that God has planned for each of us through His wonderful process of salvation by faith. (For more information on this process of spiritual growth see my book *Revelations That Will Set You Free*.)

What is the Problem?

Before attempting to understand this process of salvation by faith in more depth, we must first identify the problem to be solved. The biblical answer to this question is clear. The problem is sin or, as the Greek word *hamartia* so clearly says, "missing the mark." The problem is that we are not whole: body, mind, emotions, will or spirit. The Bible tells us in Romans 3:23, "For all have sinned, and come short of the glory of God." The apostle Paul tells us in 1st Timothy 1:15, "This [is] a faithful saying, and worthy of all acceptation, that Christ Jesus came into the world to save sinners; of whom I am chief." In John 10:10b we are told directly by Jesus, "I am come that they might have life, and that they might have [it] more abundantly." Consequently, it is clear that the problem is that we are all inadequate in some way, due to our choices, and that through the process of salvation, we are to be brought into a place of wholeness that results in the abundant life that God has given us.

We must understand that God is a holy, righteous God and that He hates sin. Sin is what mars and corrupts His wonderful creation. The penalty for the choices that we make, which lead to sin, is death. Because God is just, someone had to pay the penalty for sin. Because only He could obey the law perfectly, God, Himself, in the form of Jesus, chose to die upon the cross to pay for our sins. Clearly, God hates the sin that required Jesus to die upon the cross, but loves the sinner—you and me—so much. Jesus was willing to die for us, so that He could have a relationship with us.

Until we have a revelation of how much God hates sin and how much He sacrificed to pay the price for sin, we will not have an adequate appreciation for what God has done for us. Although it might seem somewhat trite in comparison with what Jesus did for us, my revelation of this came through the death of our family's cat. Chrissy had been in our family for 12 years and after our children left for college; she became a very close member of our empty-nest family. She was an outdoor cat, and she loved it that way. She would be sitting outside the window of our door when we would get up and let her come into our bedroom to hang out, sleep, or just to be petted. After she had enough attention, she would go to the door asking to be let out. She would roam the neighborhood and come back in again and again. In this way, we became very attached to her. Then, one day, one of our neighbors called and told us that Chrissy had been attacked by some roaming dogs. When I came home, there was Chrissy and she was dead. I went over to the neighbor's back yard and from the tracks in the snow, I could see she had put up a good fight, running and trying to escape in every imaginable way, until they finally surrounded and killed her. How I hated those dogs! In my heart I said, "If I had been there, I would have done anything, even risked my life, to save her from those vicious dogs." Just then, God spoke to me and said, "But I just had to watch those Roman dogs surround and kill my precious Son, Jesus." I can hardly imagine how much this must have hurt God the Father as He watched, and how much effort it took for Him to restrain Himself and accept Jesus' sacrifice for our sins.

The recent movie, "The Passion of the Christ," has helped many of us to understand better how much Jesus sacrificed for us, and how much God hates sin, but loves the sinner.

How is the Problem Resolved?

First, let us see what the Bible has to say about salvation and about the requirements for its accomplishment. The Greek word *sozo* means, "to save, keep safe and sound, to rescue from danger or destruction, injury or peril, to make well, heal, restore to health." I cannot think of any different word that could possibly describe the goal of Christian counseling better than "salvation." From the Bible, we see that:

1. It is based on the gospel, which is the power of God unto salvation or wholeness for everyone. This salvation is based on what God accomplished, through the death and resurrection of Jesus. Since what Jesus did is a completed work, then everything necessary for salvation has already been provided and is available to everyone who chooses to believe the gospel, or good news. We also see that something in this process of salvation has its fundamental root in believing, or having faith, in the gospel.

    Ro 1:16 For I am not ashamed of the gospel of Christ: for it is the power of God unto salvation to every one that believeth; to the Jew first, and also to the Greek.

2. There is no other way to complete wholeness—body, soul, spirit. The following verse clearly states that no matter how effective secular psychology might be, without this process of salvation, which is based on faith in Jesus, something is missing. I think this becomes completely clear when we realize that, without Jesus, we are spiritually dead, have no power to combat our sin or selfish nature, and that the best we can hope for is to be a well-balanced and socialized sinner destined for eternal damnation. Because all that is required for salvation has already been accomplished—including the provision for the healing of our entire bodies, mind, will, emotions and spirit—this process can provide the foundation for all necessary counseling.

    Ac 4:12 Neither is there salvation in any other: for there is none other name under heaven given among men, whereby we must be saved.

    It is also clear that we can neglect this great salvation, and if we do, there is no other way to complete wholeness or escape from our dysfunction and sin.

    Heb 2:3 How shall we escape, if we neglect so great salvation; which at the first began to be spoken by the Lord, and was confirmed unto us by them that heard [him];

3. One of the ways to neglect this process of salvation is to fail to meet its requirements. These requirements are most clearly described in Romans:

    Ro 10:9 That if thou shalt confess with thy mouth the Lord Jesus, and shalt believe in thine heart that God hath raised him from the dead, thou shalt be saved.

    a. Believe with the heart: In the Bible, the Greek word for heart is *kardia*. It means, "the center of all physical and spiritual life." Verses can be found where it refers to the mind, emotions, will, or spirit, or any combination of these. To be saved, we must believe in our hearts that God raised Jesus from the dead. We must have faith that Jesus was "to be the firstborn of many brethren" (Romans 8:29), and that God will also resurrect us, meet our needs and make us completely whole. The Greek word believe here is *pisteuo,* which means, "to think to be true, to be persuaded of, to credit, place confidence in; to trust in Jesus or God as able to aid either in obtaining or in doing something: saving faith; to entrust a thing to one or to be entrusted with a thing." It is the same root word, as the word translated as faith. Therefore, believing is a lot more than mental assent of the mind to agree about something. At issue here is that we must actually place our confidence in, rely on and trust God to aid, obtain or do what we need, and to have enough confidence to commit our needs to Him.

    b.   <u>Confess with our mouth what we believe</u>. The Greek word for confess is *homologeo,* which means, "to say the same thing as another, i.e. to agree with, assent, to promise, not to deny, to declare openly, speak out freely, to profess one's self the worshipper of one, to praise, and celebrate." The meaning here is to openly and outwardly speak and act in accordance with what we believe—that God has and will meet our needs through Jesus' death and resurrection. In James Chapter 2, it is clear that faith without works or action is dead, and salvation will not work if we fail to act according to our trust in Him.

    c.   <u>Confess Jesus as Lord</u>. The Greek word for Lord here is *kurios* which means, "he to whom a person or thing belongs, about which he has power of deciding; master, lord; the possessor and disposer of a thing; or the owner; one who has control of the person, the master.

The issue here is submission and control. If we refuse to cooperate with God's day-by-day direction of our lives, God's plan of salvation can be thwarted. The child who will not obey his parents makes the wonderful life they intend for him impossible or at least significantly more difficult. Either God is our boss, or we are our boss. God will not be our genie and just bless whatever we selfishly want to do! To the extent, we seek His direction for our lives, to that extent salvation or the process of moving toward wholeness will be working in our lives. By my own experience, I have found that my desire to direct my own life and not seek His direction is one of the greatest hindrances to "working out my own salvation." (Philippians 2:12b) In Jeremiah Chapter 10, the importance of this submission to the lordship of Jesus is clear:

Jer 10:23 O LORD, I know that the way of man [is] not in himself: [it is] not in man that walketh to direct his steps.

When we try to direct our own steps, even if we ask Him to bless our efforts, we are walking around like a man in fog, without a compass. We may try hard, but we have no idea where we are going and specifically what we are called to do.

The Bible goes on to clarify what has already been stated in Romans 10:9: it is faith that produces righteousness, it is acting on that faith which brings real change and it is real change that delivers us from the shame of our sin.

Ro 10:10 For with the heart man believeth unto righteousness; and with the mouth confession is made unto salvation.

11 For the scripture saith, Whosoever believeth on him shall not be ashamed.

The Bible tells us that our salvation is complete. When we accept Christ, we are born of the Spirit, our spirit is regenerated, we receive a new nature and are forgiven. Christ's spirit comes to dwell within us so that we can have fellowship with Him. Through salvation, in this lifetime, our soul becomes progressively more whole, as we yield to the Holy Spirit and renew our mind (which controls our emotions and will, and which, in turn, results in right actions). Complete healing is available for our bodies through faith, but our bodies will never finally "put off corruption" until they are renewed in the resurrection. Consequently, salvation includes complete wholeness in its fullest sense!

In the book of Galatians, it is made very clear that we cannot bring this salvation or wholeness about by trying to do what is right (the law) in our own strength (through the flesh).

Ga 3:1 O foolish Galatians, who hath bewitched you, that ye should not obey the truth, before whose eyes Jesus Christ hath been evidently set forth, crucified among you?

2 This only would I learn of you, Received ye the Spirit by the works of the law, or by the hearing of faith?

3 Are ye so foolish? having begun in the Spirit, <u>are ye now made perfect by the flesh?</u>

4 Have ye suffered so many things in vain? if it be yet in vain.

5 He therefore that ministereth to you the Spirit, and worketh miracles among you, doeth he it by the works of the law, or by the hearing of faith?

The scriptures declare that God has provided all that is necessary, through faith in His promises, to overcome our lusts as we cooperate with Him in this progressive process of salvation with a final end of glory, virtue, and the nature of Christ.

2 Pe 1:4 Whereby are given unto us exceeding great and precious promises: that by these ye might be partakers of the divine nature, having escaped the corruption that is in the world through lust.

We must remember that we have a significant part to play in cooperating with the Holy Spirit in order to make our election or salvation sure.

How is Wholeness Achieved?

Before proceeding further, it is important to understand what is the basis of our dysfunction (or sin nature), and how salvation is actually achieved. We cannot hope to build a counseling theory on a problem and a solution that we do not understand.

The Bible sees man as a creature controlled by sin or, in counseling terms, dysfunction. In the simplest terms, our sin nature is a selfish desire to do things our way, direct our own life and meet our own needs. When we begin the process of salvation, God's Spirit takes up residence within us to motivate us to do right; and a battle begins. The Bible tells us that the Spirit wars against the flesh, which is controlled by selfishness. This battle is for the control of our soul—our mind, emotions and will—which, in turn, controls our actions. To be whole from the inside out, the sin nature within us must die. How is this to be done?

First, we must realize that our sin nature has already been defeated at the cross. Romans Chapter 6 declares that our "old man" or sin nature was crucified with Christ "that the body of sin might be destroyed, that henceforth we should not serve sin." (verse 6) Although this is an accomplished fact, we must reckon or count it as accomplished—that is, believe and act like the power of sin has been broken. We are now free to choose whether to sin or refrain from sinning. (verse 11)

Ro 6:6 Knowing this, that our old man is crucified with [him], that the body of sin might be destroyed, that henceforth we should not serve sin.

7 For he that is dead is freed from sin.

8 Now if we be dead with Christ, we believe that we shall also live with him:

9 Knowing that Christ being raised from the dead dieth no more; death hath no more dominion over him.

10 For in that he died, he died unto sin once: but in that he liveth, he liveth unto God.

11 Likewise reckon ye also yourselves to be dead indeed unto sin, but alive unto God through Jesus Christ our Lord.

12 Let not sin therefore reign in your mortal body, that ye should obey it in the lusts thereof.

13 Neither yield ye your members [as] instruments of unrighteousness unto sin: but yield your-selves unto God, as those that are alive from the dead, and your members [as] instruments of righteousness unto God.

14 For sin shall not have dominion over you: for ye are not under the law, but under grace.

This is summed up clearly in the book of Galatians:

Ga 2:20 I am crucified with Christ, nevertheless I live; yet not I, but Christ liveth in me: and the life which I now live in the flesh I live by the faith of the Son of God, who loved me, and gave himself for me.

It is clear that although this victory over our sin nature has already been accomplished, the reality of this fact in our lives comes through faith. Our deliverance begins by believing that the overwhelming power of sin in our lives has been broken and that we are now free to choose whether we will yield ourselves to serve sin or to serve Spirit of Christ within us. (v. 12-16) Although Christ has provided everything that we need to be set free from sin, in our selfishness we can still choose to "serve sin." Although the Spirit of God influences us to do right, somehow we must now defeat the selfishness within us in order to live a righteous life.

Defeating the Selfishness Within

We already have had many indications that faith is the key ingredient in this process of salvation, but how does it work and how does it result in the complete wholeness of a person? How do we use the slingshot of faith to hit the mark in order to bring down the giants in our lives? Although the statement from which this series of books has been titled is repeated word for word four times throughout the Bible, I will quote it here from Hebrews:

Heb 10:38 <u>Now the just shall live by faith:</u> but if [any man] draw back, my soul shall have no pleasure in him.

39 But we are not of them who draw back unto perdition; but of them that believe to the saving of the soul.

These verses make several things clear. Somehow, faith is the basis of being just or righteous, and it is possible to draw back from faith, which results in hell (perdition). Furthermore, faith, or believing, is the basis of the healing or salvation of the soul. We must understand what it means, to be just (or righteous as this word is translated in the New International Bible). Our English dictionary states that to be just means "to be fair, evenhanded, and impartial in acting or judging." (Standard College Dictionary, 1963) In order to do this, we must not have any vested interests or biases, as explained in the book of John:

Jo 5:30. I can of mine own self do nothing: as I hear, I judge: and my judgment is just; because I seek not mine own will, but the will of the Father which hath sent me.

Let me make this clear by using an analogy:

Let us suppose that you have a grievance against the company for which you work and that you take them to court. When you come before the judge, you find that he is part owner of that company. Do you expect that you will receive a <u>just</u> hearing? You would probably say that you doubt that you will, and the law would require that the judge disqualify himself for that case. If he did not disqualify himself, the judge would clearly be influenced by outside forces. Either he would be tempted by his interest in the company to insure that they did not lose the case and be fined, or he would be biased in your favor, so that no one would think that he had favored the company that he partly owned. In fact, it would be impossible to determine how his case might be influenced due to his bias. Clearly, a person with a vested interest can never assure anyone that he can be just. **When that vested interest is to meet our own needs, it is called selfishness, because we are attempting to meet the needs of our "self."**

Since in this life we can never be absolutely safe, have all we want, or be all we want; it is clear that all of our needs cannot and will never be met in the flesh. As long as we believe that our needs will not be met and we attempt to meet them, we will have a vested interest in what we do to meet these needs and we will be selfish in some way in our actions. In fact, the more desperate we are to meet these needs, the more biased or selfish we will usually be. Most of the time we might not even recognize that we are being selfish, because the whole world is motivated by these same needs and our attempts to meet our most basic psychological needs are almost automatic, and thus sometimes very hard to detect. The truth is that everyone is motivated primarily by his own personal needs. Almost everything we do in this life is motivated by the effect it will eventually have on us. We will be nice to others so that they will be nice to us. We will try to please others so that they will like us, and we can feel good about ourselves. We will perform well at work so we can feel we did something important, earn money to meet our needs, and feel significant. This problem of selfishness is such a strong trait in all people that the Bible says in Isaiah 64:6 that "all our righteousnesses are as filthy rags." This is because even the "good" things we do are all tainted by our selfish motives. When we try to meet our own needs with this faulty, biased motivation, we inevitably sin by not being fair and evenhanded in our dealings with others. Let me use another example:

If I am $10,000 in debt and I am selling you my car, how concerned do you think I will be that you get a good deal? I will probably be more concerned that I get the very highest price possible, even if my car is not worth that much. If I have a good job and plenty of money, there is a better chance that I will not be so concerned about getting more for my car than it is worth from you. The difference is based on how needy I am, and, therefore, how much of a vested interest I have. This vested interest results in missing the mark of what I should be and what I should do as a human being. Therefore, this is what the Bible calls sin.

God's goal for us is real righteousness or wholeness in our actions, which reflect our mind, emotions, will and spirit. This requires overcoming this world system that is based on selfishness. The Bible tells us that the issues of life come out of the heart. (Proverbs 4:23) How then, are we to achieve this wholeness? The point is that **we cannot do it**. The more we try to meet our needs—including the need for wholeness—the more biased and selfish we become. In fact, the harder we try to be unselfish, so that we can be righteous, the more selfish we have become. This is because, in trying to be unselfish, we are still trying to meet our own need of the self to be worthwhile. Only through the process of salvation by faith can we overcome selfishness and achieve complete wholeness!

> 1 Jo 5:4 For whatsoever is born of God overcometh the world: and this is the victory that overcometh the world, [even] our faith.
>
> 5 Who is he that overcometh the world, but he that believeth that Jesus is the Son of God?

If it is true that as long as we are selfish, we can never be just, righteous or whole, then only the power of God can deliver us from our selfishness. This happens through the process of salvation that works by faith. This is explained again in Romans:

> Ro 1:16 For I am not ashamed of the gospel of Christ: for it is the power of God unto salvation to every one that believeth; to the Jew first, and also to the Greek.
>
> 17 For therein is the righteousness of God revealed from faith to faith: as it is written, The just shall live by faith.

The New International Version translates "faith to faith" as "faith from first to last" which makes the point even clearer. The way to become righteous is through, and only through, faith. This is because the only way to be delivered from our selfish interests is to believe that all our needs are or will be met. The only way this can happen—past, present and future—is by faith in Jesus Christ. Since we do not know the future, we can never guarantee that we will be absolutely secure, worthwhile, significant and loved, unless we know and trust the One Who controls the future.

In order to be delivered from our selfishness, we must experientially believe what the Bible says, that God has and will always meet all our basic needs for security, significance, love and worth, and whatever else we may need in the future:

1. <u>He has and will supply all our needs</u>.

    Php 4:19
    19 But my God shall supply all your need according to his riches in glory by Christ Jesus.

2. <u>He has and will protect us</u>.

    Isa 41:13 For I the LORD thy God will hold thy right hand, saying unto thee, Fear not; I will help thee.

3. <u>He has already met all our needs for significance since we are a son or daughter of the ruler of the universe and a joint heir with Jesus Christ</u>.

    Ro 8:16 The Spirit itself beareth witness with our spirit, that we are the children of God:

    17 And if children, then heirs; heirs of God, and joint-heirs with Christ; if so be that we suffer with [him], that we may be also glorified together.

4. <u>God's love is so great that nothing can separate us from His love</u>.

    Ro 8:38 For I am persuaded, that neither death, nor life, nor angels, nor principalities, nor powers, nor things present, nor things to come,

    39 Nor height, nor depth, nor any other creature, shall be able to separate us from the love of God, which is in Christ Jesus our Lord.

5. <u>He has made us in the image of God and has valued us enough to send His Son to die for us</u>. Consequently, we are worthwhile, in spite of our mistakes.

    Ge 1:27 So God created man in his [own] image, in the image of God created he him; male and female created he them.

To the extent that we actually believe and act like all our needs are and will be met, to that extent, we will be less biased and selfish in all we do. God's goal is for us to treat others fairly and to be set free to have His kind of unbiased love toward everyone. This is only possible when we are set free from the bondage of our needs.

The Bible is so strong in declaring salvation by faith that it unequivocally states that everything that is not motivated by faith inevitably results in sin. As we have already seen, this is true because everything we do in a biased or selfish way will be unjust in some way.

Ro 14:23 And he that doubted is damned if he eat, because [he eateth] not of faith: For <u>whatsoever [is] not of faith is sin</u>.

In this particular instance, if a person believed that eating something sacrificed to an idol was wrong, and he did it, he would be doing it to meet his own needs and would violate his conscience. The saints of old pleased God and received a good report because what they did was based on their faith that God would meet their needs. Therefore, these actions were unselfish.

Heb 11:1. Now faith is the substance of things hoped for, the evidence of things not seen.

2 For by it the elders obtained a good report.

They believed that God was going to take care of them, so they were released to judge and act for the benefit of everyone. In order to please God, we must believe that He exists and that He will also meet our needs.

Heb 11:6 But without faith [it is] impossible to please [him]: for he that cometh to God must believe that he is, and [that] he is a rewarder of them that diligently seek him.

In fact, God already counts us as righteous, even before we have overcome our selfishness. The way He does this is through our identification with Christ and through what He accomplished on the cross—the forgiveness of our sins. The Bible says that Abraham believed God and it was counted unto him as righteousness (Romans 4:3). In Abraham's case, God did this by looking forward to what Christ would do on the cross. This is like going to the bank and after all the paperwork is done for a home loan, the banker throws the loan application in the trash, hands you the money, and says your older brother already paid for the loan. This is what is called imputed righteousness. It is given to us through faith without works.

Ro 3:28 Therefore we conclude that a man is justified (in right standing with God) by faith without the deeds of the law.

The Bible tells us that we were crucified and we have risen with Christ. We are saved by grace or God's unmerited favor. Through what Jesus did, God has forgiven all of our sins, has declared us in right standing with Him and has placed the Spirit of Christ within us. Because of what Christ did, God sees us as already righteous, without regard to our good or evil actions. Because of our position as adopted children, He promises always to meet all of our needs. The revelation in our hearts of His unmerited favor and our position in Him provide the basis to believe that He has, is currently, and will forever love us unconditionally and provide for us.

As we start really believing that He will meet all of our needs, we will rely less and less on our own efforts. We will trust more and more in the power of the Spirit within us, focus more on spiritual answers and direction, tap into the power of the life of God within us, and as Romans suggests, walk in accordance with the Spirit.

As faith grows, we will begin to be able to delay our need for immediate gratification. This is what the Bible calls "dying to self" or "crucifying the flesh." Dying to self is also based on faith. We will never be disposed to want to put off our immediate gratification or do His will, if we are not influenced by His Spirit. We must believe He loves us, and know that He will meet our needs. As our love for God grows, we more and more appreciate what he has done for us, and we are led more by the Spirit. Our desire for furthering His kingdom will make our needs of less importance as we set our focus on His call and His kingdom. As we do this, we will be motivated by love to love others unconditionally as He has loved us.

Finally, we begin to "reap what we have sown." As we unconditionally and unselfishly love others, they begin to respond in love. When our needs begin to be met by others, our faith in God grows and we begin to feel better and more confident about who we are in Christ. Consequently, an ever-increasing cycle of blessings comes into play causing more healing from our selfishness, which, in turn, results in more faith, and causes us to have an increased revelation of God's unconditional love. The final result is a mature Christian life, motivated by and filled with the love of God.

Other Biblical Verification of the Process of Salvation by Faith

If this process of salvation by faith is so important, we should expect to find it also described in a similar manner in other portions of the Bible. We have already seen it illustrated step-by-step in 2nd Peter Chapter 1 and in the life of Abraham. In 1st John Chapter 5, we have another clear explanation of the entire process, but this time it is presented by deductive reasoning. The author begins with the fact that his intended readers really love God. If a person really loves God, he will obey God's commandments and will do God's will instead of his own. That means that he must have already overcome the world's lusts and the only way that this could have been done is through faith.

> 1 Jo 5:2 By this we know that we love the children of God, when we love God, and keep his commandments.
>
> 3 For this is the love of God, that we keep his commandments: and his commandments are not grievous.
>
> 4 For whatsoever is born of God overcometh the world: and this is the victory that overcometh the world, [even] our faith.

In 1st Peter Chapter 1, we find it described again. From these verses, we can verify that God's power comes through faith and that faith results in salvation, which is fully revealed at a future time. We also see that there is a struggle or process of trials of faith and temptation that result in honor and glory to God. Finally, we see that the final conclusion of the matter is the salvation (wholeness) of our souls.

> 1 Pe 1:5 Who are kept by the <u>power of God through faith unto salvation</u> ready to be revealed in the last time.
>
> 6 Wherein ye greatly rejoice, though now for a season, if need be, ye are in heaviness through manifold temptations:
>
> 7 That the <u>trial of your faith,</u> being much more precious than of gold that perisheth, though it be tried with fire, might be <u>found unto praise and honour and glory</u> at the appearing of Jesus Christ.
>
> 8 Whom having not seen, ye love; in whom, though now ye see [him] not, yet believing, ye rejoice with joy unspeakable and full of glory:
>
> 9 Receiving the <u>end of your faith, [even] the salvation of [your] souls</u>.

In Hebrews Chapter 11, the Apostle Paul gives us a list of many of the people in the Bible, whose lives were transformed through this process of salvation by faith. This chapter also tells us how to become a hero of faith.

How to Become a Hero of Faith

Although, by now, I hope it is clear to the reader that salvation is accomplished totally by faith in God, this fact does not deny that we have a part in this process. We have already seen that Abraham played a significant role in his salvation (or wholeness) by the choices that he made and by the victories that he won or lost in the trials of his faith. In Hebrews Chapter 11, and in the first few verses of Chapter 12, we can find our part in this process clearly spelled out for us.

1. <u>We need to desire a life of faith</u>.

> Heb 11:1 Now faith is the substance of things hoped for, the evidence of things not seen.
>
> 2 For by it the elders obtained a good report.
>
> 4 By faith Abel offered unto God a more excellent sacrifice than Cain, by which he obtained witness that he was righteous, God testifying of his gifts: and by it he being dead yet speaketh.
>
> 5 By faith Enoch was translated that he should not see death; and was not found, because God had translated him: for before his translation he had this testimony, that he pleased God.

2. <u>We need to build our faith in order to please God</u>.

Heb 11:6 But without faith it is impossible to please him: for he that cometh to God must believe that he is, and that he is a rewarder of them that diligently seek him.

3. <u>We must rely on God for our needs</u>.

    Heb 11:7 By faith Noah, being warned of God of things not seen as yet, moved with fear, prepared an ark to the saving of his house; by the which he condemned the world, and became heir of the righteousness which is by faith.

4. <u>We need to obey, knowing that God has our best interest in mind</u>.

    Heb 11:8 By faith Abraham, when he was called to go out into a place which he should after receive for an inheritance, obeyed; and he went out, not knowing whither he went.

    9 By faith he sojourned in the land of promise, as in a strange country, dwelling in tabernacles with Isaac and Jacob, the heirs with him of the same promise:

    10 For he looked for a city which hath foundations, whose builder and maker is God.

5. <u>We must rely on God for strength, even when we know we cannot do it</u>.

    Heb 11:11 Through faith also Sara herself received strength to conceive seed, and was delivered of a child when she was past age, because she judged him faithful who had promised.

    12 Therefore sprang there even of one, and him as good as dead, so many as the stars of the sky in multitude, and as the sand which is by the sea shore innumerable.

    13 These all died in faith, not having received the promises, but having seen them afar off, and were persuaded of them, and embraced them, and confessed that they were strangers and pilgrims on the earth.

    14 For they that say such things declare plainly that they seek a country.

6. <u>We must offer ourselves and everything we have, to God as a sacrifice, no matter what the cost</u>.

    Heb 11:17 By faith Abraham, when he was tried, offered up Isaac: and he that had received the promises offered up his only begotten son,

    18 Of whom it was said, That in Isaac shall thy seed be called:

    19 Accounting that God was able to raise him up, even from the dead; from whence also he received him in a figure.

7. <u>We should expect a wonderful future because we know how much God loves us</u>.

    Heb 11:20 By faith Isaac blessed Jacob and Esau concerning things to come.

    21 By faith Jacob, when he was a dying, blessed both the sons of Joseph; and worshipped, leaning upon the top of his staff.

    22 By faith Joseph, when he died, made mention of the departing of the children of Israel; and gave commandment concerning his bones.

8. <u>We must put the Kingdom of God first, before earthly things</u>.

    Heb 11:24 By faith Moses, when he was come to years, refused to be called the son of Pharaoh's daughter;

25 Choosing rather to suffer affliction with the people of God, than to enjoy the pleasures of sin for a season;

26 Esteeming the reproach of Christ greater riches than the treasures in Egypt: for he had respect unto the recompence of the reward.

27 By faith he forsook Egypt, not fearing the wrath of the king: for he endured, as seeing him who is invisible.

9.   <u>We must win the trials of our faith, expecting God to do great things through us.</u>

Heb 11:28 Through faith he kept the passover, and the sprinkling of blood, lest he that destroyed the firstborn should touch them.

29 By faith they passed through the Red sea as by dry land: which the Egyptians assaying to do were drowned.

30 By faith the walls of Jericho fell down, after they were compassed about seven days.

31 By faith the harlot Rahab perished not with them that believed not, when she had received the spies with peace.

32 And what shall I more say? for the time would fail me to tell of Gideon, and of Barak, and of Samson, and of Jephtha; of David also, and Samuel, and of the prophets:

33 Who through faith subdued kingdoms, wrought righteousness, obtained promises, stopped the mouths of lions,

34 Quenched the violence of fire, escaped the edge of the sword, out of weakness were made strong, waxed valiant in fight, turned to flight the armies of the aliens.

10. <u>We should lay aside every weight and sin, and patiently wait for God to change us by faith.</u>

Heb 12:1 Wherefore seeing we also are compassed about with so great a cloud of witnesses, let us lay aside every weight, and the sin which doth so easily beset us, and let us run with patience the race that is set before us,

11. <u>We are to make Jesus our model and example.</u>

Heb 12:2 Looking unto Jesus the author and finisher of our faith; who for the joy that was set before him endured the cross, despising the shame, and is set down at the right hand of the throne of God.

12. <u>We must not quit even if it seems hard!</u>

Heb 12:3 For consider him that endured such contradiction of sinners against himself, lest ye be wearied and faint in your minds.

4 Ye have not yet resisted unto blood, striving against sin.

But someone might object, "I thought you said that salvation is totally by faith and not by works, and now you have given us a list of works that you say are our part of the process." Go back and reread the verses that we have just covered and make a note of how many of them begin with the words "by faith" and "through faith." The Bible tells us that "faith without works is dead." (James 2:17) Therefore, we still have to conclude that our salvation or wholeness is by faith (even though we must use our faith to manifest the works in our lives that bring about the abundant life that God has promised us). It is faith that provides the catalyst for our works, which can qualify us to be listed in God's heroes of faith. Because salvation depends primarily on faith, all of us can become heroes simply by trusting God to provide the strength to do what only heroes of faith can do.

So what is the bottom line? The conclusion of this matter is that God has extended his salvation to everyone, through His Son, Jesus Christ. Because our salvation is by faith in God and not by our own works, we all can qualify to become listed in the new role call of the heroes of faith. We simply need to trust and rely on God to transform us into what He has called us to be. Because it is by faith, none of us can say that our struggles or problems are too great or that we are not smart enough or rich enough. We do not have to try harder, but simply trust harder. Our faith will provide the strength to enable us to do what we need to do. Later in this book, we will learn how to increase our faith and win the trials of our faith. These things are the building blocks of our transformation.

Finally, I need to make it very clear that, although we do have a part in our salvation, it is God, through the Holy Spirit, Who orchestrates this entire process from beginning to end. It is God Who sent His Son to die for our sins and provide everything that we need for "life and Godliness," so that we could be delivered from our selfishness. It is God Who, through His everlasting grace and patience, drew us to Himself so that we can believe and be saved. It is God Who brings us in contact with just the right church, pastors, counselors, friends, sermon or teaching to build our faith and heal our psychological and spiritual problems in order to make us whole. It is God Who works behind the scenes to use the trials of our faith, the struggles of our lives, and the consequences of our choices to develop our character. Consequently, it is God Who alone deserves the credit for bringing us from where we were, destitute in our selfishness and sin, into the wonderful wholeness of His abundant life, through His phenomenal process of salvation through faith!

How to Become a Hero of Faith

1. Want a life of faith that pleases God.

2. Build our faith in order to please God.

3. Rely on God for our needs.

4. Obey, knowing that God has our best interest in mind.

5. Rely on God for strength, even when we are not sure we can do it.

6. Offer ourselves and everything we have to God as a sacrifice, no matter what the cost.

7. Expect a wonderful future, knowing how much God loves us.

8. Put the Kingdom of God first, before earthly things.

9. Win the trials of our faith, expecting God to do great things through us.

10. Lay aside every weight and sin and patiently wait for God to change us.

11. Make Jesus our model and example.

12. Do not quit even if it seems hard!

Chapter 5

Salvation by Faith from a Psychological Perspective

In the last chapter, I described how God uses the process of salvation by faith to make us whole. In this chapter, I will re-examine this process from a psychological perspective. Although it is the Holy Spirit who orchestrates the entire process, He, at times, enlists pastors and counselors to assist in helping His people progress or overcome roadblocks in this healing process.

In order to illustrate how this process of salvation by faith works psychologically, I have developed the chart entitled "Christian Development Leading to Love" on the following page. It is a more advanced development of some similar charts presented by Dr. Crabb in *Effective Christian Counseling* (1977). In that book, he provides a reasonably simple explanation of psychological problem development in two charts.

Dr. Crabb's first chart is labeled, "Normal Development Leading to Emptiness" (Crabb, 1977, p.136). With it, he explains that we all have basic psychological needs. When we perceive that these needs are not met, we are motivated to meet them. Based on our basic assumptions as to how these needs can be met, we produce goal-oriented behavior. When we achieve our goal, we temporarily feel satisfied but are left with a vague sense of emptiness. This is because worldly ways of meeting our needs never completely fulfill us and are temporary in nature. We must meet our needs over and over again. This is why life in our society has been called the "rat race" of life. Dr. Crabb suggests that even if we are a person who has experienced "worldly success," we will eventually realize that all our efforts are vain and worthless (as King Solomon states in Ecclesiastes). At this point, we may experience despair and could even become suicidal.

His second chart, labeled "Abnormal" Development Leading to Psychological Disorder, expands the model to show what happens when our goal-oriented behavior is consistently blocked. He suggests that if we experience an obstacle to meeting our needs and see it as an unreachable goal, we feel guilt. If we see the obstacle as an external circumstance, we feel resentment. If we believe we have failed, we feel anxiety. After many obstacles, frustration can lead us to settle for just being safe. This is called neurosis. If we cannot even succeed at being safe, we may lapse into unreality, which is called psychosis. Using this same pattern, we can develop a chart describing the process of salvation by faith.

Dr. Crabb's first chart provided the basis for the chart on the following page. He states, "God, who sees to the innermost depths of our hearts, cannot commend or accept behavior that is in any way selfishly motivated. Theoretically, Christians are in a position to be free of deficit motivation. To the degree that a Christian believes these verses about God meeting our needs, he is freed from a life of self-centered concern with whether or not his own needs are met." (pp. 82-83). Expanding on these ideas on this new chart, I again begin with the basic unfulfilled needs. These needs are part of our "self" or person. As stated before, these primary psychological needs are the need to be secure, loved, worthwhile and significant (Dr. Crabb suggests only security and significance, or love and purpose as borrowed from Maslow's list, p. 79). When these needs are not met, the Christian, just like the non-Christian, is motivated to meet them. However, to the extent that we are submitted to the Spirit, we will attempt to meet these needs

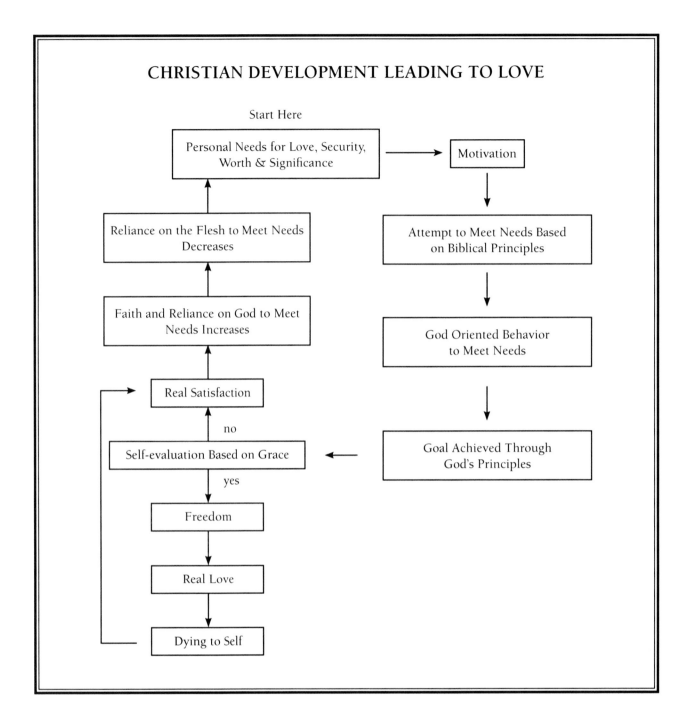

through biblical principles and God-oriented behavior. If we are successful, we will receive blessings and satisfaction that do effectively meet our needs, but which are still temporary in nature. This is where faith comes in. Can we trust that God will meet our needs for tomorrow or will we continue in the "rat race?"

If we choose to try to meet our needs ourselves through worldly means and principles, we will find ourselves exiting to one of Dr. Crabb's previous two charts (due to a lack of faith) and receiving the resulting consequences just like those experienced by an unbeliever. If we trust God to meet our needs, our reliance on Him will increase and our reliance on the flesh will decrease. To the extent that we, as Christians, rely on God and actually trust God to meet our needs, our faith will grow and continually increase. As our faith continues to grow, we will be filled with confidence that God loves us unconditionally. We must remember that we are worthwhile in spite of our performance and what people think of us. If we evaluate ourselves from the perspective of God's grace, we will be set free from the "rat race" of life. We will no longer be driven to have to perform, please others, or prove ourselves, since we will rely on God more and more for our direction and needs.

When we exit the "rat race" of life to true freedom, we enter "the rest of God" described in Hebrews 4:8-11. Being set free has an interesting result. Since we no longer have to perform to please God in order to get our needs met, we can now choose to do what is right because we want to do the right thing, out of love and appreciation for what God has done for us. We no longer have a vested interest to do anything other than please God and do what is just and right in every case. We have now moved through the developmental phases described in 2nd Peter 1:3-5 and are able to express love for others and God with no strings attached. This is true unconditional love! When we give unconditional love, we eventually receive unconditional love back, and our basic needs are really met. Because we are now more interested in meeting the needs of others, we experientially "die to ourselves." In other words, we are no longer as concerned about our own needs. When we get our eyes off of ourselves and love others, this leads to real satisfaction. As we continue around this chart, our selfishness (attempts to meet the needs of the self) decreases and we experience greater and greater freedom from the concern to meet our own needs. We also experience increased love and desire to meet the needs of others. Eventually, our entire life is motivated by love and a desire to serve the One who set us free—God.

Simplex Blockages to Salvation

The reader might object that he knows few Christians who have truly arrived at this state of freedom and love. We must all realize by now that there can be many roadblocks along this highway of salvation by faith. While it is the Holy Spirit's job to orchestrate this process of salvation by faith, it is Satan's objective to frustrate this plan of salvation at every turn; and he is quite effective in accomplishing this in many of our lives.

Referring to the chart on the following page (which expands on the chart entitled Christian Development Leading to Love that we have just reviewed), some of the most effective blockages (represented by X's) are unresolved emotional problems, fears of rejection, failure, shame, and punishment, and ego defenses established to alleviate the accompanying negative emotions. The motivation to meet our needs is diverted into a desire just to be emotionally safe. This is neurosis, as described on Dr. Crabb's second chart. Any potential that we have for growing in God or achieving God's call in our lives is effectively blocked.

At the next juncture, these fears and ego defenses can draw us off the road of salvation by faith, by influencing us to try to meet our needs through the worldly means of the flesh. We might attempt to meet our needs by trying to secure a lot of money, a college education or the right mate. The result is a return to one of Dr. Crabb's worldly charts, but worldly methods cannot bring long-term wholeness. The result will be identical to that of the consequences produced by the world's methods—despair, dysfunctional relationships, selfishness and addictions.

Even after we have reached our goal of meeting our needs through God's principles, we can be tempted with pride to take credit for our accomplishments. If we fall to this temptation, we will find that our accomplishments will no longer provide the real satisfaction that we are seeking.

Relationships problems are another source of blockages to wholeness. In 1st John 4:20 it asks the question, "How is it possible that we can say that we love God and hate our brother?" Our relationship with the body of Christ here on earth is our main support system for the process of salvation. If we forsake the church, we will no longer have the support of other Christians or God's method of perfecting the saints. The Bible suggests that even our prayers are hindered when we hold onto offenses (1 Peter 3:7) and that we will not be forgiven if we refuse to forgive (Matthew 6:15). The majority of instruction in the Bible deals with relationships. Faith itself is a trusting relationship with God. Unfortunately, for some, each of us starts with an image of God primarily based upon our relationship with our parents. When our relationships with our parents were negative ones, developing faith in God can be difficult. Whatever the case, our Godly achievements feel hollow and fail to satisfy us if we are embroiled in relationship problems.

Worry is simply an attempt to feel in control by focusing our thoughts on our problems. It is really unbelief expressed in our thoughts. The Bible contains numerous injunctions concerning the need to renew our minds and to have the mind of Christ. (Romans 12:2, 16) We are not affected by our experiences but by how we evaluate them. "For as he thinketh in his heart, so [is] he:..." (Proverbs 23:7) Worry can dampen any satisfaction that we feel in life.

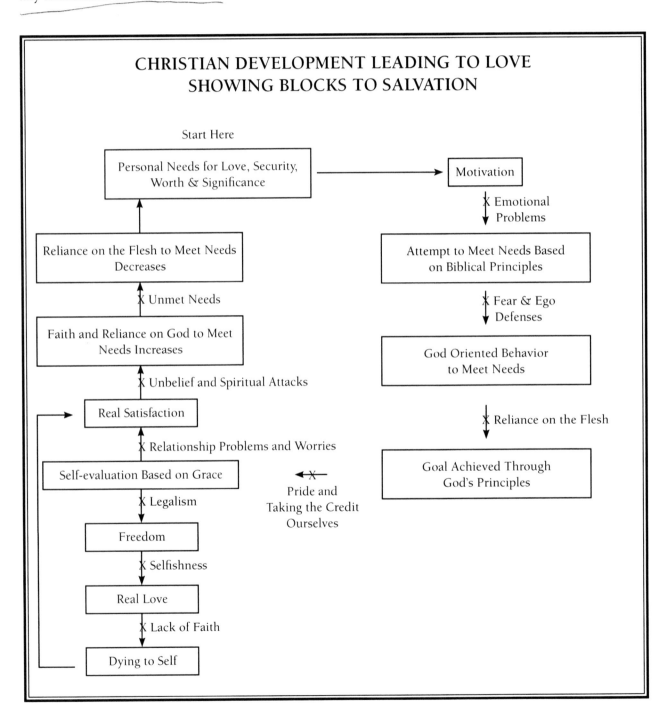

CHRISTIAN DEVELOPMENT LEADING TO LOVE SHOWING BLOCKS TO SALVATION

Start Here

Personal Needs for Love, Security, Worth & Significance → Motivation

X Emotional Problems

Reliance on the Flesh to Meet Needs Decreases

X Unmet Needs

Faith and Reliance on God to Meet Needs Increases

X Unbelief and Spiritual Attacks

Real Satisfaction

X Relationship Problems and Worries

Self-evaluation Based on Grace

X Legalism

Freedom

X Selfishness

Real Love

X Lack of Faith

Dying to Self

Attempt to Meet Needs Based on Biblical Principles

X Fear & Ego Defenses

God Oriented Behavior to Meet Needs

X Reliance on the Flesh

Goal Achieved Through God's Principles

X Pride and Taking the Credit Ourselves

Next, our salvation can be blocked by spiritual attacks. In most cases, this area of attack is stronger in people who have opened themselves up to attack through involvement in New Age or occult practices. We must remember, "We fight not against flesh and blood" (Ephesians 6:12) and that most psychological problems also have a spiritual component. The different weaknesses of the flesh make us more vulnerable to spiritual attack. Unbelief and spiritual attacks can challenge our trust and reliance on God. If we can no longer trust God because we feel He has let us down, our spiritual growth stops. Without faith, we are no better off than an unbeliever is.

The key to finding real freedom and love is our ability to perceive ourselves through the eyes of God and see ourselves as He does—with unmerited favor and love. Legalism is an attempt to gain God's favor through our works for Him. If we try again to please Him by what we do and fail to accept His unconditional love for us, we fall from grace and will again find ourselves in bondage to the law. This precludes any possibility of freedom and the experience of real love. Of course, fearing that our own needs will not be met and focusing on them will stop any progress in the process of dying to our selfish nature and thus dash any hope of a full and abundant life.

Complex Blockages to Salvation

Probably the most difficult blockages to the process of salvation by faith are complex ones. These are problems that block the process of salvation at a number of points and, in some cases, pervade the whole person. Dealing with these problems is extremely difficult unless they are understood in depth. I believe that this is one of the major weaknesses of biblical counseling today. Unfortunately, in most cases, these problems are not easily treated by the application of simple biblical truth. In some cases well-meaning pastors or biblical counselors, who do not really understand the issues involved, send wives back to "submit" to violent husbands or tell addicts just to try harder. With a deeper understanding of the Scriptures as provided by biblical models, domestic violence can be resolved and addicts can effectively recover.

Unfortunately, the church today knows little about many of these complex difficult-to-solve blockages to the process of salvation. One of these prevalent in America today is codependency. I define codependency as "excessive dependence or independence on people or things." It accounts for most of the problems in families today. It varies from mild dysfunction to the full range of mental illness, especially personality disorders. The Bible calls codependency idolatry, because these people are relying too much on themselves or others to meet their deepest needs instead of God. Based on my experience, this root problem accounts for over half of all current divorces, causes untold damage in our churches, and is the foundation of most addictions. Yet some even view many of the symptoms of codependency as Christian virtues. This is because codependents are many times the hardest and most talented workers in the church. It is probably the most predominant complex problem discussed in the Bible, yet most pastors do not even have a clear understanding of what codependency means. Lust, especially as it is carried out in fornication and sexual addiction, is another major problem in the church. Homosexuality, which I understand as a combination of identity confusion and sexual addiction, is difficult for most pastors to deal with, because it has such a strong spiritual force associated with it. In attempting to assist individuals dealing with grief, most Christians do exactly what the Bible tells us not to do: they attempt to defend God. (For more information on Bible models for dealing with these and many other complex problems, see my book *Transformation!*)

Finally, the most difficult problems to treat are mental disorders, especially those categorized as psychosis. These are not well understood even among psychiatrists and psychologists who specialize in treating them. I have found that many of these disorders are more severe cases of some of the complex problems already listed. Others originate from actual physical damage to the brain or significant imbalances in brain chemistry. Because many of these disorders are biologically based, improvement is usually only possible through long-term counseling, medication, and the power of the Spirit. "For with God nothing shall be impossible." (Luke 1:37)

Deeply-rooted Problems

We must remember that underlying our sin problem (or lack of wholeness) as well as most blockages to the process of salvation by faith, is our desire to meet our basic psychological needs through the flesh. At the root of these problems is simply our attempt to meet our need for worth, significance, security and love, without God. I define deeply rooted problems as those that are directly related to need deficits in the life of the client. These problems are extremely resistant to change unless the underlying root of the problems is dealt with directly. Otherwise, it is like trying to kill a dandelion by stomping on the leaves. As long as the root remains, it will rapidly blossom again and eventually permeate the entire lawn. As we shall see in the chapters to come, the solution for all of these problems requires meeting these basic psychological needs through faith.

PART III

Understanding Biblical Faith

Chapter 6

The Principles of Faith

As we have already seen, faith is the very basis of the salvation process, and the means for activating the spiritual power for change. As we observed in the life of Abraham, each of us progresses from "glory to glory" as we win the trials of faith in our lives. (2 Corinthians 3:18) At the very bottom of every solution is faith that God will meet our needs and deliver us from our fears. Faith is the "credit" limit on our Christian "credit card." We can only expect God to meet our needs to the degree we are willing to trust Him. Consequently, a clear understanding of the principles of faith and the development of faith is essential.

Many excellent books have been written in the past discussing the issues of faith. It is not my intent to cover all aspects of this extremely important topic in this book, but to provide a summary of the principles of faith directly from the Bible. Unfortunately, many discourses on faith have left us without a simple, clear understanding of what faith is and how it can be concretely applied in the lives of believers. We have already learned that the process of salvation is dependent on faith and that our progress depends on winning the trials of our faith in our lives. In the remainder of this chapter, I will present a brief explanation of the biblical principles of faith and suggest an analogy of a courtroom trial that I believe will make this sometimes-confusing subject clearly understood.

The Bible suggests a powerful analogy concerning faith, which is based on legal proceedings. Our fight to develop and maintain faith in our lives is similar to the struggle of a jury (our mind, emotions, will and spirit) to reach a verdict. In this trial, we have an advocate (defense lawyer—Jesus) and an accuser (prosecutor—Satan). Please refer to the chart at the end of this section for a correlation of the principles of faith and the steps that are taken in the legal process.

1 Pe 1:7 That the trial of your faith, being much more precious than of gold that perisheth, though it be tried with fire, might be found unto praise and honour and glory at the appearing of Jesus Christ:

1 Jo 2:1 My little children, these things write I unto you, that ye sin not. And if any man sin, we have an advocate with the Father, Jesus Christ the righteous:

Re 12:10 And I heard a loud voice saying in heaven, Now is come salvation, and strength, and the kingdom of our God, and the power of his Christ: for the accuser of our brethren is cast down, which accused them before our God day and night.

1. Faith is the inner conviction that something will happen or that it has already occurred. The Bible says that faith is the "substance of hope" and the "evidence of things not seen." It is because of our faith that we believe that something is true. It is the conviction of the reality of something that has not been seen and is based on evidence similar to that presented in a courtroom. Some types of court evidence include a person's testimony of what they have seen or experienced, something written down or recorded, or physical exhibits. The role of a lawyer is to convince the jury about things that they have not seen.

Heb 11:1 Now faith is the substance of things hoped for, the evidence of things not seen.

2. <u>Natural evidence can lead us to believe after the fact, but God desires for us to have faith based on His Word, before something actually occurs.</u> Faith can be based on our senses or it can be based on the Word of God. One might be termed natural faith and the other supernatural faith. Natural faith is limited by the things we can sense. It is okay, unless it contradicts the Word of God, which must provide the strongest type of evidence in our lives since God cannot lie. An example of natural faith is the faith we exercise when we sit in a chair. We believe it will hold us because we have previously experienced that type of chair holding our weight.

Jo 20:27 Then saith he to Thomas, Reach hither thy finger, and behold my hands; and reach hither thy hand, and thrust it into my side: and be not faithless, but believing.

28 And Thomas answered and said unto him, My Lord and my God.

29 Jesus saith unto him, Thomas, because thou hast seen me, thou hast believed: blessed are they that have not seen, and yet have believed.

3. <u>Supernatural faith in God's Word allows us to act before we see the result hoped for, trusting in God for the outcome.</u> Supernatural faith is based on the Word of God or supernatural revelation and believes that it is possible to accomplish things that supercede natural laws. An example of supernatural faith was demonstrated when Peter, the disciple of Jesus, walked on water. If our faith in the Word of God is strong enough, it may cause us to act in the face of contrary physical evidence. Supernatural faith counts things done, before they are actually manifested in the physical realm.

Ro 10:14 How then shall they call on him in whom they have not believed? and how shall they believe in him of whom they have not heard? and how shall they hear without a preacher?

15 And how shall they preach, except they be sent? as it is written, How beautiful are the feet of them that preach the gospel of peace, and bring glad tidings of good things!

16 But they have not all obeyed the gospel. For Esaias saith, Lord, who hath believed our report?

17 So then faith [cometh] by hearing, and hearing by the word of God.

Heb 11:17 By faith Abraham, when he was tried, offered up Isaac: and he that had received the promises offered up his only begotten son,

18 Of whom it was said, That in Isaac shall thy seed be called:

19 Accounting that God was able to raise him up, even from the dead; from whence also he received him in a figure.

4. <u>Faith is the means of receiving salvation.</u> We should avoid the common misinterpretation of Ephesians 2:8 that God gives us a gift of faith to be saved. The gift that God gives us in this verse is salvation, not faith. This is clear from the context (printed along with this verse) and from the New Living Translation (NLT) of this same verse. God sends preachers who give us His Word and the Holy Spirit draws us to believe the Word, but we must choose to have faith and to grow and strengthen our faith. Of course, there is a supernatural gift of faith, one of the nine gifts of the Spirit. (1 Corinthians 12:9) In this discussion, I wish to make it clear that if our faith is weak or fails, it is our responsibility, not God's responsibility.

Eph 2:4 But God, who is rich in mercy, for his great love wherewith he loved us,

5 Even when we were dead in sins, hath quickened us together with Christ, (by grace ye are saved;)

8 For by grace are ye saved through faith; and that not of yourselves: [it is] the gift of God: (AV)

Eph 2:8 God saved you by his special favor when you believed. And you can't take credit for this; it is a gift from God. (NLT)

5. <u>Faith is the key to supernatural manifestations and answered prayer</u>.

Mt 21:21 Jesus answered and said unto them, Verily I say unto you, If ye have faith, and doubt not, ye shall not only do this [which is done] to the fig tree, but also if ye shall say unto this mountain, Be thou removed, and be thou cast into the sea; it shall be done.

22 And all things, whatsoever ye shall ask in prayer, believing, ye shall receive.

6. <u>Righteousness or wholeness is through faith</u>.

Ro 3:22 Even the righteousness of God [which is] by faith of Jesus Christ unto all and upon all them that believe: for there is no difference:

For all have sinned, and come short of the glory of God;

7. <u>Victory over our problems comes through faith</u>.

1 Jo 5:4 For whatsoever is born of God overcometh the world: and this is the victory that overcometh the world, [even] our faith.

8. <u>Without faith, we cannot please God</u>. This is because in order to please Him, we must trust Him. Without trusting Him to meet our needs, we will be motivated to meet our own needs; and that which is motivated by selfishness can never please God.

Heb 11:6 But without faith it is impossible to please him: for he that cometh to God must believe that he is, and that he is a rewarder of them that diligently seek him.

9. <u>Everything that is not of faith is sin</u>. As we have discussed before, without faith, our motivation will be biased toward ourselves, and this bias will lead us to judge and act to meet our needs, not the needs of others. Any coming short of doing what is right is sin.

Ro 14:23 And he that doubteth is damned if he eat, because [he eateth] not of faith: for whatsoever [is] not of faith is sin.

10. <u>The promises of God are received through faith and patience</u>.

Heb 6:12 That ye be not slothful, but followers of them who through faith and patience inherit the promises.

11. <u>Faith is the beginning of the process of Christian maturity</u>.

2 Pe 1:4 Whereby are given unto us exceeding great and precious promises: that by these ye might be partakers of the divine nature, having escaped the corruption that is in the world through lust.

5 And beside this, giving all diligence, add to your faith virtue; and to virtue knowledge;

6 And to knowledge temperance; and to temperance patience; and to patience godliness;

7 And to godliness brotherly kindness; and to brotherly kindness charity.

8 For if these things be in you, and abound, they make you that ye shall neither be barren nor unfruitful in the knowledge of our Lord Jesus Christ.

12. <u>Faith begins when we hear the promises of the Word of God spoken to us</u>. In the verse below, the Greek that is translated as hearing is *rhema*, the spoken Word. It means, "that which is or has been uttered by the living voice." This is like the giving of evidence in a courtroom. First, we must learn to trust in God's Word, the Bible. As we read it, we begin to understand what God is saying to us. When this is quickened by the Holy Spirit, it becomes *rhema* to us. Of course, God also speaks to us through spiritual intuition, visions, prophecy and those in authority over us in the church. The Word of God is the strongest evidence that exists in the universe. In our courtroom analogy, it is the law. Whatever the God or King of the universe says, in verbal or written form, is His law. The Word of God is this law on which the case for faith must be built.

Ro 10:8 But what saith it? The word is nigh thee, [even] in thy mouth, and in thy heart: that is, the word of faith, which we preach;

17 So then faith [cometh] by hearing, and hearing by the word of God.

13. <u>We must accept what is spoken and believe it, or it will do us no good</u>. God may speak to us in many ways, but we must know that He has spoken a particular word to us so that we have a foundation on which to base our faith. It is not good enough to simply read a promise in the Bible and decide we want it. We must be convinced that this particular promise from God applies to us in particular. When we know that God has spoken this word to us and it applies to our situation, it becomes *rhema* to us. In a court case, we must first find a law, and then prove that the law applies to our case, or we do not have any legal basis for the trial.

Heb 4:2 For unto us was the gospel preached, as well as unto them: but the word preached did not profit them, not being mixed with faith in them that heard [it].

14. <u>It is the drawing of the Holy Spirit and what Jesus has done for us that helps us want to accept and believe the Word of God</u>. Our members of the jury (our mind, emotions, will and spirit) must choose to want to do the will of God and bring a valid, just verdict to God, the judge.

Jo 6:44 No man can come to me, except the Father which hath sent me draw him: and I will raise him up at the last day.

12:32 And I, if I be lifted up from the earth, will draw all [men] unto me.

15. <u>But we are the ones who must decide to believe and to live by faith</u>. We are the jury that must decide the verdict concerning our lives and each specific case. <u>Our spirit is the foreman of the jury and our mind, emotions and will are the members of the jury that help decide the case.</u>

Heb 10:38 Now the just shall live by faith: but if [any man] draw back, my soul shall have no pleasure in him.

39 But we are not of them who draw back unto perdition; but of them that believe to the saving of the soul.

16. <u>We must believe in our heart</u>. For the jury to convict, ideally, it should reach a unanimous decision. At the very least, all members of the jury should be convinced "beyond a reasonable doubt."

   Ro 10:9: That if thou shalt confess with thy mouth the Lord Jesus, and shalt believe in thine heart that God hath raised him from the dead, thou shalt be saved.

   10 For with the heart man believeth unto righteousness; and with the mouth confession is made unto salvation.

17. <u>The heart consists of the inner-most being of the man</u>. The heart can refer to the mind, emotions, will and/or spirit. These make up the jury. The agreement of these four provides a solid foundation for faith. The verses below make it clear that our heart can consist of any or all of the four parts of our inner being.

   a. <u>Mind</u>. Matthew 13:15 For this people's heart is waxed gross, and [their] ears are dull of hearing, and their eyes they have closed; lest at any time they should see with [their] eyes, and hear with [their] ears, and should <u>understand with [their] heart,</u> and should be converted, and I should heal them.

   b. <u>Emotions</u>. Mark 12:33 And to <u>love him with all the heart,</u> and with all the understanding, and with all the soul, and with all the strength, and to love [his] neighbour as himself, is more than all whole burnt offerings and sacrifices.

   c. <u>Will</u>. Hebrews 4:12 For the word of God [is] quick, and powerful, and sharper than any twoedged sword, piercing even to the dividing asunder of soul and spirit, and of the joints and marrow, and [is] a discerner of the thoughts and <u>intents of the heart</u>.

   d. <u>Spirit</u>. Romans 2:29 But he [is] a Jew, which is one inwardly; and circumcision [is that] of the heart, in the spirit, [and] not <u>in the letter;</u> whose praise [is] not of men, but of God.

   1 Jo 3:20 For if our <u>heart condemn us,</u> God is greater than our heart, and knoweth all things.

18. <u>It is absolutely critical that we "know" in our spirit, in order to receive from God</u>. Although it is important that we believe it in our mind, emotions, and will, faith in these members is not sufficient to bring results. None of these, by themselves, is enough to bring supernatural results. Our spirit, the foreman of the jury, must be convinced.

   1 Co 2:10 But God hath revealed [them] unto us by his Spirit: for the Spirit searcheth all things, yea, the deep things of God.

   11 For what man knoweth the things of a man, save the spirit of man which is in him? even so the things of God knoweth no man, but the Spirit of God.

   12 Now we have received, not the spirit of the world, but the spirit which is of God; that we might know the things that are freely given to us of God.

   13 Which things also we speak, not in the words which man's wisdom teacheth, but which the Holy Ghost teacheth; comparing spiritual things with spiritual.

19. <u>In order to acquire faith in our spirit, we must persevere in prayer until we know that we have the answer</u>. Our job here is to gather and present evidence to the jury—the mind, emotions, will and spirit—until it is convinced. This gathering of evidence is what John Avanzini has called "faith extenders" (1988). Persevering in praying has previously been referred to as "praying through." The process, here, is getting our faith from our mind, emotions and will into our spirit where it will

bring supernatural results. For some, this may require only one prayer. For others it might require a significant period of "praying through."

Lu 11:5 And he said unto them, Which of you shall have a friend, and shall go unto him at midnight, and say unto him, Friend, lend me three loaves;

6 For a friend of mine in his journey is come to me, and I have nothing to set before him?

7 And he from within shall answer and say, Trouble me not: the door is now shut, and my children are with me in bed; I cannot rise and give thee.

8 I say unto you, Though he will not rise and give him, because he is his friend, yet because of his importunity he will rise and give him as many as he needeth.

9 And I say unto you, Ask, and it shall be given you; seek, and ye shall find; knock, and it shall be opened unto you.

10 For every one that asketh receiveth; and he that seeketh findeth; and to him that knocketh it shall be opened.

18:1 And he spake a parable unto them to this end, that men ought always to pray, and not to faint;

2 Saying, There was in a city a judge, which feared not God, neither regarded man:

3 And there was a widow in that city; and she came unto him, saying, Avenge me of mine adversary.

4 And he would not for a while: but afterward he said within himself, Though I fear not God, nor regard man;

5 Yet because this widow troubleth me, I will avenge her, lest by her continual coming she weary me.

6 And the Lord said, Hear what the unjust judge saith.

7 And shall not God avenge his own elect, which cry day and night unto him, though he bear long with them?

8 I tell you that he will avenge them speedily. Nevertheless when the Son of man cometh, shall he find faith on the earth?

20. We can win any case in which we are accused of inadequacies or sins, because when Jesus died upon the cross, He paid the price for all of them. As our final witness, we can call Jesus to the stand to testify that all of our sins have already been paid for, since He died for them. In court terms, we cannot be tried and convicted of the same crime twice, especially if we have pleaded guilty and the fine has already been paid (by Jesus).

21. We can win even the hardest case with insurmountable evidence against us, by using what the Word of God says concerning our position in Christ. After all the evidence against us has been presented, we can declare that the person on trial has died! According to Romans Chapter 6, we have been crucified with Christ, the old person that we were is dead, and we are now part of the body of Christ. Therefore, any evidence that is presented against us concerning what we have done before we were saved can only be used to convict our "old man." But if our old man has died, these things cannot be used against our new man who is in Christ. Furthermore, Christ has not and cannot sin, so there is no evidence that can be presented against Him, and we are in Him and He is in us.

Ro 6:6 Knowing this, that our old man is crucified with him, that the body of sin might be destroyed, that henceforth we should not serve sin.

7 For he that is dead is freed from sin.

8 Now if we be dead with Christ, we believe that we shall also live with him:

9 Knowing that Christ being raised from the dead dieth no more; death hath no more dominion over him.

22. <u>After we are convinced that we know something is true in our spirit, we need to openly confess what we believe</u>. In the courtroom analogy, this is declaring the verdict. Once the jury is convinced, it will vote to convict or acquit the case. At this point, we have successfully "prayed through." Therefore, we should quit praying and start thanking God for the answer that we know we will receive, in expectation of the manifestation of the answer in the natural realm, until we finally see it. In the courtroom analogy, this manifestation is the carrying out of the sentence. Confusion seems to exist on this point. Confession is simply declaring what we believe in our spirit to be true. It is not denying that we currently have a problem, but that we have confidence that what the Word of God says is true and our problem will somehow be overcome. Negative confessions or declaring that what God said will not come to pass can undermine our faith. A careful use of the words that we speak can alleviate many misperceptions and snares to our faith. As an example, we can confess that although we still have the symptoms of a sickness, we know that we are healed. We are simply thanking God for our healing until it fully manifests in our life.

2 Co 4:13 We having the same spirit of faith, according as it is written, I believed, and therefore have I spoken; we also believe, and therefore speak;

Pr 6:2 Thou art snared with the words of thy mouth, thou art taken with the words of thy mouth.

Mr 9:24 And straightway the father of the child cried out, and said with tears, Lord, I believe; help thou mine unbelief.

23. <u>We need to act according to the faith we have</u>. If we truly believe that we have something, we will act accordingly; or we really do not have faith. If the verdict has been declared, the judge will give the sentence or penalty. If we act according to our faith, our actions put a firm foundation under this faith that will help us resist the storms that challenge our faith.

Jas 1:22 But be ye doers of the word, and not hearers only, deceiving your own selves.

2:17 Even so faith, if it hath not works, is dead, being alone.

18 Yea, a man may say, Thou hast faith, and I have works: shew me thy faith without thy works, and I will shew thee my faith by my works.

19 Thou believest that there is one God; thou doest well: the devils also believe, and tremble.

20 But wilt thou know, O vain man, that faith without works is dead?

26 For as the body without the spirit is dead, so faith without works is dead also.

Mt 7:24 Therefore whosoever heareth these sayings of mine, and doeth them, I will liken him unto a wise man, which built his house upon a rock:

25 And the rain descended, and the floods came, and the winds blew, and beat upon that house; and it fell not: for it was founded upon a rock.

26 And every one that heareth these sayings of mine, and doeth them not, shall be likened unto a foolish man, which built his house upon the sand:

27 And the rain descended, and the floods came, and the winds blew, and beat upon that house; and it fell: and great was the fall of it.

24. <u>We need only enough faith to overcome our unbelief</u>. Conviction in a court of law only requires that there must be a preponderance of evidence "beyond a reasonable doubt."

    Mt 17:20 And Jesus said unto them, Because of your unbelief: for verily I say unto you, If ye have faith as a grain of mustard seed, ye shall say unto this mountain, Remove hence to yonder place; and it shall remove; and nothing shall be impossible unto you.

25. <u>Our faith will be tried</u>. Circumstances, symptoms, negative reports from doctors, etc., may bombard our senses. These can challenge the faith that we have in our mind, emotions, will and spirit. They are simply different forms of evidence that is being presented against us. We must insure that the evidence that we have gathered for our faith is enough to overcome this negative evidence. This struggle to believe God, in spite of the negative evidence presented against us, is called the good fight of faith. Our confession and actions help us in this fight against Satan's attacks.

    Ro 4:18 Who against hope believed in hope, that he might become the father of many nations, according to that which was spoken, So shall thy seed be.

    19 And being not weak in faith, he considered not his own body now dead, when he was about an hundred years old, neither yet the deadness of Sara's womb:

    20 He staggered not at the promise of God through unbelief; but was strong in faith, giving glory to God;

    21 And being fully persuaded that, what he had promised, he was able also to perform.

26. <u>Our faith must not waver</u>. A double-minded man is one that is in conflict about what he believes between his soul—the mind, emotions or will—and his spirit. This is a locked jury or one that is constantly changing its mind about the verdict as new evidence is presented, old evidence is reviewed in the jury room, or different jury members give their input concerning the case. If the jury is unable to make a decision, it will result in a hung jury and the case may have to be retried.

    Jas 1:6 But let him ask in faith, nothing wavering. For he that wavereth is like a wave of the sea driven with the wind and tossed.

    7 For let not that man think that he shall receive any thing of the Lord.

    8 A double minded man [is] unstable in all his ways.

    4:8 Draw nigh to God, and he will draw nigh to you. Cleanse [your] hands, [ye] sinners; and purify [your] hearts, [ye] double minded.

27. <u>Our lack of faith can be based on a lack of knowledge or having inadequate evidence</u>.

    Hosea 4:6 My people are destroyed for lack of knowledge: because thou hast rejected knowledge, I will also reject thee, that thou shalt be no priest to me: seeing thou hast forgotten the law of thy God, I will also forget thy children.

28. <u>Our unbelief can be based on the hardening of our hearts</u>. When our hearts are hard, we allow our own biases to prevail and stubbornly refuse even to consider the evidence that has been presented because our mind is already made up.

    Heb 4:2 For unto us was the gospel preached, as well as unto them: but the word preached did not profit them, not being mixed with faith in them that heard it.

6 Seeing therefore it remaineth that some must enter therein, and they to whom it was first preached entered not in because of unbelief:

7 Again, he limiteth a certain day, saying in David, To day, after so long a time; as it is said, To day if ye will hear his voice, harden not your hearts.

29. Unbelief can be based on trusting our physical senses more than we trust the Word of God. This is actually a lack of faith in God's Word and demonstrates a lack of trust in God Himself.

   Jo 20:24 But Thomas, one of the twelve, called Didymus, was not with them when Jesus came.

   25 The other disciples therefore said unto him, We have seen the Lord. But he said unto them, Except I shall see in his hands the print of the nails, and put my finger into the print of the nails, and thrust my hand into his side, I will not believe.

30. We might not believe because we feel we are too unworthy for God to meet our needs or answer our requests. Peter saw himself as a sinful man, but Jesus accepted him as he was. God accepts us and meets our needs based on what Jesus did for us on the cross, not on the basis of our own works or performance.

   Lu 5:8 When Simon Peter saw it, he fell down at Jesus' knees, saying, Depart from me; for I am a sinful man, O Lord.

31. Faith can be confused with hope. Hope expects something to occur in the future, while faith expects it to happen now. The following verse makes it clear that we are to expect the grace of God right now but that we are to hope to be fully conformed to the glory of God in the future. Some people are always hoping for something to happen in the future, but not expecting it today. If we never move from hope to faith, we will never acquire the promises of God.

   Ro 5:2 By whom also we have access by faith into this grace wherein we stand, and rejoice in hope of the glory of God.

32. A supernatural battle occurs between the time we have heart faith and when we see the manifestation of what we have believed for in the natural realm. This is the time of the appeal. It is Satan's plan to try to get us to doubt our faith so that what we have believed for will never happen. Even after we know that we have the answer, if we lose faith that it will happen, it will never occur. The verdict in this case has been successfully appealed. We see an example of this delay between the time Daniel prayed and when he received the answer to his prayer. This is the time delay between the sentencing, and when the sentence is actually carried out.

   Da 10:12 Then said he unto me, Fear not, Daniel: for from the first day that thou didst set thine heart to understand, and to chasten thyself before thy God, thy words were heard, and I am come for thy words.

   13 But the prince of the kingdom of Persia withstood me one and twenty days: but, lo, Michael, one of the chief princes, came to help me; and I remained there with the kings of Persia.

33. At some point, we must reach an assurance that the manifestation of our faith goal will occur at a particular time or when a particular event occurs. This has been called the "point of contact." In the court analogy, this occurs when, after all appeals have been exhausted, the judge declares that the sentence will begin. In the case of the woman with the issue of blood, her point of contact was touching the hem of Jesus' garment.

Mt 9:20 And, behold, a woman, which was diseased with an issue of blood twelve years, came behind him, and touched the hem of his garment:

21 For she said within herself, If I may but touch his garment, I shall be whole.

22 But Jesus turned him about, and when he saw her, he said, Daughter, be of good comfort; thy faith hath made thee whole. And the woman was made whole from that hour.

34. Even after the manifestation has occurred, we must still hold onto our faith and act on it by giving witness to what God has done; or the manifestation can be lost. Although Peter's faith had clearly manifested in his ability to walk on water, when it was challenged by the natural circumstances of the storm and waves, he sank. Just because the convicted person begins a jail sentence does not necessarily mean that he will have to remain in jail for the entire sentence. Periodically, parole hearings are held, requiring the hearing of evidence that the conviction and sentence should be fully executed.

Mt 14:29 And he said, Come. And when Peter was come down out of the ship, he walked on the water, to go to Jesus.

30 But when he saw the wind boisterous, he was afraid; and beginning to sink, he cried, saying, Lord, save me.

31 And immediately Jesus stretched forth [his] hand, and caught him, and said unto him, O thou of little faith, wherefore didst thou doubt?

35. Our faith increases when, after patiently waiting for the manifestation of what we have prayed for, we receive what was promised. When the apostles asked Jesus how to increase their faith, he did not suggest they pray for it. Through a parable, He suggested that they do their duty as servants first and trust Him to pay them later. Just as employers expect us to work before we are paid, God expects us to step out and act according to our faith before it is manifested. After we do this, we will see the manifestation of our faith, and our faith will be increased. When our legal system justly tries, sentences, and carries out the penalty, our faith in the judge and our justice system is increased.

Lu 17:5 And the apostles said unto the Lord, Increase our faith.

6 And the Lord said, If ye had faith as a grain of mustard seed, ye might say unto this sycamine tree, Be thou plucked up by the root, and be thou planted in the sea; and it should obey you.

7 But which of you, having a servant plowing or feeding cattle, will say unto him by and by, when he is come from the field, Go and sit down to meat?

8 And will not rather say unto him, Make ready wherewith I may sup, and gird thyself, and serve me, till I have eaten and drunken; and afterward thou shalt eat and drink?

9 Doth he thank that servant because he did the things that were commanded him? I trow not.

10 So likewise ye, when ye shall have done all those things which are commanded you, say, We are unprofitable servants: we have done that which was our duty to do.

36. We have dead faith when our will stops us from acting in accordance with the faith in the rest of our heart.

Jas 2:17 Even so faith, if it hath not works, is dead, being alone.

8 Yea, a man may say, Thou hast faith, and I have works: shew me thy faith without thy works, and I will shew thee my faith by my works.

19 Thou believest that there is one God; thou doest well: the devils also believe, and tremble.

20 But wilt thou know, O vain man, that faith without works is dead?

21 Was not Abraham our father justified by works, when he had offered Isaac his son upon the altar?

37. <u>We have perfect or mature faith when we are able to act on our faith and our confidence does not waver</u>.

Jas 2:22 Seest thou how faith wrought with his works, and by works was faith made perfect?

38. <u>We have little faith when the faith in our spirit is easily overcome by our circumstances and the fear in our soul</u>.

Mt 6:30 Wherefore, if God so clothe the grass of the field, which to day is, and to morrow is cast into the oven, [shall he] not much more [clothe] you, O ye of little faith?

8:26 And he saith unto them, Why are ye fearful, O ye of little faith? Then he arose, and rebuked the winds and the sea; and there was a great calm.

14:31 And immediately Jesus stretched forth [his] hand, and caught him, and said unto him, O thou of little faith, wherefore didst thou doubt?

39. <u>We have great faith when our faith is so strong that no circumstance or natural evidence can shake it</u>.

Mt 8:8 The centurion answered and said, Lord, I am not worthy that thou shouldest come under my roof: but speak the word only, and my servant shall be healed.

9 For I am a man under authority, having soldiers under me: and I say to this man, Go, and he goeth; and to another, Come, and he cometh; and to my servant, Do this, and he doeth it.

10 When Jesus heard [it], he marvelled, and said to them that followed, Verily I say unto you, I have not found so great faith, no, not in Israel.

15:25 Then came she and worshipped him, saying, Lord, help me.

26 But he answered and said, It is not meet to take the children's bread, and to cast it to dogs.

27 And she said, Truth, Lord: yet the dogs eat of the crumbs which fall from their masters' table.

28 Then Jesus answered and said unto her, O woman, great [is] thy faith: be it unto thee even as thou wilt. And her daughter was made whole from that very hour.

40. <u>We have sufficient faith when we have at least enough faith to overcome our unbelief</u>. A grain of mustard seed is an extremely small seed.

Lu 17:6 And the Lord said, If ye had faith as a grain of mustard seed, ye might say unto this sycamine tree, Be thou plucked up by the root, and be thou planted in the sea; and it should obey you.

41. <u>Saving or effective faith is faith that meets all the requirements already discussed and brings the desired result</u>.

Ro 10:9 That if thou shalt confess with thy mouth the Lord Jesus, and shalt believe in thine heart that God hath raised him from the dead, thou shalt be saved.

10 For with the heart man believeth unto righteousness; and with the mouth confession is made unto salvation.

11 For the scripture saith, Whosoever believeth on him shall not be ashamed.

12 For there is no difference between the Jew and the Greek: for the same Lord over all is rich unto all that call upon him.

13 For whosoever shall call upon the name of the Lord shall be saved.

42. <u>We have no faith when we do not believe in the soul—mind, emotions, will—or the spirit</u>. Instead of faith in this instance, the disciples were filled with fear and doubt. Another way to look at it is that they had no faith in Jesus and a tremendous amount of faith that the storm would result in their deaths.

Mr 4:38 And he was in the hinder part of the ship, asleep on a pillow: and they awake him, and say unto him, Master, carest thou not that we perish?

39 And he arose, and rebuked the wind, and said unto the sea, Peace, be still. And the wind ceased, and there was a great calm.

40 And he said unto them, Why are ye so fearful? how is it that ye have no faith?

43. <u>When we lack faith, fear will overwhelm us; and we will be unable to carry out the directions of God</u>.

Nu 13:31 But the men that went up with him said, We be not able to go up against the people; for they [are] stronger than we.

32 And they brought up an evil report of the land which they had searched unto the children of Israel, saying, The land, through which we have gone to search it, [is] a land that eateth up the inhabitants thereof; and all the people that we saw in it [are] men of a great stature.

33 And there we saw the giants, the sons of Anak, [which come] of the giants: and we were in our own sight as grasshoppers, and so we were in their sight.

44. <u>We are to use faith, not performance, approval, or worldly gain as the measuring rod of our value to the Kingdom of God</u>. Because of the confusing way that the King James Translation renders the following verse, it has led to an unfortunate misunderstanding even among well-respected pastors. The context of the rest of this verse is clearly that of measuring our value to God, not obtaining a small bit (measure) of faith to be saved (as many use this verse). The word translated as measure is *metron*, which means primarily, "an instrument for measuring." The New Living Translation interprets it this way, "As God's messenger, I give each of you this warning: Be honest in your estimate of yourselves, measuring your value by how much faith God has given you."

Ro 12:3 For I say, through the grace given unto me, to every man that is among you, not to think [of himself] more highly than he ought to think; but to think soberly, according as God hath dealt to every man the measure of faith.

45. <u>Jesus is the one who pioneered the life of faith and is the example we should follow</u>. The following verse has often been misinterpreted from the King James Translation to suggest that it is Jesus' responsibility to begin and perfect our faith. Even some pastors and teachers have falsely interpreted this verse to mean that God is responsible for initiating and providing faith from beginning to end. The word interpreted as author is *archegos*, which means, "one that takes the lead in any thing and thus affords an example," and the word interpreted as finisher is *teleiotes*, which means,

"a perfector or one who has in his own person raised faith to its perfection and so set before us the highest example of faith." The Amplified Bible translation, which I have included below, helps to clarify the true meaning of this verse. This unfortunate interpretation of this verse by some pastors and teachers has been used by a few clients to avoid their own responsibility to develop and increase their faith and to blame God when their faith was not sufficient to provide victory in their lives.

Heb 12:2 Looking unto Jesus the author and finisher of [our] faith; who for the joy that was set before him endured the cross, despising the shame, and is set down at the right hand of the throne of God. (AV)

Heb 12:2 Looking away [from all that will distract] to Jesus, Who is the Leader and the Source of our faith [giving it maturity and perfection]. He, for the joy [of obtaining the prize] that was set before Him, endured the cross, despising and ignoring the shame, and is now seated at the right hand of the throne of God. {AMP)

If you have not already done so, please examine the chart on the following page, where I have graphically presented these truths concerning faith as they relate to the timeline of a court trial and the subsequent proceedings. It is my hope that this chart will help clarify many of these issues and help you, the reader, see the trial of your faith from a fuller perspective. It is also my hope that by now you are convinced that having faith and developing it is one of the most critical tasks that all of us have in this life. Without it, we cannot please God or be transformed and made whole. But even if you are now convinced that you have a responsibility to increase your faith in God, how is this to be done? This is the subject of the next chapter.

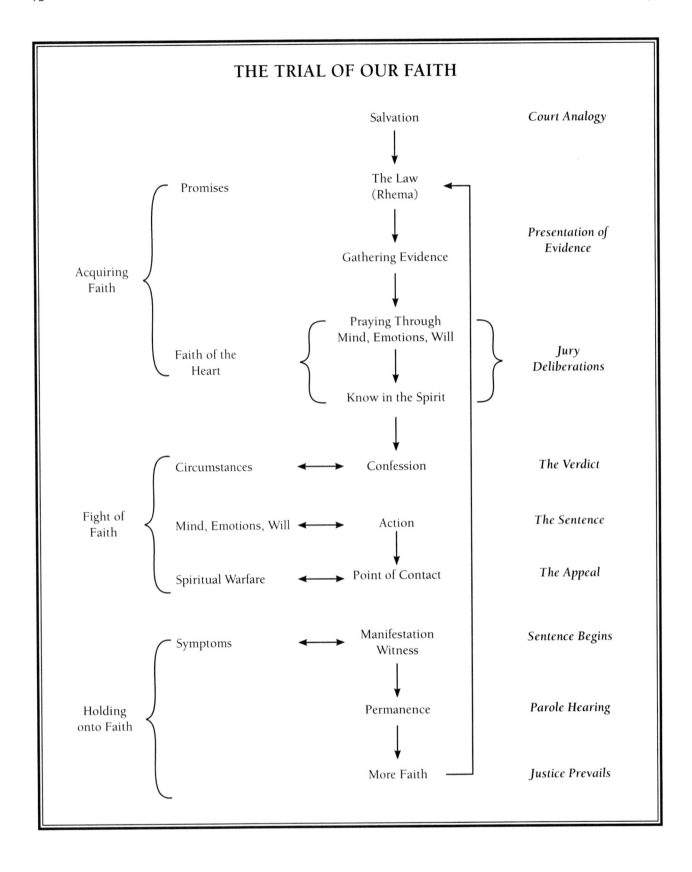

THE TRIAL OF OUR FAITH

The Principles for Increasing Faith

The Bible makes it clear that not only does God want our faith to grow, but also He wants it to grow exceedingly. Increasing our faith is especially important in our lives, because our level of faith limits what we can receive from God. It is the foundation of the entire process of salvation. It leads to our Christian maturity and it results in our ability to express unconditional love, which is the very essence of God Himself.

2 Th 1:3 We are bound to thank God always for you, brethren, as it is meet, because that your faith groweth exceedingly, and the charity (love) of every one of you all toward each other aboundeth;

If we accept that our salvation and wholeness occurs primarily by faith, then it follows that at least part of the counselor's job is building faith in the client. In the story of the exodus from Egypt, Aaron and Moses attempted to build faith in the children of Israel so that they might be able to enter the Promised Land. When their faith failed after the return of the ten spies, the children of Israel were unable to enter or conquer the land. In the same way, it is impossible for our clients to face and overcome the more significant psychological problems of their lives without sufficient faith.

Principles for Increasing Our Faith

When dealing with the growth of faith, we must realize that faith is three-dimensional: 1. We can grow our faith in intensity and strength from having no faith, to hope for the future, to weak faith, to sufficient faith, to strong faith, to great faith. 2. We can increase our faith from believing that God will work in one area of our lives to believing that He will meet all our needs. 3. We can increase our faith from residing in one part of our heart (mind, emotions, will or spirit) to filling our entire heart. Some methods for growing our faith will be primarily effective in only one dimension, while others will have a more general effect on our life of faith.

1. The primary and most important way to increase faith is to build a deep, trusting relationship with God. Sometimes people view building a personal relationship with God as a mysterious and difficult task, while, in fact, it is extremely simple. Whatever works in developing relationships with people works in our relationship with God, and whatever works with God, works with people. As an example, words of affection will help us get closer to our spouses in the same way that praise and worship moves us closer to God. In order to have a closer relationship, we have to talk to and spend time with another person. In order to get closer to God, we must spend quiet time with Him and give ourselves to prayer. Jesus made the importance of spending time in a personal relationship with Him clear when he rebuked Martha for her excessive focus on serving Him and commended Mary for just wanting to be with Him.

   Lu 10:38 Now it came to pass, as they went, that he entered into a certain village: and a certain woman named Martha received him into her house.

39 And she had a sister called Mary, which also sat at Jesus' feet, and heard his word.

40 But Martha was cumbered about much serving, and came to him, and said, Lord, dost thou not care that my sister hath left me to serve alone? bid her therefore that she help me.

41 And Jesus answered and said unto her, Martha, Martha, thou art careful and troubled about many things:

42 But one thing is needful: and Mary hath chosen that good part, which shall not be taken away from her.

Relationships are also built by working together for a common cause. This is the primary way that most men build relationships. Working with and experiencing God in the work of His kingdom helps us to get to know Him and develop a closer relationship with Him. This type of relationship development is illustrated by Jesus' training of His disciples and the principles outlined in the best selling book, *Experiencing God* (1990). In it, Blackaby explains the process of developing faith in God through working with God. When we realize that the roots of faith are trust and that trust is build most effectively through the experiences of a loving, personal relationship, it becomes clear that the development of a personal relationship with God is critical to our faith walk.

2. <u>Building a faith foundation in God's Word is required to begin a life of faith</u>. Unless the client has a strong faith in the reliability of God's Word, he will have little more than sense-based physical evidence for what he believes. Some denominations rely more heavily on the priest or pastor to interpret the Bible to the congregation than on having each member "be fully convinced in their own minds" (Romans 14:5) through personal study of the Bible. This leads to confusion because not every priest or pastor interprets every aspect of the Bible in the same way even when discussing basic Christian doctrines. Clients need something more than opinions on which to base their faith. In order to build a basic faith in the reliability of the Bible, I use the writings of Josh McDowell, especially *Evidence That Demands a Verdict, Volumes I and II* (1972, 1975). The direct physical evidence presented in these books helps the client realize that, in the Bible, he is dealing with reality, not just some unsupported myth and that he can believe what he reads.

3. <u>The client must be taught the principles of faith</u>. Faith is the evidence of things not yet seen. (Hebrews 11:1b) As we have previously discussed, this evidence can take physical, experiential, written, verbal and spiritual forms, but all evidence must be based on something. The client must be led to understand that the most reliable form of evidence is what God Himself says, since He knows everything and cannot lie. God's Word is even more reliable than what a person sees, experiences, or is told. Without this foundation, changes in circumstances will overwhelm his faith, and he will be limited in what he can receive from God.

4. <u>He must learn how to hear the voice of God and not be confused with thoughts that come from his own mind or from Satan</u>. The Bible is clear that faith comes from hearing the Word of God. (Romans 10:17) In this well-known verse, the Greek word translated as "word" is *rhema*, a specific spoken revelation from God. Some people become confused, thinking that this verse says that faith comes simply by reading the words of the Bible. Instead, this verse makes it clear that in order to build faith, the words that we read must become a revelation from God to our spirit.

5. <u>The client must make himself available to hear and receive additional revelation from God</u>. New revelation comes through hearing, studying, and meditating on the Word of God through a variety of sources. I have found that listening to audio compact disks or tapes of the Bible is especially productive for new believers. Quiet time with God and meditating on His Word are the first steps to greater faith.

6. <u>The client must understand that it is his job to build his faith</u>. Sometimes clients become confused about what they are required to do to build their faith and what God has already done for them. I remember one client who emphatically stated that God is the only one who can give faith and since his wife had died of cancer, it was God's fault for not giving them enough faith. Following this train of thought, the fact that she was not healed was God's fault and he was powerless to do anything about it. We must be reminded that potentially God has provided everything we need, but that we are required to "work out our own salvation" first in order for God to "work in us both to will and do of his good pleasure." (Philippians 2: 12, 13) God has chosen to provide salvation, to draw us by His Holy Spirit, and to bring us His Word. It is our job to believe what He has said and increase our trust and faith in Him.

7. <u>The client must gather evidence to support the faith that he wishes to have</u>. The client must bring his mind, emotions, will and spirit into agreement with what he is attempting to believe. Faith extenders are simply methods for gathering evidence to support his faith. Below is a partial list of seven useful faith extenders in each area. (For a more in-depth understanding of faith extenders see the book *Faith Extenders* (1988) by John Avanzini.)

   a. Evidence for Mental Faith
      1. Studying and building confidence in the reliability of God's Word
      2. Studying the Word of God
      3. Articles about faith that are written in books, magazines, newspapers, etc. that are thought to be reliable
      4. Records of past victories, especially answered prayers
      5. Possibility thinking
      6. Physical evidence
      7. Models, pictures, maps

   b. Evidence for Emotional Faith
      1. Our past experience and the experiences of others (e.g. support groups)
      2. Theophostic experiences that change our perceptions of the past
      3. Trusting relationships with people
      4. Agreement with others that what we believe will happen
      5. Imagining the faith event happening
      6. Reading about the victories of others; especially heroes of faith
      7. Prayer

   c. Evidence for Volitional faith (or Faith in Our Will)
      1. Fellowship with those who have faith
      2. Speaking what we believe
      3. Remembering the actions of others who believe
      4. Anticipating what God will do
      5. Studying biographies of famous Christians
      6. Acting according to the level of faith that we have
      7. Acting on our faith and attempting more difficult things in other areas

   d. Evidence for Spiritual Faith
      1. Revelation including dreams, prophecy, visions, words from God
      2. Developing a close experiential relationship with God
      3. Experiencing God's presence
      4. Meditation on the Word of God.
      5. Walking in the Spirit
      6. Praise and worship
      7. Fasting

8. <u>The client must object to and not allow negative evidence to be presented to his heart</u>. Many Christians assist Satan in destroying their faith through negative self-talk, focusing on past failures, or putting themselves down. Doing this is as foolish as presenting or allowing others to present evidence in a trial that supports the case against us. The evidence presented against our faith needs to be limited as much as possible because it leads to unbelief and doubt. In a courtroom, attorneys have a right to object to any evidence that either does not apply to the case, is clearly baseless or would unnecessarily prejudice the jury. All evidence against God's Word is erroneous and, therefore, we have a right to object to its presentation. I am not suggesting that we are to ignore reality or refuse to face the negative issues in our lives. We are simply to concentrate on all the wonderful things that God has done for us in the past and the fantastic future that is before us.

9. <u>The client should speak what he believes is true</u>. Confession is a form of acting on the Word of God and it makes the truth more real to us. When we speak the Word of God to ourselves and others, we are presenting evidence to the jury. The more we present our evidence for faith in varied and different ways, the more our mind, emotions, will and spirit will remember and accept it as fact.

Mr 11:22 And Jesus answering saith unto them, Have faith in God.

23 For verily I say unto you, That whosoever shall say unto this mountain, Be thou removed, and be thou cast into the sea; and shall not doubt in his heart, but shall believe that those things which he saith shall come to pass; he shall have whatsoever he saith.

24 Therefore I say unto you, What things soever ye desire, when ye pray, believe that ye receive [them], and ye shall have [them].

We cannot act one way and believe the opposite for long, so this method can change our minds; and our minds can affect our emotions and our will. Kenneth Hagin Sr. states, "If your confession is wrong, your believing is wrong. If your believing is wrong, your thinking is wrong. If your thinking is wrong, your understanding of the Word is wrong. Confession is faith's way of expressing itself. Faith never grows beyond your confession. Wrong confession is taking sides against God's Word. Confessing that the Word of God is not true sets up defeat at the most basic level. Right confession is witnessing for a truth that we have embraced, testifying of something we know and affirming something we believe." (Hagin, 1996) I caution clients to be careful how they confess things. Do not tell lies about your symptoms or circumstances, but tell the truth about what God has done and is doing. As an example, "I have the symptoms of a cold, but God has already provided for my healing. I'm waiting for my healing to be fully manifested."

12. <u>The client should act on the faith that he has, before expecting to see it manifested</u>. Jesus made this clear when He responded to the apostles' request to increase their faith in Luke 17:5. He stated that sufficient faith could be as small as a mustard seed—just enough to overcome unbelief. To increase faith the client must do his part first and be willing to act on what he believes before he see it. Jesus used the example of a hired servant. The servant has to do his part and do what his master asks (act on his faith) before he will have his needs met (the manifestation of his faith). The client must do the work before he gets paid.

13. <u>The building block approach to faith allows the client to begin with limited faith and develop more as the project continues</u>. Just as a building is not built in one day and by a single act of faith, faith projects can be divided into faith-sized bites. It is interesting to note that nothing is ever built without at least natural faith. First, the builder has to believe that he can build the building. Then, he must act on his faith to find investors and write a contract with an architect. Once the plans are done, he must again act on his faith to sign the contract to buy the land and build the building. If, at any point, he is not convinced the project will actually happen and he does not act, the project will stop. Finally,

in faith, he must believe that the project will be completed by a certain date and start advertising for tenants. In the same way, we can see God accomplish great things in our lives by using our faith one-step at a time and acting on it until that phase has been manifested. With a stronger faith, based on a recent victory, we can expand our vision and again act on our faith. One faith victory sets the stage and provides additional evidence to believe for the next step. (Avanzini, 1988)

14. <u>The client can join in agreement with others to strengthen his faith</u>. In more important court cases, other affected entities (such as the Federal Government, institutions that will be affected or have an interest in the outcome of the case, or others involved in the case) are allowed to file briefs as "friends of the court." These briefs give additional evidence or arguments that might influence the case. In the same way, we need to surround ourselves with church leaders and friends that are full of faith that can be trusted to strengthen our hearts and present additional evidence for our faith. Of course, we also need to avoid those who are filled with unbelief, who will work against our faith and object to any evidence they wish to present that will undermine our faith.

15. <u>He must stand in that faith even in the face of adverse circumstances or physical evidence, until he receives the manifestation of his faith</u>. This is "the good fight of faith" already discussed. When what God says contradicts what is currently manifested in his life, he must choose to believe what God says over what he sees with his eyes. This can be very difficult, but he must have faith victories in order for his faith in God to continue to increase.

In summarizing these principles, there are four basic ways to increase faith: 1. We can increase our faith through a personal relationship and an ever increasing knowledge of God. 2. We can hear, study or meditate on the Word of God until it becomes a revelation to us. 3. We can gather evidence to support or develop faith for a particular area of our lives or for a particular part of our heart. 4. Finally, we can develop faith through experience. Every time we confess our faith, act on it, and receive what we have believed God for, our faith is strengthened.

As we are assisting the client to do his part to increase his faith and to rely on God to meet his needs, it is important that we have some method for assessing the client's level of faith as it applies to a particular need and as it relates to the members of his heart: mind, emotions, will and spirit. I will develop methods for the assessment of faith in the next chapter.

How to Increase Faith

1. Build a deep, trusting relationship with God.

2. Build faith in the infallibility of God's Word.

3. Learn the principles of faith.

4. Learn to discern God's voice from other voices, thoughts, or suggestions from Satan.

5. Make ourselves available to hear and receive additional revelation from God.

6. Gather evidence to support the faith that we wish to have.

7. Do not allow negative thoughts, self-talk, or evidence.

8. Confess what we believe is true.

9. Act first, according to our faith, expecting the result.

10. Believe for smaller things first to have faith for greater things.

11. Join with others to strengthen our faith.

12. Stand in our faith against adverse circumstances until we receive our answer.

Chapter 8

Faith Assessment

When assisting our clients to develop and increase their faith, it is helpful to have some means for assessing the level of faith each client possesses at a given time. This is not as simple as it sounds because each person may possess differing amounts of faith in their mind, emotions, will and spirit for any number of subjects or circumstances. This is clear when we realize that some healing evangelists have differing amounts faith for particular illnesses and some prophets have more faith to step out in prophecy than others do.

Ro 12:6 Having then gifts differing according to the grace that is given to us, whether prophecy, let us prophesy according to the proportion of faith;

The Analysis of the Heart

Faith analysis examines problems of faith according to the area of the heart affected. This method consists of asking critically worded questions to help the client identify which part of his heart lacks adequate evidence to have the required faith. When these areas are identified, it helps the counselor to know what kind of evidence will be useful to the client to bring his heart into full agreement, in order to strengthen his faith in that particular area. This assessment will help us understand why a client is "double minded." Double-mindedness is one of the primary hindrances to the manifestation of faith. As I stated before, I believe that this term refers to a person who believes either in his spirit or soul, but not with all of his heart. I believe that the spirit and the soul are the two "minds" or areas of decision making referred to in James.

Jas 1:6 But let him ask in faith, nothing wavering. For he that wavereth is like a wave of the sea driven with the wind and tossed.

7 For let not that man think that he shall receive any thing of the Lord.

8 A double minded man is unstable in all his ways.

This need to address our whole heart becomes clear when we apply common terms to the faith problems of the soul. A person who attempts to act only according to his will is called presumptuous. A person who acts only according to faith in the emotions is said to have "feeling faith." A person who only believes in his mind has "mental ascent." All of these are well-known hindrances to seeing the manifestations of what we believe. Of course, it is possible that the client has no faith at all in a particular area.

Mind: <u>Do you logically think that it will really happen?</u> If this is not true, the client does not have faith in his mind. Lack of boundaries, low self-image, strife or injustice can provide major problems in this area. He needs to consider logically the evidence presented, especially the validity of the Word of God and his past faith victories.

Emotions: <u>Do you feel like it is true and that it will happen?</u> If the client does not believe something in his emotions, it will tend to make faith in other areas more difficult, because the faith will not seem real. This is especially true with females who are many times influenced more by their emotions. Negative experiences, fear, depression and grief can become major obstacles in this faith area. Evidence to assist in the development of feeling faith may include biographies or true stories of famous Christians, uplifting Christian movies, and praise and worship songs.

Will: <u>Are you willing to act on what you say you believe?</u> If the client is not willing to act on what he says he believes, a problem can exist in any of the areas of the heart. This is because action usually requires the full agreement of the entire heart. It is clear from his inaction that his motivation not to act exceeds his motivation to act. Consequently, in order to conclude that the primary problem is solely volitional, we must first establish that the person has solid faith in the remaining areas of their heart. One of the greatest enemies of action is the fear of failure or rejection. The most effective evidence to increase our desire to act comes from the lives and faith victories of others and from the influence of the Holy Spirit in the client's life.

Spirit: <u>Do you intuitively know and expect that it will happen?</u> If the client answers "no," we know that he is not yet convinced in his spirit. The dominance of the flesh is the major enemy to spirit faith and is many times manifested through struggles for prominence, abuse, addictions, lust or selfish desires. In these cases, the client will need to overcome the lust of the flesh and acquire more spiritual evidence and experience through fasting and the other spiritual disciplines.

Faith Ladder Analysis

The faith ladder is an effective way to measure faith versus hope. Since believing something will happen is merely hope until it is brought into the present, we can measure how close we are to having faith by measuring how soon we expect our hope to be manifested. This point is made clear by a sign in a restaurant window, which reads, "Free food tomorrow." Of course, if we enquire tomorrow, they will simply tell us to go read the sign again. Since the sign always says tomorrow, we will never get the free food. That is how hope is. Until it turns into faith that it will happen now, the manifestation never occurs.

The faith ladder provides a method of evaluating the development of faith in any component of our heart simply by rephrasing the question as I have just discussed in the previous section. However, since faith of the spirit is the critical factor that results in supernatural manifestations of faith, evaluating where the client is spiritually is usually most important. I first began using this method of evaluating faith with drug and alcohol clients. For addicts, their chance of recovery is strongly related to whether they believe they will recover and whether they were willing to do whatever it takes to recover. To evaluate an individual's faith, a faith ladder can be used. At one end of the faith ladder spectrum, we have hope. Kenneth Hagin Sr. suggested that faith is grasping the unrealities of hope and bringing them into the realm of reality (1998, page 5). After faith is achieved that one will recover, the ladder continues to measure faith for believing that sobriety, once achieved, will continue in the future. I ask a series of questions to which the client is to tell me if they "have a gut level expectation that a particular event will happen within a given time frame." I will use the addiction example.

Do you believe that God can deliver people from an addiction like yours?

Do you believe that God wants to deliver people from addictions like yours?

Do you believe that God wants to deliver you?

Do you believe that you will be delivered in 20 years?

Do you believe that you will be delivered in 5 years?

Do you believe that you will be delivered in one year?

Do you believe that you will be delivered in 6 months?

Do you believe that you will be delivered in 2 months?

Do you believe that you will be delivered in 1 month?

Do you believe that you will be delivered in 2 weeks?

Do you believe that you will be delivered tomorrow?

Do you believe that you will be delivered now?

Do you believe that you are delivered now?

Do you believe that you will remain sober for two days?

Do you believe that you will remain sober for one week?

Do you believe that you will remain sober for one month?

Do you believe that you will remain sober for six months?

Do you believe that you will remain sober for 1 year?

Do you believe that you will remain sober for 5 years?

Do you believe that you will remain sober forever?

Only when the client reaches a level of faith that he believes that the manifestation of recovery is permanent can we say that he has sufficient faith. As discussed under the principles of faith and the trial of faith, the client's faith will be tested. Strong faith is usually developed only through significant periods of testing.

Comprehensive Faith Assessment

As a more comprehensive means of analysis, we can use the faith assessment tool described at the end of this chapter. Faith Assessment is a broad, overall tool that incorporates the previous methods to determine the amount and type of faith a person has, and to identify areas which limit an effective faith walk. The amount of faith a person has may vary greatly between areas. As an example, a person might have faith to be blessed financially, yet have difficulty in believing for a physical healing. Every Christian has areas of stronger and weaker faith. To evaluate these strengths and weaknesses, we must first have a way of measuring faith. As we have already discussed, it is faith in the human spirit that is required to see results. However, our spirits are so intertwined with our souls that an in-depth understanding of faith requires examining it in all aspects of the heart. This assessment tool gives us a three-dimensional picture of the client's faith, which includes:

1. The area in which he is attempting to believe.
2. The level of the development of his faith in that area
3. If he does not have sufficient faith in that area, the component of the heart in which faith is lacking.

In my experience, the faith life of some clients is so low that they are unable to hear from God or see any manifestation of faith in their lives. This can lead to devastation, especially when we realize that it is the "shield of faith" that should provide a hedge of protection around them and stop the arrows of their negative thought-life. This Faith Assessment is provided here so that it can be easily reproduced for use. I sometimes use it when I suspect that a lack of faith is one of the major factors underlying dysfunction. I repeat its use to track clients' progress as their faith grows. Please examine the Faith Assessment in detail on the following page.

Faith Assessment

Assess the strength of your faith by answering the following questions using the faith ladder below. As an example, if you <u>know in your heart</u> and expect that an event will be physically manifested in one month, you should enter 6, or if an event has already occurred and you know that it will continue for your lifetime you should enter 10. Answer the questions based on what you know in your heart, not what you only hope will happen (presumption), believe in your mind (mental ascent), or feel (feeling faith). To "know" means that <u>when you think about that physical event in that particular time period</u> you expect the event to have physically occurred by that time. Do not answer questions as to what God says or "speaking that which is not as through it were," but what <u>you anticipate actually manifested</u> in your life at a particular time. For those questions where you could not answer a 10, indicate which area or areas of your heart is lacking in faith agreement: S = don't "know it" in your spirit. M = don't think it will happen. E = don't <u>feel</u> it will happen. W = faith not strong enough to act on. On lines 23 – 25 fill in any additional areas of faith that are important to you but have not been covered.

0. It will never happen
1. God can make it happen.
2. God wants to and does it for people.
3. In 20 years, it will happen.
4. In 5 years, it will happen.
5. In 1 year, it will happen.
6. In one month, it will happen.
7. It has happened now.
8. It has happened and will continue to be true one month from now.
9. It has happened and will continue to be true 5 years from now.
10. It has happened and it will always be true.

_____ 1.   I am saved and consequently will go to Heaven.
_____ 2.   I am worthwhile even if I have accomplished nothing or others hate me or treat me badly.
_____ 3.   God will meet all my needs even if I lose my job or the economy fails.
_____ 4.   God loves and favors me no matter what I have done or how I have acted.
_____ 5.   I am important no matter how bad I fail or even if people disapprove of me.
_____ 6.   I am out of debt and prospering financially.
_____ 7.   I am in good health and have no significant health problems.
_____ 8.   I am protected from danger and significant calamities in life.
_____ 9.   I will have a long and prosperous life.
_____ 10. If I am married, my marriage will be prosperous and happy.
_____ 11. My children are saved and successful in life.
_____ 12. I have overcome my besetting sins.
_____ 13. I have overcome any and all addictions in my life.
_____ 14. I have good relationships with everyone.
_____ 15. I have received my specific call from God and am prospering in my call.
_____ 16. I have the baptism of the Holy Spirit and operate in at least one spiritual gift.
_____ 17. God has forgiven me and I have forgiven myself and others for all offenses.
_____ 18. I am favored and blessed of God in everything I do.
_____ 19. I have all the power I need, to do everything God calls me to do.
_____ 20. Anything I ask for according to God's will in Jesus' name, God will do.
_____ 21. I know that no matter what happens, or what mistakes I make, God will work it for good.
_____ 22. With God's help, I have and can overcome every problem in my life.
_____ 23. _____
_____ 24. _____
_____ 25. _____

PART IV

Understanding Root Problems

Chapter 9

Analyzing Root Problems

At the very center of our being, self or psyche are our psychological needs for self-worth, significance, security and love. Abraham Maslow is well known for his proposed hierarchy of needs. Although research has brought into question his suggestion that a person must first fulfill more basic needs, before being motivated to meet higher needs, his studies of historical and famous individuals do provide some validation of the basic needs of humans. His list includes physiological needs, safety needs, belongingness needs, esteem needs and self-actualization needs. (Morris, 1973, p. 431) His physiological needs and safety needs fall into the basic category of a need for security. His need for belongingness is primarily a need to be unconditionally loved and accepted. His esteem need is a need to see oneself as worthwhile. Finally, his self-actualization need is a need for significance in life.

In 1st John, we are told that our desire or love for earthly things and the things of God are diametrically opposed. Either we love God or we love the world with its lusts or selfish desires. We will either meet our needs through the Spirit or the flesh. One leads to doing God's will, the other passes away and is worthless.

1 Jo 2:15 Love not the world, neither the things [that are] in the world. If any man love the world, the love of the Father is not in him.

16 For all that [is] in the world, the lust of the flesh, and the lust of the eyes, and the pride of life, is not of the Father, but is of the world.

17 And the world passeth away, and the lust thereof: but he that doeth the will of God abideth for ever.

These verses also identify our basic needs. The lust of the flesh, which is our sensuous nature, is our attempt to meet our desire for love wrongly. The lust of the eyes is our desire to have worldly things and use them in an attempt to make ourselves feel secure. The pride of life is our misguided attempt to feel worthwhile and significant through our own efforts. These desires also result in most of the temptations in our lives. Eve ate of the tree of the knowledge of good and evil because it was good for food (physical need), it looked good (security need), and she thought she would be a better person if she was "wise" like God (self-worth and significance). Possibly, Adam ate of the tree out of a need for Eve's acceptance and love.

Ge 3:6 And when the woman saw that the tree was good for food, and that it was pleasant to the eyes, and a tree to be desired to make one wise, she took of the fruit thereof, and did eat, and gave also unto her husband with her; and he did eat.

No matter how we might choose to categorize these basic needs, they lie at the very center of all that motivates us and at the very heart of our self-bias or selfishness. It is our attempt through the flesh to meet these needs that leads to the desire that we have for the things of this world.

Root problems, which underlie almost all psychological problems, have a number of dimensions. On one dimension is the unmet need. Is it love, security, worth, or significance? On the second dimension is strength of the unmet need. This strength is usually determined by our perception of our need and the degree it went unfulfilled in childhood. The third dimension is the reason for the deficit. This reason can be due to neglect, active abuse, attachment style, parenting, life experiences or other issues. A series of past experiences that have gone unresolved, like abandonment, can result in strong fears and a feeling of low self-worth. Because experience is one of the strongest factors in faith, these experiences convince us that not only will we be abandoned again but that the results of that abandonment will be catastrophic. If we perceive the probable result to be catastrophic, we will act in catastrophic ways. Of course, all of us have some unmet needs in our lives, but usually these are not strong enough to paralyze us with fear or drive us to dysfunctional actions.

Our lack of faith also has a number of dimensions. First, there is the primary member of the heart that is filled with unbelief: the will, mind emotions or spirit. The problem is that we are unable to cope, due to a lack of faith that God has and will meet this need. The second is the level of hope that the problem will be successfully resolved. For example, we might have a deep need for love, which is primarily affecting our emotions, and we do not feel that we will ever or could ever become worthy of anyone else's love.

It should be made clear that our emotions are based on what we believe is true about a particular event in the past, present or future. Consequently, our emotions are usually the first tip-off that a significant problem exists. This is especially clear if we allow our emotions to affect our actions in a dysfunctional way.

Layer Caking: Determining Which Basic Needs are Involved

Layer caking is the most effective method that I use in the analysis of problems in order to understand them and find their root cause. It is based on the fact that our emotions are not derived from the first perception that we have concerning a circumstance, but by layer after layer of perceptions about what we have concluded about the previous perceptions. To "layer cake," the counselor simply asks how the client looked at the situation or what it meant to him. When the client gives his perception, the counselor asks the same basic question again to find out what the client now concludes about the last perception. Some clients have difficulty figuring out how they actually evaluated each situation. In these cases, the counselor can guess what they may have thought and ask if that is true until the client fully agrees.

I use an example to teach this process. What would usually happen if, at dinner, a wife asked her husband, "How are the peas?" Most husbands have learned from experience that this can be a dangerous question. One husband I counseled said he would lie rather than tell his wife that the peas were cold and pulpy! The problem is that typically his wife would evaluate his response as follows: Since he does not like my peas, he does not like my meal, and if he does not like my meal, he thinks I am a poor cook and does not like me. If he does not like me, he does not love me, and if he does not love me, I am worthless. Consequently, the husband may not know why, but his wife may leave the room crying if he gave her his true evaluation of the condition of the peas. In order to answer the question truthfully and not receive a negative emotional reaction, the husband needs to learn how to answer the question in a way that heads off the invalid layers of the layer cake. He should say something like this: "Honey, I love you very much and you are a great cook, but for some reason this time the peas are a bit cold and pulpy."

It is absolutely amazing how almost every situation eventually leads to one of the basic needs: worth, love, security or significance. One other aspect of this process is that layer caking can be used to find triggers for unresolved issues from the family of origin or past marriages. If a particular layer is similar to past emotional trauma, all the emotions from the past will be brought into the present and will increase the intensity of the current situation. Once the layer cake is complete, significant progress can be made by challenging the truth of each layer until the client perceives the situation in a more valid way. Consequently, this method of analysis identifies both the root cause and the lies that the client believes, which have resulted in the client's emotional response.

Identifying the Need and its Strength from Defenses

As a counselor, I have an interesting way of looking at life. I start with the presenting personality of the client. Personality is simply the sum of the methods the person has adopted to cope with the challenges of life, as he perceives them. After identifying the way the client is attempting to cope, I try to determine its function. If a man comes for counseling dressed perfectly in a $300, three-piece suit without a spot or wrinkle, I automatically ask myself the question, "What is the underlying issue that drives him to dress so perfectly?" Perfectionism is an almost automatic tip-off to a problem with worth. The level of the perfectionism is usually a measure of the strength of the underlying problem of low self-worth. The more worthless the person feels inside, the more he will do everything to perfection beyond what the average person would do. Of course, this man's perfectionism might also be due to working at a company or job that demands this level of appearance. Being critical, jealous, or judgmental also suggest someone with problems of worth. If the client feels inferior and less than others, he will try to make himself feel better by warping his perceptions about other people in an attempt to bring them down to his level. If we judge others as wrong or inferior to ourselves, we are telling ourselves that we are at least as good as or better than they are. Bragging or an excessive need for approval from others usually also indicates self-worth problems. It is also interesting when a client manifests a more twisted type of coping mechanism, where he will constantly put himself down in order to get others to tell him that he is really okay.

If we are struggling for significance, we may become very competitive or driven to accomplish things in order to prove that we are better than others are. We might envy what others have and do everything we can to get possessions or money in order to show that we are successful. Climbing to the top of the ladder to feel more important will usually manifest itself in a lack of concern for the needs of others, a disregard for their feelings and the poor treatment in close relationships. Many driven people are unable to relax even on a vacation.

Those who struggle with insecurity many times have problems with worry, anxiety, panic attacks or phobias. They may cope through an excessive need for control, a rigid life structure, or by acting as if they have all the answers. They might also become very religious and legalistic in their approach to Christianity. They usually desire to live in a black and white world without any ambiguity.

Problems with love tend to manifest themselves in codependency, jealousy, fear of abandonment, lust and the addictions of romance, relationships or sex. Attention getting, not wanting to be alone, desperation in relationships and projecting excessive neediness are also characteristic of those who are trying to cope with emptiness resulting from a perception of a lack of love. Unfortunately, attempting to analyze emotional defenses can become complex, especially in cases where the person has a number of conflicting deficits. For example, clients with a deep love deficit, but who perceive themselves as unworthy to be loved, may become loners.

The second part of this type of analysis is to determine the strength of need. Clearly, the strength of the need is usually directly related to the amount of effort expended to meet the need and the intensity of the defenses developed to protect the client from feeling unfulfilled. As an example, the codependent who has to talk with someone every day for hours, probably has a stronger need for love than one who calls her mother twice a week; and someone who becomes suicidal when her husband is going on a weeklong trip is more needy than one who has to call him every day of the trip. The stronger the defense and coping, the stronger the probable need deficit.

Determining the Cause of the Need Deficit—Historical Analysis

Probably the most usual method for determining the cause of a need deficit is the assessment of the client's early formative years in their family of origin. This type of analysis is not an attempt to find persons to blame, but it is the simple recognition that most of our personality is formed during the early years of our life. A family history or Genogram will many times reveal incidents or specific deficits that have led to the need. For example, verbal abuse or put downs, never getting the approval of a parent, favoritism in the family or rejection at school, in most cases, lead directly to problems with self-image. A child who felt abandoned, was adopted, desperately longed for parental attention or was sexually abused will usually have issues with love, acceptance or low self-worth. In almost all cases, the specific root problem or unmet need can be derived directly from neglect or active abuse in childhood, negative life experiences or from excessive attempts to meet that specific need.

Faith Focus Analysis

Once the basic need, its strength and its possible cause are determined, we can identify the area of the heart where the faith deficit exists. This is important in order to determine the approach or solution. Faith in God is always the answer, but building faith in our mind, will, emotions and spirit may take different approaches. If we lack faith in our minds, we need to identify the lies and teach ourselves biblical truth. Problems in our emotions may reflect how we perceive life or past life experiences. Our lies and perceptions require teaching, while our experiences must be overcome by re-experiencing our past through the illumination of the Holy Spirit (Theophostic Ministry) or through having new experiences that change our perceptions of these events. Our spirit can only be ministered to through spiritual means, and, of course, all of these have an effect on each other.

In the next chapters, we will discuss methods for addressing each of these need deficits through faith. Even though we humans are extremely complex, all of our behavior can ultimately be explained layer by layer as originated and motivated by our attempts to meet our four basic needs or root causes.

Chapter 10

Faith and Self-worth

An invalid evaluation of our self-worth is the root problem, or at least a major contributing factor, in almost all psychological disorders. Low self-worth results in the development of facades, hypocrisy, bragging, timidity, shyness, criticalness, large emotional swings or explosive anger. It is the underlying cause in most conflict, bitterness, lack of forgiveness, striving for supremacy, as well as some of the most devastating emotional pain. At the other extreme, thinking too highly of ourselves (which is usually an attempt to cope with low self-worth), results in pride, arrogance, feelings of entitlement and a lack of empathy toward others. The issues of self-worth are so serious that Jesus, in the Sermon on the Mount, compared verbally degrading another's worth to murder.

Mt 5:21 Ye have heard that it was said by them of old time, Thou shalt not kill; and whosoever shall kill shall be in danger of the judgment:

22 But I say unto you, That whosoever is angry with his brother without a cause shall be in danger of the judgment: and whosoever shall say to his brother, Raca, shall be in danger of the council: but whosoever shall say, Thou fool, shall be in danger of hell fire.

Unfortunately, the concepts of self-worth, self-esteem, significance and self-image have become very confused. Worth means, "the quality that renders a thing desirable or of value." Self-worth is our evaluation of our inherent value. As an example, a diamond ring has a certain inherent value even if it is broken or does not fit. A synonym might be "potential value." This should not be confused with the term self-esteem "which means, a good opinion or an overestimate of oneself," and significance which means, "having or expressing a meaning or fulfilling the intent or purpose of something." Finally, self-image is how we perceive ourselves, which may include our self-worth, significance and even how we think others evaluate us. (The Standard College Dictionary, Funk & Wagnalls, 1963)

Low self-worth affects what we will do, limits what we will try to do, and takes away the strength to do most things. I remember a story related to me by a professor at a major university. Just before graduation, a Ph.D. candidate came to the faculty and stated that she could not accept the Doctoral Degree that she had earned because she knew that she must have cheated in some way. No, she had not plagiarized her dissertation or cheated on any of the tests, but she knew that somehow she must have cheated because "she knew that she was not capable of achieving a Doctoral Degree." She was too worthless to accomplish what she had done. Although she did not say it, somehow she had to fail since that was the only way she could fulfill her inner evaluation of herself. She had made the mistake of succeeding! In a similar situation, a woman I have counseled refused to take the final course required for her Master's Degree and, therefore, was able to fail in accordance with her low self-image.

One of the most heart-wrenching instances of low self-worth that I have encountered was the wife of a verbally abusive client whose mother had been very over-protective. This client constantly looked down to avoid eye contact. She saw herself as so incompetent that she still had to have her mother come over to do her housework for her. She was still bathing her eight-year-old daughter who was now having problems in school. Without her mother's advice, she would not make any decisions. She refused to drive a car even though she had a driver's license. Although this client was clearly codependent on her mother from whom she had never separated, her feelings of inadequacy were even more predominating. Although there were no physical or mental abnormalities; because of low self-worth, her ability to cope with life was extremely impaired.

How We Develop Worldly Self-worth

Our concept of our own worth begins at a very early age. It starts with our initial contact with our mothers and is significantly impacted by how we are treated, what others say about us and how we view our performance as we compare it with others. If we are told by others how wonderful we are and we feel loved and secure, we will perceive ourselves as persons of value. If we are ignored and told that we are "idiots," we will accept that evaluation as fact. As a child, we have no other frame of reference. To us, our parents are as god and their evaluations are, without doubt, true. This is especially the case during the concrete period of development (ages 7-11) when we egocentrically believe that we control the events of our lives. If we are mistreated, we believe that we must have done something wrong. In our minds, we do not even consider the possibility that we may have an abusive or prejudiced parent, or that the problem resides in the other person.

Of course, children do not hesitate to demean their playmates in the most degrading ways and certain children inevitably become the targets of bullies, especially if they have some defect or handicap. Each class has its popular clique and its outcasts. If we are the last to be picked on a team or do not seem to have many friends, evidence mounts that we are in some way inferior to others in the class. As a general rule, the more we feel inferior, the more withdrawn we will become and the fewer friends we will have. It is a well-known fact that the more anxious we are about failing, the poorer we will perform. All this becomes a self-fulfilling cycle where those who feel valued grow in confidence and capability, and those who see themselves as worthless become more and more inadequate to face the challenges of life. Some of the worst emotional pain that we can experience comes from seeing ourselves as worthless and inferior to others.

These feelings of worthlessness automatically lead to the development of a myriad of defenses and attempts to over-compensate through perfectionism, performance and people pleasing, in order to become worthwhile in the eyes of others. These are the beginning of the patterns of dysfunction, codependency or neurosis that can even lead to mental illness. The need for worth is at the core of our being and without it, we will do whatever it takes to avoid the excruciating pain of feeling worthless.

The World's System

Unfortunately, most people struggle with self-worth problems to some degree. Many times, low self-worth underlies an excessive drive to succeed, exaggerated attempts to please people, and the overwhelming stress of life. Most secular answers provide little relief. Playing audio tapes over and over affirming that the client is a person of worth provides little help. Trying to learn to love ourselves can just lead to more self-centeredness. Helping the client understand that, just because someone treats them badly does not make them worthless, can help only to a limited degree. Support groups that provide us with reality checks and affirmation can be of some help. Developing capability and performance in a specific area can also be useful, but only to the degree that we are continually successful.

Jay Adams points out many of the pitfalls of these secular methods in his book *The Biblical View of Self-esteem, Self-love, Self image* (1986). He particularly challenges the secular idea that we must first love ourselves before we can learn to love others (as suggested by Adler and Maslow). Adams is concerned that we might go so far as to excuse ourselves from loving God and our neighbor simply because we have not been loved or have not learned to love ourselves. He quotes Matthew 6:33 to show that we are to seek first the Kingdom of God and that then all our needs will be met. He points out that seeking to love the self leads to more selfishness and more problems. The biblical implication about loving others as we love ourselves is that everyone actually does love himself already. Although a person might say that he hates himself, in fact, he is really just attempting to deflect shame.

All of us, to some degree, believe in the world's system of worth and have variations of how we evaluate the worth of others and ourselves. Some of us value position, possessions or money as trophies of our accomplishments. Other people value power, strength or beauty, and still others value moral character. All of these relate to our performance or what we believe will result in the approval of others. The Bible warns us that we will be judged by the same measure that we judge others. (Matthew 7:2) It is interesting to note how true this seems to be. Those that feel bad about themselves, usually value what they do not have and criticize others for the very faults that they have. As long as we believe the world's system, we will be driven to build our self-worth through performance, seeking the approval of others, or trying to be good. This will place us at the mercy of how we perform, how others view us and the circumstances of our lives. In fact, the world's system of worth and the things we value in others can be summed up in some fashion into a single formula: **Self-worth = performance + approval + morals**.

The Consequences of the World's System—All Feel of Little Worth Sometimes

The Bible makes it clear that the world's system is fundamentally flawed, is a lie, and does not even make logical sense. The fact that most of us have unwittingly bought into this system and live our life by it, does not make it true. Let us examine the logical consequences of this system if we believe and try to live by it.

1. The perception of our worth or value will be extremely unstable and volatile. In order to see that this is true, consider the example of President George Bush Sr. immediately after the first Gulf War. He had just defeated the fourth largest army in the world with the loss of only about 250 soldiers, he had an unheard of worldwide approval rating of 90% and he had acted so morally that he had even invited Evangelist Billy Graham to pray with him at the White House during the war. According to the world's formula for worth, he would have been considered at the least one of the most worthwhile persons on earth at that moment. However, when he lost the next election, according to this formula he would have plummeted to near the bottom of the world's self-worth ladder since he had failed to perform and had lost the approval of a majority of the American voters. Either there is something wrong with this system or we must accept the fact that our value is an extremely insecure proposition.

2. All of us will feel worthless and of little value at times in our lives. This is clear from the fact that none of us is perfect and lives our lives without experiencing some failure. In fact, it is our failures that teach us how to succeed better the next time. According to this formula, if we fail to perform or receive the approval of others, we are of little worth. Even Jesus, who was perfect, was rejected by most of the people of His time. The Bible says that we have all sinned, are unable to keep the law perfectly and have failed morally in some way. Therefore, according to the world's system, all of us are worthless at least during some periods of our lives. The result of these failures is guilt and for many, bouts with depression.

3. All of us will eventually become worthless in the eyes of the world. If our worth is dependent primarily on our performance, then it must also be true that as we age, become sick, retire or spend the remainder of our days in a nursing home, we are of little value. According to this formula, even the beloved President Ronald Reagan became worthless when he developed Alzheimer's disease. He did not even remember that he had been president and his wife, Nancy, had to break the bottle of champagne for him to launch the ship named after him. In fact, if this world system is true, then euthanasia of elderly persons, the holocaust, abortion, the killing of unwanted babies, and the elimination of homeless persons makes sense because those that we evaluate as worthless are simply a burden to society. We usually discard things that we think are worthless. Finally, when we die, according

to this system, we have definitely become worthless because we can do nothing, cannot take our possessions with us, and even our relative's memory of us begins to fade.

4. <u>We will never be able to escape the emotional turmoil and stress in our lives</u>. If we believe the lie that when we accomplish something or bask in the approval of others, we are more worthwhile, then we must also believe that when we fail or others reject us, we are of little worth. We will then naturally attempt to rebuild our worth through performance, people pleasing and ego defenses (to deny our moral failures). By doing so, we place our worth at the mercy of our own capabilities, the opinions of others, and the circumstances of our life. This leads to fear of rejection, fear of failure, fear of punishment and fear of shame. (*Search for Significance,* 1990). These fears result in extreme emotional swings, defenses to moderate these swings and psychological problems. This, unfortunately, is the situation with every human being who accepts the world's system for evaluating worth.

5. <u>We will have to live with contradictions and internal inconsistency in how we relate to others</u>. One of the measures of the validity of a system is internal consistency. If something is true, than it should be applicable to all aspects of the lives of those who believe it. In order to see how ridiculous the lie is that we have believed for so long, simply ask any mother—even those who believe in the world's system of worth—"Which of your children are worth the most?" With only the possible exception of those who are mentally ill or extremely dysfunctional, every one will state that all of their children are of equal value! They love and value each equally even if one is a straight "A" student and the other is mentally challenged. However, if we ask an employer which of his employees are worth the most to him, we will almost always get a ranking based on their performance. Clearly, there must be something wrong with a system that is not even consistent within itself.

God's System of Self-worth

In order to understand the foundational issue involved in evaluating our worth, we must return to the Garden of Eden before the fall of man. If we accept the worldly point of view that our self-worth is a combination of approval, performance and morals, then we need to ask ourselves these questions: What was it that Adam did that made him so worthwhile? Who were the people who provided approval for Adam in the garden? What were the moral values of good and evil to which he adhered? Of course, there were none; he had nothing to do but to name the animals, there were no people to give approval, and no moral excellence or even rules until the single command was given not to eat of the tree of the knowledge of good and evil. If this is true, then where did Adam get this all-important feeling of worth? He received it from God! God had made him in His image and God had said that he and all the creation were very good! His worth was based on God's unconditional love and acceptance. If this is true, then it is also true that there is nothing that we can do to make ourselves more or less worthwhile. This fact is extremely important.

The fall of Adam and Eve in the garden has added a lot of confusion and has obscured this fact that we are all of equal value. How was our worth affected by the fall? Malcom Smith gives us part of the answer in his tape series on codependency and self-worth (not dated). He points out that it was the fall that changed our way of looking at our worth. Before the fall, Adam's wife was called *Isha* or woman, indicating that her worth was based on her creation to be like Adam, one made in God's image. After the fall, she was called Eve, the mother of all the living—her function. Before the fall, obtaining another's approval was not important. But after the fall of Adam and Eve, because man had chosen to be independent from God and his sin had separated him from God, what others thought became extremely important. He no longer heard God's voice saying that he was very good. Therefore, he sought another voice to affirm his worth. Finally, before sin came into the world, shame did not exist. Now that Adam and Eve had eaten of the tree of the knowledge of good and evil, they had the potential for moral judgment. Because of their shame, Adam and Eve hid themselves from God, sewed fig leaves to cover themselves, and blamed God, each other, and Satan. In this one stroke, an ungodly method of evaluating our image was so thrust into prominence, that even most Christians today do not question it. The "rat race" of life is a race to meet our needs for worth and significance at the expense of others. It has become the very expression of selfishness, which, even when modified by socialization, only results in making us more sophisticated, clever, selfish rats.

The Results of God's System of Self-worth—All Are of Great and Equal Value

Unfortunately, even among Christian circles, there is disagreement as to what the Bible actually says about how sin has affected our self-worth. Jay Adams (1986) correctly points out that our creation in God's image did not vanish with the fall. This is clear in Genesis 9:6 and James 3:9. However, Jay then states, "intrinsically man is worth little." He attempts to prove that "man is of value only to other men, and not to God at all." (pp. 82-86) By this argument, he is trying to avoid the conclusion that it was because of man's worth that Jesus died on the cross, rather than because of His mercy and grace. To Jay Adams, man's image has been tarnished by sin, and, therefore, he is of little value. I agree that our image has been tarnished by sin, but I do not agree that this makes us of little value or worth. Christ died for us when we were helpless sinners or enemies, because he loved us (Romans 5:6-10), and because He loves us, we have value or worth. Jay Adams asks the question, "Of what worth is a weak, sinful enemy of God to Him?" The key to his confusion here is clear when he states, "To be of value is to be valuable for something." As most writers in this area, he has not differentiated the concept of worth from that of significance. As I have stated before, ask any father or mother if their child is worthless because he flunked a math test or hit his sister. Our child's worth is based on the fact that he is our child and that we love him, and not on how well he has obeyed us, or how much he has accomplished in life. It was not our inherent worth that was affected by the fall, but our significance or meaning—the carrying out of our potential which will be discussed in the next chapter. Adam was made in God's image and his inherent design is "very good." Nothing has changed or can ever change that!

What people think of us, and even how we choose to utilize our lives, does not change our inherent value. As in the case of the auction of a Rembrandt painting, the value is established by what a rational person is willing to pay for it. God was willing to give His Son in payment for humanity. In doing so, He placed the very highest value on man and did this while we were still sinners. **Either God paid too much for us and got a bad deal, or we have as much inherent value to God as Jesus. In fact, to God, all of His children are of equal value.** It is the love of God that provides the basis of our worth. In Romans Chapter 8, He has promised that nothing can ever separate us from His love. Seeing ourselves as worthless or having a "worm" theology is not required in order to recognize that we are sinners who have fallen far short of our potential. The fulfilling of our potential is what was lost at the fall and is being restored through the process of salvation, but not our value or inherent worth.

We also must be careful not to under-value God's love for us. It is not just that we are okay in God's eyes. We must understand that we are greatly loved and valued above the rest of God's creation, just a little lower than the angels (Psalms 8:3-5) and we are destined to judge the angels. I am loved and accepted just the way I am, not just tolerated. I am His especially loved child, and because I am loved, I can know that He will always have my very best interest in mind. God will never leave me nor forsake me, I have infinite value in His eyes and what He thinks of me is the only thing that really matters. No matter how much I may fail in the eyes of the world, or how much I might find success in the eyes of the world, I am still greatly loved along with every other person. That is why He wants me, through faith, to be freed of my selfish motivations, so that I can truly love my fellow man as He does. He has provided it <u>all,</u> not just a minimal level of acceptance. No matter what, <u>I am loved</u>!

The Process of Transformation by Faith

This root problem of low self-worth is primarily based on accepting the lie that a person's value depends on his performance, approval or morals, and using the experiences of our life to evaluate our worth. The primary battle for our worth is in our mind. We have all fallen to some extent into the trap visited by Adam and Eve. Because they attempted to be their own God and determine their worth by their performance, the approval of others and their adherence to their values; they became worthless in their own eyes and shame overcame them. Helping a client escape from the world system for evaluating his self-worth requires a number of steps, because this system is so strongly entrenched in the lives of most clients.

I have met few people who have not, at least to some extent, accepted the world's system of evaluating worth. Most of those with a reasonably healthy self-worth developed it through worldly achievement and a healthy loving family. Even this provides an extremely shaky foundation since all of us eventually fail at something and no one will always bask in the approval of others.

Overcoming the world's system requires both debunking the lies of the world system by showing our clients that the world system of worth does not make sense and establishing the client's worth based on the Word of God.

1. <u>The client must honestly evaluate the world's system of worth from a logical and biblical perspective and convince himself that it is a lie.</u> Let us evaluate what the Bible says about the characteristics that we value so much in others and ourselves.

    a. <u>Wealth</u>. We often ask, "how much is he worth?" We sometimes think that because a rich person must have done something to acquire his riches or that because of his riches he might have more influence, he is in some way more worthwhile. But if we believe that this is true, than it must also be true that this same person is worthless when the stock market crashes and he loses all of his wealth. Believing this lie led to a number of suicides after the stock market crash in the United States in the 1920's and during the recent economic downturn in Japan. Jesus said that he was particularly called to preach the gospel to the poor and that God greatly values the poor. (Luke 4:18, 6:20) Jesus specifically refuted this belief with a parable that demonstrates how foolish we are to believe in riches. We must also realize that we cannot take our money with us when we die.

        Lu 12:16 And he spake a parable unto them, saying, The ground of a certain rich man brought forth plentifully:

        17 And he thought within himself, saying, What shall I do, because I have no room where to bestow my fruits?

        18 And he said, This will I do: I will pull down my barns, and build greater; and there will I will bestow my fruits and my goods.

        19 And I will say to my soul, Soul, thou hast much goods laid up for many years; take thine ease, eat, drink, [and] be merry.

        20 But God said unto him, [Thou] fool, this night thy soul shall be required of thee: then whose shall those things be, which thou hast provided?

        21 So [is] he that layeth up treasure for himself, and is not rich toward God.

    b. <u>Intelligence</u>. I counseled a man who took IQ tests almost every six months because his parents had given him the idea that, unless he was a genius, he was worth little. Each time he tried to get the examiner to agree that if he were less anxious and had fewer psychological problems, he probably would have scored 20 points higher. Does it make sense that if we have a low IQ, are learning disabled or get Alzheimer's, we become worthless?

    c. <u>Education</u>. College degrees are seen by some as making a person more worthwhile. The Bible tells us that God has chosen to use the foolish things of this world for His purpose, not the wisdom of this world.

        1 Co 1:26 For ye see your calling, brethren, how that not many wise men after the flesh, not many mighty, not many noble, [are called]:

27 But God hath chosen the foolish things of the world to confound the wise; and God hath chosen the weak things of the world to confound the things which are mighty;

28 And base things of the world, and things which are despised, hath God chosen, [yea], and things which are not, to bring to nought things that are: That no flesh should glory in his presence.

After obtaining a number of degrees, I have concluded that a degree might be of help in getting a better job, but the information learned provides only a foundation for the job. It is seldom used on that job. It is mostly those without degrees who see university degrees of great value. In any case, what value will our degrees have after we are admitted as a nursing home resident?

d. <u>Approval</u>. One of Aesop's fables describes how a father and son did everything they could to be pleasing to everyone. As they were leading a donkey along a road, they were criticized for not riding the donkey, so the father began to ride. As the father rode the donkey, he was criticized for making his son walk, so he got off the donkey and his son began to ride. As the son rode, he was criticized for making his father walk. Finally, they both rode the donkey and were criticized for abusing the donkey, making it carry such a heavy load. (Tan, 1979) The message is clear. We can never please everyone, no matter what we do. In fact, approval is probably one of the most fleeting events in life. Ask any war hero how long his great honor lasted?

e. <u>Honor</u>. A number of years ago, the United States Chief of Naval Operations put a gun to his chest and killed himself. He was about to be exposed for wearing "V's" on his military ribbons, which he did not have the paperwork to back up. Most agreed that he had qualified for the awards. He was the first Chief of Naval Operations ever to achieve that position by rising from the rank of seaman. Did he actually become so worthless, due to this one minor violation of honor, that his life was no longer worth living? His actions seem to indicate that he must have felt that this was true. According to John 5:44, seeking honor from men detracts from faith in God, "How can ye believe, which receive honor one of another, and seek not the honor that [cometh] from God only?"

f. <u>Performance</u>. Man believes that performance is most important. Saving face after a failure was so important to the crew of a Korean Airlines Boeing 747 that crashed short of the runway that they chose to burn to death rather than to face their failure. Is a man only worthwhile because he accomplishes something? Solomon, the wisest and most accomplished man on earth, gave us his opinion of this subject, based on his experience.

Ec 2:11 Then I looked on all the works that my hands had wrought, and on the labour that I had laboured to do: and, behold, all [was] vanity and vexation of spirit, and [there was] no profit under the sun.

g. <u>Possessions</u>. The hidden meaning behind many advertising campaigns is that if people saw us in that new sports car or new suit they would think that we must really be somebody. What happens when our car gets a small dent in the door or the suit gets a rip in it? Did our worth just decrease? Matthew says it this way:

Mt 16:26 For what is a man profited, if he shall gain the whole world, and lose his own soul? or what shall a man give in exchange for his soul?

h. <u>Power and prestige</u>. Some seek to have a place of power in our society and to have the prestige of being one of the "honored guests" at state events. This is also an illusion. God states that it is He Who directs the affairs of men and that the more He gives us the more He and others will require of us. It is those who do not seek position or authority who make the best leaders.

Ps 75:6 For promotion cometh neither from the east, nor from the west, nor from the south.

7 But God is the judge: he putteth down one, and setteth up another.

Lu 12:48b …For unto whomsoever much is given, of him shall be much required: and to whom men have committed much, of him they will ask the more.

i. <u>Physical strength and athletics</u>. The Olympics are a good example of how much people will sacrifice in order to win in competition. We honor the world's greatest athletes when they win, but are those who fail to win a medal actually worth less? Timothy, one of the youngest of the pastors in the early church, gives bodily exercise a much lower priority.

1 Ti 4:8 For bodily exercise profiteth little: but godliness is profitable unto all things, having promise of the life that now is, and of that which is to come.

2. <u>The client must be convinced that God's evaluation of him is vastly more important than his accomplishments or what men say and think about him</u>. Think of it this way. Let us suppose that you have become the most important man in America because you discovered the cure for AIDS. Your picture is in every paper and on the cover of every news magazine. People even want to name a highway after you and declare your birthday a national holiday. Now let us evaluate how important you really are. Momentarily, you may be the most popular person in the United States, but the United States has less than 350 million people compared to approximately 6 billion people on the whole earth. If you compare our earth to our sun, over 1 million earths would fit inside the sun. Pluto, the farthest planet from our sun, is about 3,670 million miles from the sun. Yet, compared to the known universe, our solar system is like one single grain of sand out of all the sand on all of the seashores of the entire world. (We still have no idea how big the rest of the universe is.) (Compton's, 1996, Tan, 1979) If our entire solar system was destroyed, the fact that it was missing, would not even be noticeable in that great expanse. Yet somehow we people think that our accomplishments, or that the opinion of just a few other human beings is really important. Without God, we are truly worthless and insignificant. However, the perfect God, Who cannot lie, Who made us and the entire universe, has clearly stated that He made us in His image, that we are very good, that He loves us, that He has chosen us to be on the team that is to rule the universe, that we are His adopted children, that we are joint heirs with His Son Jesus Christ, and that we will sit beside Him on his throne forever. It is these facts that make us truly worthwhile and significant.

Ps 8:3 When I consider thy heavens, the work of thy fingers, the moon and the stars, which thou hast ordained;

4 What is man, that thou art mindful of him? and the son of man, that thou visitest him?"

3. <u>He must establish a close, intimate, experiential relationship with God, in order to trust God's Word more than man's world system</u>. In order to hear the voice of God as Adam did, the client must achieve a close experiential relationship with God. Without it, he will be unable to feel and accept the love of God and achieve the peace that Adam experienced. He must accept himself as God does. Here is what God says about our position and our value to Him:

Lu 12:7 But even the very hairs of your head are all numbered. Fear not therefore: ye are of more value than many sparrows.

Ps 8: 5 For thou hast made him a little lower than the angels, and hast crowned him with glory and honour.

6 Thou madest him to have dominion over the works of thy hands; thou hast put all things under his feet:

4. <u>The client must clearly understand, meditate, and act on the fact that he is of great worth no matter how successful he is or how badly he fails, until it becomes a revelation in his spirit</u>. As we clearly saw in the previous chapters on faith, it is critical that he is fully convinced in all of his heart, not just in his mind. He must move what he believes from his mind to his spirit or sub-conscious mind. To do this, I teach clients what I call the "If it is true…" method. The client simply states what the Bible says about his self-worth, and then asks the question, "If this is true, how would I act?" Consistently acting correctly, according to the Word of God, will eventually provide the experiential evidence to develop the faith needed in his spirit. As an example, the client would state, "If it is true that my worth is based on the love that God has for me and not on how I perform or the approval I might get from taking on this new project, how would I act?" In most cases, this truth will assist the client to act according to what he has stated and his actions will result in a positive experience, which will strengthen his faith in what he believes. Of course, all of the other means for increasing the client's faith that have previously been discussed should also be applied.

5. <u>The client must consistently deal with the shame in his life, in order to maintain a healthy emotional "bank account.</u>" The story is told illustrating this fact about a young man who had been delinquent and living in debauchery. He was converted, but continued to be moody, ruminative, unpredictable in interpersonal responses, and never sure he would not backslide. Finally, on advice from an elder, he changed his strategy of hiding his mistakes and the sins of the past and confided in two trusted members of the congregation. There was a striking change noted by everyone. He stated this principle as follows: "When we tell or brag about some accomplishment or favor we've done someone, we exchange the 'credit' for immediate satisfaction that is we 'spend' it. And, in the same way, when we confess an evil, something we feel guilty about, we likewise get rid of it, dissipate it…like those things I did and thought I wasn't ashamed of, but was. Now that I have admitted them, they aren't a part of me any more—they just don't seem very important. By admitting these things, I have 'spent' my guilt. And now the same principle seems to work the other way 'round. Just as the wrong kind of 'credit,' if accumulated, will eventually destroy you, so good 'credit,' if not used up, gives you strength and inner confidence. The net effect is that you are, in any case, what you keep back or save: strong and self-accepting, if what you hide and keep back is good, and weak and self-hating, if what you keep and hide is bad. It is, quite simply, to reverse this whole strategy: admit and thus divest oneself of one's weaknesses, errors, follies, and hide one's charities, good deeds, virtues." Simply, pay your debts and save your income." (*The Magnificent Obsession*, 1929, Lloyd Douglas)

I am not suggesting that this is a way that we can build our worth, but is it a way to rid ourselves of toxic shame. The Bible makes it clear that if we do things to receive praise of men, we receive no further reward from the good we do. This is how we use up our assets.

Mt 6:1 Take heed that ye do not your alms before men, to be seen of them: otherwise ye have no reward of your Father which is in heaven.

2 Therefore when thou doest [thine] alms, do not sound a trumpet before thee, as the hypocrites do in the synagogues and in the streets, that they may have glory of men. Verily I say unto you, They have their reward.

3 But when thou doest alms, let not thy left hand know what thy right hand doeth:

4 That thine alms may be in secret: and thy Father which seeth in secret himself shall reward thee openly.

On the other hand, the Bible tells us that if we confess our sins, God forgives and cleanses us of them. This is how we liquidate our debts.

1 Jo 1:9 If we confess our sins, he is faithful and just to forgive us [our] sins, and to cleanse us from all unrighteousness.

6. <u>He must quit striving to improve his self-worth through performance, seeking approval, or trying to obey the moral law</u>. Most persons struggling with low self-worth have become excellent performers and are driven in life to accomplish things. They usually have to be doing something all of the time to be happy. They have become human doers instead of human beings. In order for them to find God's abundant life and escape the stress of the "rat race," they must replace this drivenness with the peace that only comes from resting in what God has already done for us. Many times, I suggest they say to themselves over and over again when they have the urge to have to perform: "You don't have to do anything! God will still love you."

7. <u>He must evaluate and treat others according to God's truth</u>. To be delivered from the problems created by the world's system for evaluating self-worth, he must totally embrace God's truth and act accordingly in the way he evaluates and treats others. He cannot continue to evaluate others according to the world's system and evaluate himself by God's system. Just as his inherent worth is based on God's love for him, so is the worth of every other person, no matter how badly they have performed. God's love never changes. God said it and the client must believe that he and everyone else is made in God's image, that they are very good, and that nothing they do or can do can even change this truth. God is more concerned for the one lost sheep than the ninety and nine that are not lost. (Matthew 18:12). Even Saddam Hussein has as much inherent worth to God as the client does, and the client has no less worth than any of the heroes of faith like Abraham, Moses or Elijah. If the client truly believes this, he will treat and value everyone else as equal to himself.

8. <u>The client must fully accept the worth that God has provided for him, see himself as worthwhile, and accept himself as God does—His beloved and favored child</u>. When we finally realize experientially, how much God loves and favors us, we can believe that God has and will always meet all of our needs—including that of our self-worth—and enter into His rest and cease from our own attempts to make ourselves valuable. Unfortunately, for some, a child's original concept of God is that of his parents. If, when the client was a child his self-worth was damaged by parental abuse or neglect, he will have difficulty experiencing God's unconditional love. A simple exercise of comparing the characteristics of the client's father and mother with how he perceives God can help him see the fallacy in the way he perceives God. An intensive study of the grace and the love of God in the Bible, or other books such as *Knowing God* by Packer (1973) can help. I have found the book *Search for Significance* useful in helping clients recover from low self-image. I often use the four fear tests (pp. 46, 66, 90, 105) to help the client understand the underlying problem of fear. I then use McGee's method for dealing with false premises (pp. 158-159) to help the client change his thinking process, which has resulted in his warped concept of God and his low self-worth.

9. <u>He must learn to appreciate all that God has done for him and replace the motivation to fix his own deficit with the desire to serve God and others out of love</u>. Until we have replaced our motivation to fix our self-worth, with the understanding that we are already worthwhile because God loves us, and thus are motivated by our appreciation for all that He has done for us, we will still not have fully recovered from the effects of our previous feelings of low self-worth.

For further discussion of this subject and a comprehensive model for overcoming low self-image, please refer to the biblical counseling model of Barak later in this book and the discussion of self-image at the conclusion of the next chapter.

Steps for Overcoming Low Self-worth

1. We must be convinced that the world's system for evaluating self-worth is a lie. We are of value simply because God loves us, not because we perform, are approved of by men or follow the law.

2. We must be convinced that God's evaluation of us is vastly more important than man's evaluation.

3. We must establish a close, intimate relationship with God, in order to trust His Word more than man's word.

4. We must completely accept and act on the fact that we are worthwhile without regard to our successes or failures.

5. We must quit striving to improve our self-worth through performance, seeking approval, or trying to obey the moral law.

6. We must realize that all men are of great and equal value because God loved all of us and sent His son to die for us while we were sinners and enemies of God.

7. We must accept the unmerited favor (grace) that God has for us, appreciate what He has done for us and accept ourselves as His special children, who are of infinite value to Him.

8. Out of gratitude for all that He has done for us, we should be motivated by love to serve Him for the good of the Kingdom of God and love others as we have been loved.

Chapter 11

Faith and Significance

Even if we are now convinced that what God says about us is the only reasonable evaluation of our worth, we must still deal with the issue of significance. Significance has to do with carrying out the meaning that God placed in our lives when He created us. Significance, as defined in the Standard College Dictionary (Funk & Wagnalls, 1963), is that which is signified or intended to be expressed; the meaning of the object. It is the degree that the object meets its intended use or potential. A closely related issue is that of having a feeling that we are important in some way. As an example, a Rembrandt painting has certain value no matter where it is and how it is used. However, it is not very effective in improving the looks of a room when it is hung upside down on a shattered wall of a rundown slum. God is glorified when we reach our potential. Sin is missing the mark of that potential. If we never sinned, we would achieve absolute significance for a human being, just as Jesus did.

How We Develop Worldly Significance

Just as with the case of self-worth, we first develop our concept of significance in our families of origin as we grow up. From the first experiences we have as we play with other children, we begin to determine who is fastest, smartest, or best at any particular game. Once we begin to attend school, it very soon becomes evident who gets the best grades or who is the best at certain sports. This is the beginning of a pecking order of who is popular and who is not, and who is most likely to succeed in life. Even at this early age, we have entered the "rat race" of life. We are in a battle or competition for who will win the game of "king of the hill." As we discovered in the previous chapter, this information concerning our significance is also many times erroneously applied to our evaluation of our worth or value. (PARENT MIRRORING)

The World's System

From the world's point of view—without God in the picture—each of us is in competition with all others to obtain the scarce resources of life in order to meet our needs. We want to feel that we are important or significant in life and that we count for something. The problem is that the world believes that each of us, as our own god, must determine our own destiny and then compete with others in order to achieve it. Of course, in the world's system, only a few make it to the top, and those who do will soon be replaced by the generation that follows.

The world is filled with pride. Each of us wants to become somebody, be important, and do something significant in life. It should humble us to understand that almost nothing that we do or attempt to do will even be known two hundred years from now and that our entire solar system is totally insignificant in the universe. We are like ants thinking that we are so great because we can move a larger grain of sand than another ant. The Bible compares us to vapor that exists one moment and is gone. (James 4:14)

The Consequences of the World's System of Significance—All Eventually Lose

Every society has a focus that is its own particular theme or somewhat universal goal. In the Orient it is saving face, in the Middle East it is getting revenge for wrongs suffered, and in the United States and much of Europe, it is being successful. In our drive for worldly success, one of the premises of our societal system is that significance must be obtained at the expense of others in our society. We are all in competition but we cannot all be significant. This is called the "rat race." It results in a number of direct consequences for our lives.

1. We are stressed by our competitive life style. Because we view our world as a "zero sum game," we view all others in our society as competitors for a limited resource called success. A zero sum game means that to the degree one person wins, another has to lose out on that resource. Consequently, some will win, some will lose and it is our desire to do whatever it takes in order to be one of the winners. Stress results when we perceive that what is required of us may exceed our capabilities. Of course, failure is always possible in a competition and therefore, we live a life filled with stress. Because this competitive way of viewing life pervades our entire society, we are stressed about almost everything in our lives. This competitive mindset is clear from the high salaries we provide for the most successful players of our competitive sports.

2. Only a limited few achieve significance at any time and it is short-lived. In the game called "king of the hill," only one can achieve the significance of being "top dog" or king of the hill. The rest will do anything to topple the king, including stepping on others who are also trying to be king. The result is a selfish "dog fight" to be somebody and the majority who play this game do not go away without emotional bruises or worse. Of course, in our society, we prize those who know how to win in a more socialized manner, but the battle for promotion is a clear fact in most of the corporate world. There are only a few of the six billion people on this planet who can reach the top and even fewer are able to remain at the top for an entire lifetime.

3. Eventually, we all lose. It might seem negative, but it is a fact of life that eventually all lose in this worldly fight for significance. Let me explain through the example of a high jumper. If you are good at high jumping at your school, you will compete in more competitions at the state, regional, and, finally, national level. If you prove to be one of the very best, you may even make the Olympic Team. If you compete in the Olympic Games, you may even win the gold medal. If you do, you are definitely successful and significant at least for the moment. If you do not go on to win a gold medal at the next Olympic Games, you will be labeled a loser, even if you win the silver medal. If you continue to win, eventually you will grow older, and will be beaten by a younger, stronger competitor. If you set a world record, eventually someone will surpass your accomplishment, and your great success will be forgotten.

4. We are driven to take on more than we can easily accomplish. Although talent is highly rewarded in the world's system, it also has its downside. The more talented we are, the more opportunities we will be given to take on more and more difficult tasks. Figuratively, if we are a very successful fish in a small fish bowl, we will be promoted to larger and larger bowls. Unfortunately, in the larger bowls are other very talented fish and larger sharks. Because we feel each promotion makes us more significant, we are driven to take on more and more difficult tasks. One well-known statement concerning this issue is "the higher you go, the harder you fall." The problem is that there is always a higher mountain. One of my friends, caught up with this drive for significance, died in the Himalayan Mountains on Annapurna I. Another froze to death after making the summit of Mount Everest.

5. We all eventually top out at the level of our incompetence. In the corporate world, this has been called "The Peter Principle." It goes like this. In most cases as long as we are doing a good job at the current level of responsibility, we will be promoted. When we reach a level where we are no longer

competent, we will be passed over for promotion. Therefore, unless we are fired, we will finish our careers working at our level of incompetence. Of course, this also means that we will find ourselves locked into a stressful job that requires more of us than we can produce for the remainder of our careers.

6. <u>We are driven to medicate our stress with addictions, alcohol or drugs</u>. Because of the high stress environment produced by this drive for significance, we are tempted to medicate our emotional swings and our stress with some sort of addiction or drug. Drug, alcohol and other addictions are commonplace in the corporate world. It seems to be a necessary part of attempting to cope with such a competitive and stressful life.

7. <u>We are taught to sacrifice character in order to accomplish things</u>. With this as the predominant message in our society, it is not difficult to understand why the number of high-ranking politicians and corporate executives charged with ethical violations or crimes seems to be increasing.

8. <u>Anxiety has become a major factor in our failures</u>. Because we are so driven to be successful, the fear of failure is an underlying cause in many dysfunctional attempts to succeed, avoidant types of codependency and even mental illness. The anxiety from a fear of failure can prevent us from even trying something, it can lead us to an all-or-nothing mentality, and it can drive us to try too hard to be successful. All of these can lead to failure, which in turn leads to more dysfunctional attempts to succeed and more failure.

9. <u>We are losing our soul for the sake of success in this world</u>. Unfortunately, even many Christians are not aware that we have been caught up in this "rat race" of life. It can cost us our families, will do damage to the quality of our lives, and will limit our ability to be fruitful in the Kingdom of God. In the Parable of the Sower, Jesus explained that it was the cares of this world that were the weeds that choked out the plants and caused them not to produce fruit. (Matthew 13:22)

God's System of Significance

As you might have already guessed, God has a very different method of achieving significance and a successful life. Let us start our investigation by examining what the Word of God tells us about this subject.

1. <u>When the Bible speaks of significance, it generally uses the term "worthy" to evaluate our merit as compared to what God originally intended us to be</u>. The word translated from the Greek as worthy is *axios*, which means, "something having the weight of another thing of like value, worth as much, or one who has merited anything worthy both in a good and a bad sense." Those who act in a worthy way deserve rewards.

   Mt 10:37 He that loveth father or mother more than me is not worthy of me: and he that loveth son or daughter more than me is not worthy of me.

   38 And he that taketh not his cross, and followeth after me, is not worthy of me.

   22:8 Then saith he to his servants, The wedding is ready, but they which were bidden were not worthy.

2. <u>The ultimate in human functioning is called "the glory of God."</u> The word translated as glory is *doxa, which* means, "a good opinion concerning one, resulting in praise, honour, and glory; splendor, brightness, magnificence, excellence, preeminence, dignity, grace; or the absolutely perfect inward or personal excellency of Christ."

   1 Th 2:12 That ye would walk worthy of God, who hath called you unto his kingdom and glory.

Php 1:11 Being filled with the fruits of righteousness, which are by Jesus Christ, unto the glory and praise of God.

3. <u>Everything we do in our own strength is motivated by selfishness and is, therefore, filthy rags in God's eyes</u>. Before we accept Christ, we are dominated by our sin nature. Each of us has sinned. Sin simply means missing the mark of the full potential for which God has designed us. We are selfish and therefore, everything we do is motivated by that selfishness and is no better than filthy rags to God. The Bible tells us that all have sinned and come short of the glory of God. (Romans 3:23)

   Isa 64:6 But we are all as an unclean thing, and all our righteousnesses are as filthy rags; and we all do fade as a leaf; and our iniquities, like the wind, have taken us away.

4. <u>When we were saved, God began the process of delivering us from our selfishness through salvation by faith, and God has declared us to be righteous based on that faith</u>. Righteousness is another word for reaching our potential (making right judgments and carrying them out). Because God operates outside of any reference of time, when we have faith in Him, He counts us as already being righteous. This allows us to have intimate fellowship with Him.

   Ro 4:3 For what saith the scripture? Abraham believed God, and it was counted unto him for righteousness.

   5 But to him that worketh not, but believeth on him that justifieth the ungodly, his faith is counted for righteousness.

5. <u>As our faith grows, we are transformed more and more into our full potential</u>. Through the process of salvation, we become more and more righteous and we sin less and less. In direct proportion to our faith, we learn to love others unselfishly and we are conformed into the image of Christ Jesus—our full potential.

   Ro 8:29 For whom he did foreknow, he also did predestinate to be conformed to the image of his Son, that he might be the firstborn among many brethren.

   30 Moreover whom he did predestinate, them he also called: and whom he called, them he also justified: and whom he justified, them he also glorified.

6. <u>When we sin, our sin is covered by the blood of Jesus' sacrifice and so, in God's eyes, we remain righteous.</u>

   Col 1:14 In whom we have redemption through his blood, even the forgiveness of sins.

7. <u>Jesus resolved the problem of shame for us when He took our shame upon Himself as He died on the cross</u>. Since Adam and Eve ate of the tree of the knowledge of good and evil, we have had the capacity to judge our actions; therefore, we feel guilt or shame when we sin. This shame leads us to negative evaluations of ourselves, especially when we try to hide the shame or blame others. Shame and guilt must be dealt with effectively or they will result in toxic shame—a pervasive feeling that we are bad.

   Heb 12:2 Looking unto Jesus the author and finisher of our faith; who for the joy that was set before him endured the cross, despising the shame, and is set down at the right hand of the throne of God

Isa 50:6 I gave my back to the smiters, and my cheeks to them that plucked off the hair: I hid not my face from shame and spitting.

Ro 10:11 For the scripture saith, Whosoever believeth on him shall not be ashamed.

8. <u>Even with all that Christ has done for us, the Bible tells us that we are still powerless to do anything of merit for God, without doing it in His power and strength.</u> Everything we attempt to do in our own strength will be deficient in some manner and will be rejected.

Jo 15:4 Abide in me, and I in you. As the branch cannot bear fruit of itself, except it abide in the vine; no more can ye, except ye abide in me.

5 I am the vine, ye are the branches: He that abideth in me, and I in him, the same bringeth forth much fruit: for without me ye can do nothing.

9. <u>The Bible makes it clear that we cannot do anything in our own efforts (the law) to make ourselves better people or more significant.</u>

Ga 3:1 O foolish Galatians, who hath bewitched you, that ye should not obey the truth, before whose eyes Jesus Christ hath been evidently set forth, crucified among you?

2 This only would I learn of you, Received ye the Spirit by the works of the law, or by the hearing of faith?

3 Are ye so foolish? having begun in the Spirit, are ye now made perfect by the flesh?

4 Have ye suffered so many things in vain? if it be yet in vain.

5 He therefore that ministereth to you the Spirit, and worketh miracles among you, doeth he it by the works of the law, or by the hearing of faith?

10. <u>It is God Who makes us want to do what is right, promotes us, and assists us in being successful and wealthy. Therefore, He is the one Who should get the glory for everything.</u> We have not made ourselves successful. It is God Who created us, gave us the talents we have, promoted us and gave us all the good things that we have. All the thanks and glory are to go to Him.

Php 2:13 For it is God which worketh in you both to will and to do of his good pleasure.

De 8:18 But thou shalt remember the LORD thy God: for it is he that giveth thee power to get wealth, that he may establish his covenant which he sware unto thy fathers, as it is this day.

1 Co 1:31 That, according as it is written, He that glorieth, let him glory in the Lord.

11. <u>If we think that we have accomplished anything and take the credit for it, we have fallen into the trap of pride.</u> A prideful attitude states that we do not appreciate what God has done for us, and that we do not need God. For our own good, God will resist our success and will bring us low until we realize that everything that we have is a gift from him. (See the biblical model of King Nebuchadnezzar for overcoming pride later in this book.)

Dan 4:30 The king spake, and said, Is not this great Babylon, that I have built for the house of the kingdom by the might of my power, and for the honour of my majesty?

31 While the word was in the king's mouth, there fell a voice from heaven, saying, O king Nebuchadnezzar, to thee it is spoken; The kingdom is departed from thee.

32 And they shall drive thee from men, and thy dwelling shall be with the beasts of the field: they shall make thee to eat grass as oxen, and seven times shall pass over thee, until thou know that the most High ruleth in the kingdom of men, and giveth it to whomsoever he will.

33 The same hour was the thing fulfilled upon Nebuchadnezzar: and he was driven from men, and did eat grass as oxen, and his body was wet with the dew of heaven, till his hairs were grown like eagles' feathers, and his nails like birds' claws.

37 Now I Nebuchadnezzar praise and extol and honour the King of heaven, all whose works are truth, and his ways judgment: and those that walk in pride he is able to abase.

Job 33:17 That he (God) may withdraw man from his purpose, and hide pride from man.

Ps 10:4 The wicked, through the pride of his countenance, will not seek after God: God is not in all his thoughts.

Pr 16:18 Pride goeth before destruction, and an haughty spirit before a fall.

12. <u>The fact that God has adopted us into His family makes us so significant that there is absolutely nothing that we can do to make ourselves any more significant</u>. As I have stated before, without God, we as people, are so insignificant in the universe that even if we blew up our entire solar system it would hardly be noticeable. The fact that God has already made us children of the ruler of the universe, joint heirs with Christ (we will own a huge chunk of the universe), selected us to be on the team that will rule the universe, has provided a throne for us, and has declared us to be righteous through faith elevates us far beyond anything we can do in our own efforts in this lifetime. This is our position in Christ. What can we do on this earth that is so important that it will make us more significant than this?

13. <u>We must, therefore, draw the conclusion that our significance is totally dependent on what Christ did, and that we cannot do anything in our own strength to achieve any greater success than this by ourselves</u>. It is God, through the process of salvation by faith, who delivers us from our selfishness, so that we are capable of good works. It is the blood of Jesus that provides for the forgiveness for our failures (sins). It is Jesus Who took our shame upon himself so that we would not be ashamed. It is God Who provides the strength and ability to do His will. And it is God Who, by adopting us into His family, makes us so significant that there in nothing we can do to make ourselves any more significant.

The Results of God's System—We Can All Be Significant and Successful

It is important that we understand the difference between what it is to be successful in this world and what it means to be successful from God's point of view. In the world, success is deciding what we want to do and accomplishing it in such a way that others see us as making a significant contribution to something. God's view of success and significance is very different from this.

1. <u>The Bible tells us that God has a plan for us even before we were born and that He designed us to fulfill that plan.</u>

Jer 1:5 Before I formed thee in the belly I knew thee; and before thou camest forth out of the womb I sanctified thee, and I ordained thee a prophet unto the nations.

Isa 49:5 And now, saith the LORD that formed me from the womb to be his servant, to bring Jacob again to him, Though Israel be not gathered, yet shall I be glorious in the eyes of the LORD, and my God shall be my strength.

Ga 1:15 But when it pleased God, who separated me from my mother's womb, and called me by his grace,

16 To reveal his Son in me, that I might preach him among the heathen; immediately I conferred not with flesh and blood:

2. <u>Because each of us has been designed and called for a specific purpose, we are not in competition with others, but with ourselves to become all that God has called us to be and do</u>. We are running different races; therefore, the Bible warns us that if we compare ourselves with others, we are not wise. What would happen if a racer who is running 440 yards compares his progress with one running the fifty-yard dash or the marathon?

2 Co 10:12 For we dare not make ourselves of the number, or compare ourselves with some that commend themselves: but they measuring themselves by themselves, and comparing themselves among themselves, are not wise.

3. <u>God has also chosen to give us different talents, based on our calling and He will reward us for what we do with them</u>. The more that He has given us, the more He requires of us. Since it is He Who chose to give us the specific talents that we will need for the specific mission on earth for which He designed us, we are only responsible for doing our best to find and carry out that specific calling. Notice that the man with two talents who made another two, was rewarded exactly the same as the man who had five and had made another five. Had the man with one talent made another, he also would have received the same reward. Only the servant who refused to use what God had given him was punished. God sees and rewards us according to what we have done with the capabilities He has given us. Again, we are not in competition with each other and we are not to compare ourselves with others; but only with ourselves.

Mt 25:15 And unto one he gave five talents, to another two, and to another one; to every man according to his several ability; and straightway took his journey.

19 After a long time the lord of those servants cometh, and reckoneth with them.

20 And so he that had received five talents came and brought other five talents, saying, Lord, thou deliveredst unto me five talents: behold, I have gained beside them five talents more.

21 His lord said unto him, Well done, thou good and faithful servant: thou hast been faithful over a few things, I will make thee ruler over many things: enter thou into the joy of thy lord.

22 He also that had received two talents came and said, Lord, thou deliveredst unto me two talents: behold, I have gained two other talents beside them.

23 His lord said unto him, Well done, good and faithful servant; thou hast been faithful over a few things, I will make thee ruler over many things: enter thou into the joy of thy lord.

24 Then he which had received the one talent came and said, Lord, I knew thee that thou art an hard man, reaping where thou hast not sown, and gathering where thou hast not strawed:

25 And I was afraid, and went and hid thy talent in the earth: lo, there thou hast that is thine.

26 His lord answered and said unto him, Thou wicked and slothful servant, thou knewest that I reap where I sowed not, and gather where I have not strawed:

4. <u>God has specifically placed persons with differing talents in each of His churches</u>. We, as part of the body of Christ, are not in competition with each other, but are to care for each other, complement each other, and work together for the good of that local body and to further the Kingdom of God.

1 Co 12:14 For the body is not one member, but many.

15 If the foot shall say, Because I am not the hand, I am not of the body; is it therefore not of the body?

18 But now hath God set the members every one of them in the body, as it hath pleased him.

28 And God hath set some in the church, first apostles, secondarily prophets, thirdly teachers, after that miracles, then gifts of healings, helps, governments, diversities of tongues.

5. <u>Those things that are motivated by selfishness, as well as those done in the flesh according to what we want to do, will have no value and will be rejected by God.</u>

    1 Co 3:11 For other foundation can no man lay than that is laid, which is Jesus Christ.

    12 Now if any man build upon this foundation gold, silver, precious stones, wood, hay, stubble;

    13 Every man's work shall be made manifest: for the day shall declare it, because it shall be revealed by fire; and the fire shall try every man's work of what sort it is.

    14 If any man's work abide which he hath built thereupon, he shall receive a reward.

6. <u>In God's system, we can all win and be successful in life.</u> Because God has saved us from our selfishness, has called all of us to a different specific mission and has given us all differing talents to fulfill that mission, He does not compare us with each other. Because He helps and provides all we need, absolutely every one of us can become significant, have a fully successful life, and become a hero of faith.

The Process of Transformation by Faith to Achieve Significance or Success

Although all of us are already significant in the eyes of God through our position in Christ and even though all of us can become truly successful in this life according to God's plan, the Bible warns that many of us will not actually achieve the level of success that God has intended for us. Matthew 22:14 states that, "For many are called but few are chosen." Clearly every one of us has something significant to do in this life, but all of us will probably not achieve the level of commendation that Jesus gave to John the Baptist: "…Among them that are born of women there hath not risen a greater than John the Baptist:.." (Matthew 11:11) In order to understand our part in becoming truly successful in life, let us examine the life of John the Baptist.

1. <u>We must be saved and develop a close relationship with God in order to know specifically what He has called us to do.</u> When we are saved, we all have a general call on our lives to become established in a church, read our Bible, witness to others and do what we can to further the Kingdom of God. But, as in the case of John the Baptist, God calls all of us for a particular mission even before we are born. John the Baptist's call was revealed to his father in the temple by an angel even before his mother Elizabeth, a relative of Mary the mother of Jesus, became pregnant. This was prior to Jesus' birth. Many clients I have counseled have wished that God had revealed their specific call in a similar manner. But for most, God requires us to get to know His voice and prove ourselves faithful to our general call before He reveals to us our specific call.

    Lu 1:13 But the angel said unto him, Fear not, Zacharias: for thy prayer is heard; and thy wife Elisabeth shall bear thee a son, and thou shalt call his name John.

    14 And thou shalt have joy and gladness; and many shall rejoice at his birth.

    15 For he shall be great in the sight of the Lord, and shall drink neither wine nor strong drink; and he shall be filled with the Holy Ghost, even from his mother's womb.

    16 And many of the children of Israel shall he turn to the Lord their God.

17 And he shall go before him in the spirit and power of Elias, to turn the hearts of the fathers to the children, and the disobedient to the wisdom of the just; to make ready a people prepared for the Lord.

2. <u>We must accept that we are already significant because of who we are in Christ, reject the world's system of trying to establish our significance through worldly accomplishments, and be willing to accept what God has called us to do, even if it appears worthless in the eyes of the world</u>. From a worldly standpoint, John was a loser. We are told nothing about him for the first 30 years of his life. When God directed him to begin his ministry, he is a loner in the wilderness, wearing camel's hair and eating locusts and wild honey. His mission was to preach that people should repent of their sins. From a worldly standpoint, this calling does not appear to be one that will lead to great significance. The world lies to us and tells us that we must do something "significant" in its eyes to be successful.

Mt 3:1 In those days came John the Baptist, preaching in the wilderness of Judaea,

4 And the same John had his raiment of camel's hair, and a leathern girdle about his loins; and his meat was locusts and wild honey.

3. <u>We must obey God and do what He tells us to do even if we feel unworthy, or the task seems overwhelming or insignificant to us</u>. John obeyed God and baptized Jesus, even though he felt he was unworthy to do so. Another danger in our attempt to fulfill our calling is listening to our own evaluation of ourselves when we feel unworthy, inadequate, or incompetent to accomplish what we have been called to do. As in the case of the one talent man in the parable of the talents, we can be easily diverted from our purpose by our fear of failure. (Matthew 25:25) Jonah was also temporarily diverted by his fear of failure when he was called to preach repentance to the city of Nineveh. (Jonah 1:3)

Mt 3:13 Then cometh Jesus from Galilee to Jordan unto John, to be baptized of him.

14 But John forbad him, saying, I have need to be baptized of thee, and comest thou to me?

15 And Jesus answering said unto him, Suffer it to be so now: for thus it becometh us to fulfil all righteousness. Then he suffered him.

16 And Jesus, when he was baptized, went up straightway out of the water: and, lo, the heavens were opened unto him, and he saw the Spirit of God descending like a dove, and lighting upon him:

4. <u>We must not seek to make a name for ourselves or compete with others, but do our best to fulfill exactly what God has called us to do</u>. John the Baptist did not try to make a name for himself. In fact, he said that he must decrease so that Jesus could increase. He refused the temptation to compete with Jesus when his disciples complained that Jesus was becoming more popular and was baptizing more converts. In fact, he even sent some of his disciples to Jesus. He understood that he was called only to go before Jesus to prepare the way for His ministry. He recognized that they both had distinct and different callings.

Jo 3: 26 And they came unto John, and said unto him, Rabbi, he that was with thee beyond Jordan, to whom thou barest witness, behold, the same baptizeth, and all men come to him.

27 John answered and said, A man can receive nothing, except it be given him from heaven.

28 Ye yourselves bear me witness, that I said, I am not the Christ, but that I am sent before him.

29 He that hath the bride is the bridegroom: but the friend of the bridegroom, which standeth and heareth him, rejoiceth greatly because of the bridegroom's voice: this my joy therefore is fulfilled.

30 He must increase, but I must decrease.

5. <u>We must be willing to sacrifice whatever it takes to fully fulfill our ministry and accept whatever role God has for us in this life</u>. John was condemned by the world and eventually executed after less than two years of ministry. From the world's standpoint, he was a total failure. We are not to defend our ministry or ourselves but simply do what God calls us to do.

Mt 11:18 For John came neither eating nor drinking, and they say, He hath a devil.

14:3 For Herod had laid hold on John, and bound him, and put him in prison for Herodias' sake, his brother Philip's wife.

4 For John said unto him, It is not lawful for thee to have her.

8 And she, being before instructed of her mother, said, Give me here John Baptist's head in a charger.

10 And he sent, and beheaded John in the prison.

6. <u>We must persevere in viewing our life and what is important in this world from God's point of view</u>. This will enable us to yield our lives for His glory, and trust Him to bring it to pass. Although, from a worldly standpoint, John the Baptist might be considered a loser, Christ Himself stated that from God's standpoint, up until that time, there had been none greater than John. That meant that in God's eyes, John was as great as Abraham, Moses and Elijah! If we wish to be significant in the Kingdom of God, we need to find what God has called us to do, focus on our mission, serve God and complete it, without comparing ourselves to others. The soldier who does exactly what he is called to do is the one who is great and who will be rewarded. We must make a choice between being significant in this world, which passes away, or significant in the Kingdom of God, which lasts forever. We all have the potential to become great in God's Kingdom if we will simply seek His will for our lives, do our best to carry it out, and trust God for the results. This last verse states that all of us can be even greater than John the Baptist was, because the Spirit of God is within us.

Mt 11:2 Now when John had heard in the prison the works of Christ, he sent two of his disciples,

4 Jesus answered and said unto them, Go and shew John again those things which ye do hear and see:

7 And as they departed, Jesus began to say unto the multitudes concerning John, What went ye out into the wilderness to see? A reed shaken with the wind?

11 Verily I say unto you, Among them that are born of women <u>there hath not risen a greater than John the Baptist:</u> notwithstanding he that is least in the kingdom of heaven is greater than he.

Establishing Our Self-image

Our self-image is a combination of how we evaluate our worth, our importance, or our significance in life and how we perceive that others view us. Consequently, it embraces all of the issues discussed so far in these last two chapters.

To summarize what I have just discussed concerning self-worth and significance, please examine the chart on this page. Our worth is the straight line that never changes. Our significance, as God sees it, is the top line labeled the "Glory of God." In the Garden of Eden, both our worth and significance were at their maximum. At the fall, man perceived that his self-image and worth were dependent on performance and approval. Because of this, he perceived his attempts to do better as improving his worth and his failures or sin as diminishing it. Of course, this is not true, but to a person who believes that it is, this false perception results in an emotional roller-coaster ride. Due to selfishness and sin, the unsaved person's significance is minimal, but his worth is not really affected. When we were saved, faith in Christ began to deliver us from our selfishness and as this was accomplished, we trusted God to meet our needs more and more and, therefore, sinned less and less. However, God counted our faith for righteousness just as he did for Abraham. Consequently, to Him, it is as if we are already completely righteous. If we repent when we sin (represented on the chart by the different sized "V's"), we are forgiven so that in His eyes, we are truly righteous and have attained to His glory or plan for us. It becomes only a matter of growing in faith over our lifetime and our walk in life will approach closer and closer to our position in Christ. It is important to note that it is by faith in Him, not by our works or efforts that this transformation occurs. This demonstrates the reality of Ephesians 2:8-9, "For by grace are ye saved through faith; and that not of yourselves: [it is] the gift of God: Not of works, lest any man should boast." Both our worth and our significance, and consequently, the whole of our self-image, is based on and is dependent solely on what God alone has done for us!

Finally, let us establish God's formula for a valid self-image. It is the combination of: 1. My self-worth due to the unconditional love and acceptance of God. 2. My significance because I have been adopted into His family. 3. My imputed righteousness because the blood of Jesus covers all of my mistakes, shortcom-

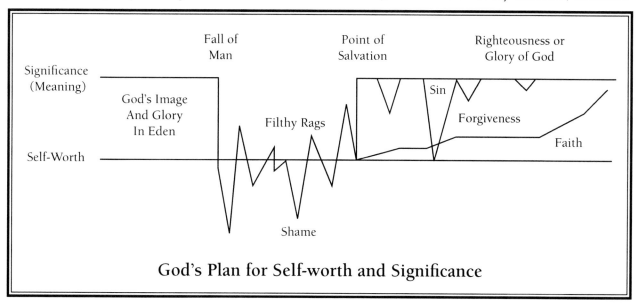

God's Plan for Self-worth and Significance

ings, and sin. 4. My imparted righteousness (or sanctification) which grows day by day as my faith in Him increases. Therefore, all of my entire self-image is based on my faith in Jesus Christ. Anything I am able to do unselfishly for Him is due solely to my faith in all that He has done for me. Therefore, it is not surprising that the Bible says we are to evaluate our self-image or ourselves by the measure of faith that we have. (Romans 12:3)

> Ro 12:3 For I say, through the grace given unto me, to every man that is among you, not to think [of himself] more highly than he ought to think; but to think soberly, according as God hath dealt to every man the measure of faith.

Please refer again to the model of Barak later in this book and the quick reference chart following this model for a list of steps for achieving a valid self-image.

Steps for Overcoming Insignificance

1. True significance comes by fulfilling what God has designed and called us to do. It is achieved by accepting our identity in Christ and doing God's will, not ours. We must find our importance in the sight of God, not in the sight of men.

2. We must be convinced that the world's system of competing with others (The "rat race") to achieve significance is a lie.

3. We must understand that we are not in competition with others, but that we are to compete against ourselves in order to run our own race and become all that God designed us to be.

4. It is God Who has chosen to give us life and the talents we have. He is the one who gave us our mission on this earth, He is the one who gave us the ability to get wealth, and He is the one Who promoted us, so we cannot take credit for anything that we have done, for what we possess, or for our success.

5. We must fight pride by being careful not to accept credit for anything we do, since without Christ, we cannot do anything of eternal value.

6. To God, all of our attempts to be righteous in our own efforts are filthy rags, because they are motivated out of selfishness. There is nothing we can do to make ourselves more significant.

7. Through the process of salvation by faith, God delivers us from our selfishness, forgives our sins, deals with our shame, and brings us into a place where we can do right motivated by unconditional love.

8. Because of what Christ has done, we have become so significant that we can not do anything on this earth to make ourselves any more important. God has adopted us into His family, chosen us to assist in ruling the universe, made us joint heirs with Jesus, and has declared us to be righteous through faith. This is our position in Christ and it cannot be improved upon. All we have to do is to accept it by faith.

Chapter 12

Faith and Security

Security is defined as, "The state of being secure; freedom from danger, poverty, or apprehension." It is our desire to be safe and have an abundant life. Security is so fundamental for survival and the enjoyment of life that it is one of our deepest needs. Fear is our natural response to a threat to our security. Fear is "an agitated feeling aroused by awareness of actual or threatening danger or trouble." It provides the energy to defend ourselves from a threat. Anxiety is a generalized fear due to a perceived or buried threat or conflict. (The Standard College Dictionary, Funk & Wagnalls, 1963) Feelings of security are fundamental to our happiness, and feelings of insecurity underlie almost all types of dysfunction and emotional torment.

How We Develop Our Feelings of Security

All of us begin life with certain basic fears: a fear of falling, noise, and maybe a fear of abandonment. During the first six to seven years of our lives, fears play a major role since children lack the means to judge or independently interpret the dangers of the world around them. Most overreactions in adult life and irrational fears come from traumatic childhood experiences. Fears are simply emotions that warn us when we may be in danger and provide the motivation and energy to escape from that danger. They activate our body to be prepared to protect itself. Our body undergoes a number of different changes as it prepares for our defense. The most noticeable changes include deeper respiration, increased pulse rate, higher blood pressure, a movement of the blood supply away from the stomach and intestines to the heart, muscles and lungs. Furthermore, all processes in the alimentary canal cease, the spleen contracts and sends corpuscles to damage control stations, adrenaline is excreted and sugar is freed from liver. (Morris, 1996)

As a child, we are just about as secure as our parents are. An infant's emotional makeup begins with that of the mother. It has been suggested that fear and anxiety can even be felt by the unborn child in the womb. As we have learned in the case of self-worth and significance, we learn about our world from our parents and accept their views as reality. An overprotective mother sends the message that the world is a dangerous and scary place. A secure mother transmits a feeling of security to the child. Of course, as the child grows, the experiences of life modify his or her view of life. Traumatic experiences can drastically alter views. As an example, men returning from war or those who have been traumatized by a great catastrophe may suffer from Post Traumatic Stress Disorder for a lifetime. Women who have been raped may suffer severe anxiety or panic attacks years after the event. Our overall outlook on life is set by these events and, because of them; we might remain a pessimist or optimist throughout the rest of our lives.

The World's System

When we realize that we live in a world filled with fearful possibilities, we naturally seek some way to make it safe. If we choose to rely on ourselves, we may work hard to cope with our fears, learn karate, lift weights, install a security system, put bars on our windows, wear a bulletproof vest or carry a gun. Other ways of coping include amassing large amounts of money, becoming powerful, or hiring somebody to protect us. Some, like the Pharisees try to be good enough to deserve God's protection. Whatever the method, we will work hard to make our world secure and prosperous.

How we view life significantly affects our emotional makeup and the intensity of our emotions, especially fear and anger. In one of my domestic violence groups, one of the men who attended described the world as "a sea of sharks that will devour you if you show any sign of weakness." Because of this perception of the world, he was a very angry person who tended to perceive almost everything that happened to him as a serious threat. Because of these perceptions, he had a significant problem with uncontrollable anger and violence.

The Consequences of the World's System for Security—Fear of Catastrophe

1. <u>We can never become absolutely safe by our own efforts</u>. We simply do not have enough information or capability. The attacks on the World Trade Center on September 11th made this very clear. Terrorist attacks, diseases, earthquakes, tornadoes and accidents can happen to all of us without warning and there is little we can reasonably do to prevent them. What could have the family driving under the overpass have done to prevent a steel beam from falling on their car at the split second that they drove by? Even if we try to be good enough to deserve protection as Job did, we will never be fully protected since we all sin.

    Ec 8:8 There is no man that hath power over the spirit to retain the spirit; neither hath he power in the day of death: and there is no discharge in that war; neither shall wickedness deliver those that are given to it.

    Job 24:22 He draweth also the mighty with his power: he riseth up, and no man is sure of life.

2. <u>The more we rely on ourselves, the more vulnerable to fear we become</u>. When we imply that we are going to rely on ourselves and be our own God, God watches until we learn that He alone can provide for our safety. The more we trust in ourselves, the more we realize how limited we really are. The result is anxiety and fear. *Problems get Bigger*

    Ps 20:7 Some trust in chariots, and some in horses: but we will remember the name of the LORD our God.

    Mic 5:10 And it shall come to pass in that day, saith the LORD, that I will cut off thy horses out of the midst of thee, and I will destroy thy chariots:

3. <u>The more we try to control people or circumstances, the more we lose our ability to control them</u>. If we try to control people, they will eventually rebel against our attempts to control them. When we try to control our circumstances, our very attempts tend to overcompensate and cause our circumstances to spiral further out of control. What we learn in the end is that we are truly powerless over most of the events of our lives. <u>The only real way to gain control of our lives is to give up trying to control our lives and yield them to God—the only One Who is truly in control of everything</u>.

    Lu 17:33 Whosoever shall seek to save his life shall lose it; and whosoever shall lose his life shall preserve it.

    Jo 12:25 He that loveth his life shall lose it; and he that hateth his life in this world shall keep it unto life eternal.

    Pr 16:25 There is a way that seemeth right unto a man, but the end thereof are the ways of death.

4. <u>The more we have or gain, the more we have to fear</u>. The more successful in life we are at playing the game of "king of the hill," the more we become a target of those hoping to replace us. The richer we are or the more we possess things that others want, the more we become a target for theft or con games. Armies, no matter how powerful, are never enough. This has become clear in Iraq. In fact, our power and abundance makes us the prime target of terrorist organizations. Today, it is much safer when traveling abroad to be a citizen of an undeveloped and impoverished country than it is to be a citizen of the sole superpower on Earth.

Isa 31:1 Woe to them that go down to Egypt for help; and stay on horses, and trust in chariots, because they are many; and in horsemen, because they are very strong; but they look not unto the Holy One of Israel, neither seek the LORD!

5. <u>The more we possess on earth, the more we have to do to maintain and protect what we have acquired</u>. Life becomes a constant fight to stay ahead. The greater our house and yard, the more we have to paint and mow. The more money we have, the more we are consumed with our investments. The larger the business, the more we have to struggle to maintain our market share. Riches do not really increase our security, but increase our responsibilities and, therefore, can make us feel even more insecure.

Mt 6:19 Lay not up for yourselves treasures upon earth, where moth and rust doth corrupt, and where thieves break through and steal:

20 But lay up for yourselves treasures in heaven, where neither moth nor rust doth corrupt, and where thieves do not break through nor steal:

6. <u>The more we focus on our fears the greater they become</u>. Sometimes we feel that by thinking about our problems we will feel more in control. The opposite is true. The more we are concerned and focus on our fears, the greater they become in our minds until we become obsessed by them. Howard Hughes, who had everything he wanted, eventually became consumed with a fear of germs and protecting himself from disease to such a degree that he isolated himself for the remainder of his life.

Job 3:25 For the thing which I greatly feared is come upon me, and that which I was afraid of is come unto me.

26 I was not in safety, neither had I rest, neither was I quiet; yet trouble came.

Ps 48:6 Fear took hold upon them there, and pain, as of a woman in travail.

Lu 21:26 Men's hearts failing them for fear, and for looking after those things which are coming on the earth: for the powers of heaven shall be shaken.

7. <u>The more successful and prominent we become, the greater our potential for having a significant failure</u>. The recent trial of Martha Stewart for lying to an investigator about inside trading is a good example. Even the prosecution agreed that if she was not so prominent they possibly would have dropped the case. The more we build our security on our performance and the approval of others, the more vulnerable we become when we fail.

Pr 29:25 The fear of man bringeth a snare: but whoso putteth his trust in the LORD shall be safe

8. <u>The level of stress that we experience in life increases as we accomplish more, achieve greater position, or have more possessions</u>. This is because with greater accomplishments and success,

come more responsibility. In fact, the more we have, the more that is required of us, and the more that is required of us, the more we will feel that all the demands on our lives exceed our capabilities. Stress results when we perceive that what we are required to do exceeds our current capabilities. I counseled an engineer who was experiencing anxiety attacks, not because he feared failure, but because of the added responsibility that went along with his continued successes.

9. Riches do not make you happy. It is interesting to note that today there are psychologists that specialize in just helping the very rich and famous cope with their anxiety and the problems associated with being rich and famous. The Bible makes it clear that leading a normal life is best.

    Pr 30:8 Remove far from me vanity and lies: give me neither poverty nor riches; feed me with food convenient for me:

    9 Lest I be full, and deny thee, and say, Who is the LORD? or lest I be poor, and steal, and take the name of my God in vain.

10. We eventually all lose the battle to make ourselves secure and die. As we become older, most people feel less and less secure, especially when they come face to face with the day of their death. We cannot take our power, accomplishments or possessions with us, and if we are without Christ, we must face the greatest of all fears alone. Ultimately, without God, there is no answer for our fears and, especially, for our security beyond the grave.

    Mt 10:28 And fear not them which kill the body, but are not able to kill the soul: but rather fear him which is able to destroy both soul and body in hell.

God's System for Security

How we view God colors our entire world and what we believe about Him determines how secure we are in life. Is He a taskmaster that demands obedience waiting for us to make a mistake so He can punish us, or is He a loving God that gives us unmerited favor and even uses our mistakes for our long term good? Does He protect us from every danger or are we just rolling the dice waiting for a catastrophe in our lives?

Because even many Christians do not totally understand what the Bible has to say concerning the protection that God provides, they are not able to live in the security and peace that He meant for us to have. Many are confused about what God promises to do to protect us, what part we play in our own protection, what we need to do or not do to remain in God's protection, and how to deal with the tragic events in our lives that do not seem to line up with what the Bible promises. A number of excellent books have been written on this subject, but let us examine briefly, what is clear from the Word of God.

1. The only way to obtain an abundant, secure life is to follow Christ.

    Mr 8:35 For whosoever will save his life shall lose it; but whosoever shall lose his life for my sake and the gospel's, the same shall save it.

    Lu 12:33 Sell that ye have, and give alms; provide yourselves bags which wax not old, a treasure in the heavens that faileth not, where no thief approacheth, neither moth corrupteth.

    Mt 7:13 Enter ye in at the strait gate: for wide is the gate, and broad is the way, that leadeth to destruction, and many there be which go in thereat:

    14 Because strait is the gate, and narrow is the way, which leadeth unto life, and few there be that find it.

2. <u>We can either try to make ourselves secure in this life through our own efforts and the world's system, or we can serve God</u>. We cannot have both. There is no security trying to ride on the fence of life.

   Mt 6:24 No man can serve two masters: for either he will hate the one, and love the other; or else he will hold to the one, and despise the other. Ye cannot serve God and mammon.

3. <u>God has promised to take care of us, just like He cares for all of creation.</u>

   Mt 6:25 Therefore I say unto you, Take no thought for your life, what ye shall eat, or what ye shall drink; nor yet for your body, what ye shall put on. Is not the life more than meat, and the body than raiment?

   26 Behold the fowls of the air: for they sow not, neither do they reap, nor gather into barns; yet your heavenly Father feedeth them. Are ye not much better than they?

4. <u>We must realize that what we can accomplish, no matter how hard we try, is extremely limited.</u>

   Mt 6:27 Which of you by taking thought can add one cubit unto his stature?

5. <u>We can never, in our own efforts, take care of ourselves as well as God can provide for us when we fully trust Him.</u>

   Mt 6:28 And why take ye thought for raiment? Consider the lilies of the field, how they grow; they toil not, neither do they spin:

   29 And yet I say unto you, That even Solomon in all his glory was not arrayed like one of these.

   30 Wherefore, if God so clothe the grass of the field, which to day is, and to morrow is cast into the oven, shall he not much more clothe you, O ye of little faith?

6. <u>We are not to worry about things like food or clothing, for God knows that we need them.</u>

   Mt 6:31 Therefore take no thought, saying, What shall we eat? or, What shall we drink? or, Wherewithal shall we be clothed?

   32 (For after all these things do the Gentiles seek:) for your heavenly Father knoweth that ye have need of all these things.

7. <u>Having our needs met and finding security in life can only be obtained indirectly, by seeking the good of God's kingdom and living right, always trusting in His power.</u>

   Mt 6:33 But seek ye first the kingdom of God, and his righteousness; and all these things shall be added unto you.

8. <u>When we have put our trust in God, we should not even be concerned about what could happen tomorrow.</u>

   Mt 6:34 Take therefore no thought for the morrow: for the morrow shall take thought for the things of itself. Sufficient unto the day is the evil thereof.

   De 31:6 Be strong and of a good courage, fear not, nor be afraid of them: for the LORD thy God, he it is that doth go with thee; he will not fail thee, nor forsake thee.

9. <u>God is not limited in power, but can help in all circumstances.</u>

    2 Chr 14:11 And Asa cried unto the LORD his God, and said, LORD, it is nothing with thee to help, whether with many, or with them that have no power: help us, O LORD our God; for we rest on thee, and in thy name we go against this multitude. O LORD, thou art our God; let not man prevail against thee.

    Job 26:2 How hast thou helped him that is without power? how savest thou the arm that hath no strength?

    Isa 40:29 He giveth power to the faint; and to them that have no might he increaseth strength.

    50:2 Wherefore, when I came, was there no man? when I called, was there none to answer? Is my hand shortened at all, that it cannot redeem? or have I no power to deliver? behold, at my rebuke I dry up the sea, I make the rivers a wilderness: their fish stinketh, because there is no water, and dieth for thirst.

    Jos 1:5 There shall not any man be able to stand before thee all the days of thy life: as I was with Moses, so I will be with thee: I will not fail thee, nor forsake thee.

    21:45 There failed not ought of any good thing which the LORD had spoken unto the house of Israel; all came to pass.

10. <u>Our security in life depends on doing what God tells us to do in the Word of God, not just hearing His Word.</u>

    Mt 7:24 Therefore whosoever heareth these sayings of mine, and doeth them, I will liken him unto a wise man, which built his house upon a rock:

    25 And the rain descended, and the floods came, and the winds blew, and beat upon that house; and it fell not: for it was founded upon a rock.

    26 And every one that heareth these sayings of mine, and doeth them not, shall be likened unto a foolish man, which built his house upon the sand:

    27 And the rain descended, and the floods came, and the winds blew, and beat upon that house; and it fell: and great was the fall of it.

11. <u>God has given us supernatural power.</u>

    Mt 10:1 And when he had called unto him his twelve disciples, he gave them power against unclean spirits, to cast them out, and to heal all manner of sickness and all manner of disease.

    Lu 10:19 Behold, I give unto you power to tread on serpents and scorpions, and over all the power of the enemy: and nothing shall by any means hurt you.

12. <u>It is in our weakness that we manifest the power of God most effectively.</u>

    2 Co 4:7 But we have this treasure in earthen vessels, that the excellency of the power may be of God, and not of us.

    12:9 And he said unto me, My grace is sufficient for thee: for my strength is made perfect in weakness. Most gladly therefore will I rather glory in my infirmities, that the power of Christ may rest upon me.

    13:4 For though he was crucified through weakness, yet he liveth by the power of God. For we also are weak in him, but we shall live with him by the power of God toward you.

13. <u>When we rely on God, His power within us makes all things possible</u>.

Eph 3:20 Now unto him that is able to do exceeding abundantly above all that we ask or think, according to the power that worketh in us,

6:10 Finally, my brethren, be strong in the Lord, and in the power of his might.

14. <u>Only God can protect us from the ultimate insecurity of death</u>.

1 Co 15:52 In a moment, in the twinkling of an eye, at the last trump: for the trumpet shall sound, and the dead shall be raised incorruptible, and we shall be changed.

53 For this corruptible must put on incorruption, and this mortal must put on immortality.

54 So when this corruptible shall have put on incorruption, and this mortal shall have put on immortality, then shall be brought to pass the saying that is written, Death is swallowed up in victory.

The Consequences of God's Plan for Security—Peace and Happiness

If we choose to end our attempts to provide our own security and rely on God for our protection and prosperity, this choice will significantly affect the quality of our lives and eventually lead to the abundant life that God has promised us.

1. <u>We will be protected from catastrophe if we rely on Him</u>.

Ps 91:1 He that dwelleth in the secret place of the most High shall abide under the shadow of the Almighty.

2 I will say of the LORD, He is my refuge and my fortress: my God; in him will I trust.

3 Surely he shall deliver thee from the snare of the fowler, and from the noisome pestilence.

4 He shall cover thee with his feathers, and under his wings shalt thou trust: his truth shall be thy shield and buckler.

5 Thou shalt not be afraid for the terror by night; nor for the arrow that flieth by day;

6 Nor for the pestilence that walketh in darkness; nor for the destruction that wasteth at noonday.

7 A thousand shall fall at thy side, and ten thousand at thy right hand; but it shall not come nigh thee.

2. <u>Everything will work for our good</u>.

Ps 91:9 Because thou hast made the LORD, which is my refuge, even the most High, thy habitation;

10 There shall no evil befall thee, neither shall any plague come nigh thy dwelling.

11 For he shall give his angels charge over thee, to keep thee in all thy ways.

12 They shall bear thee up in their hands, lest thou dash thy foot against a stone.

13 Thou shalt tread upon the lion and adder: the young lion and the dragon shalt thou trample under feet.

14 Because he hath set his love upon me, therefore will I deliver him: I will set him on high, because he hath known my name.

15 He shall call upon me, and I will answer him: I will be with him in trouble; I will deliver him, and honour him.

16 With long life will I satisfy him, and shew him my salvation.

Ro 8:28 And we know that all things work together for good to them that love God, to them who are the called according to his purpose.

3.   We will be delivered from our fears.

Ps 27:1 The LORD is my light and my salvation; whom shall I fear? the LORD is the strength of my life; of whom shall I be afraid?

27:3 Though an host should encamp against me, my heart shall not fear: though war should rise against me, in this will I be confident.

4.   We will experience the peace of God.

Ps 4:8 I will both lay me down in peace, and sleep: for thou, LORD, only makest me dwell in safety.

46:2 Therefore will not we fear, though the earth be removed, and though the mountains be carried into the midst of the sea;

56:4 In God I will praise his word, in God I have put my trust; I will not fear what flesh can do unto me.

5.   We will be prosperous and have all that we need.

Ez 34:27 And the tree of the field shall yield her fruit, and the earth shall yield her increase, and they shall be safe in their land, and shall know that I am the LORD, when I have broken the bands of their yoke, and delivered them out of the hand of those that served themselves of them.

2 Pe 1:3 According as his divine power hath given unto us all things that pertain unto life and godliness, through the knowledge of him that hath called us to glory and virtue:

Ps 34:9 O fear the LORD, ye his saints: for there is no want to them that fear him.

6.   We will be happy.

Ps 144:15 Happy is that people, that is in such a case: yea, happy is that people, whose God is the LORD.

146:5 Happy is he that hath the God of Jacob for his help, whose hope is in the LORD his God:

1 Pe 3:14 But and if ye suffer for righteousness' sake, happy are ye: and be not afraid of their terror, neither be troubled;

7.   Nothing will be able to shake our optimism about life.

Ps 23:1 The LORD is my shepherd; I shall not want.

2 He maketh me to lie down in green pastures: he leadeth me beside the still waters.

3 He restoreth my soul: he leadeth me in the paths of righteousness for his name's sake.

4 Yea, though I walk through the valley of the shadow of death, I will fear no evil: for thou art with me; thy rod and thy staff they comfort me

8. <u>We will have the great and wonderful life that God intended for us</u>.

    Ps 23:5 Thou preparest a table before me in the presence of mine enemies: thou anointest my head with oil; my cup runneth over.

    6 Surely goodness and mercy shall follow me all the days of my life: and I will dwell in the house of the LORD for ever.

    Lu 12:32 Fear not, little flock; for it is your Father's good pleasure to give you the kingdom.

9. <u>We will be delivered from the fear of death</u>.

    1Co 15: 55 O death, where is thy sting? O grave, where is thy victory?

    56 The sting of death is sin; and the strength of sin is the law.

    57 But thanks be to God, which giveth us the victory through our Lord Jesus Christ.

The Process of Transformation by Faith to Have a Secure Life

We have just examined the basic principles of security outlined in Bible. The process of developing a secure life is based primarily on knowing the truth about what God will do for us, believing His truth in our heart and acting according to it by facing our fears. In order to help my clients, I use the following steps to teach them a summary of what we have already learned and challenge them to choose which system of security they want for their lives: God's which results in peace and safety, the world's which results in a fear of catastrophe, or the devil's which will result in catastrophe.

1. <u>We must learn what the Word of God promises us concerning fear and our protection from catastrophe</u>. Because this is an essential and complex subject, I have provided an outline of these important principles and a chart labeled Protection from Catastrophe at the end of this chapter.

2. <u>Although fear is a natural response, we must learn to master it for our good</u>. Rational fears warn us about danger, but irrational fears can debilitate us. Fear can manifests itself through anxiety, panic attacks, phobias, posttraumatic stress disorder, obsessions and compulsions. If we do not master it, it will hinder our life, stop what God has called us to do and prevent us from having the abundant life that God has provided for us.

3. <u>We must quit trying in our own strength to feel secure and completely yield our lives to God, trusting in Him for our protection</u>. Because we are so limited in this life, the more we rely on ourselves, the more we will feel insecure.

4. <u>Since faith in God is the opposite of fear, we must establish a close, intimate relationship with God in order to trust Him more than our fears</u>. We must do everything we can to build and strengthen our faith since it is the key for overcoming our fears and having a happy life. (See the chapter on methods for increasing our faith.)

5. <u>We must focus on God instead of our fears</u>. The more we concentrate on our problems and fears, the more they grow in strength. The more we focus on God, the more our faith in Him will overcome our fears. This principle is clearly illustrated when the children of Israel sinned by speaking against Moses and were being bitten by snakes. The brass serpent on the pole is a type of Jesus taking our sins upon the cross. When we concentrate our focus on Him, we are healed of our fears; and when we focus on our fears, they become larger and will eventually consume us.

    Nu 21: 7 Therefore the people came to Moses, and said, We have sinned, for we have spoken against the LORD, and against thee; pray unto the LORD, that he take away the serpents from us. And Moses prayed for the people.

8 And the LORD said unto Moses, Make thee a fiery serpent, and set it upon a pole: and it shall come to pass, that every one that is bitten, when he looketh upon it, shall live.

9 And Moses made a serpent of brass, and put it upon a pole, and it came to pass, that if a serpent had bitten any man, when he beheld the serpent of brass, he lived.

6. <u>Facing our fears is the most effective way to overcome them.</u> Facing them systematically, a little at a time, is a very effective method for overcoming all types of insecurity. When the Hebrew children faced the fiery furnace, they were not harmed by its fire. (For the steps for overcoming fear, see the model of the fiery furnace later in this book.)

7. <u>God promises that, if we will put our trust in Him, we will never be tempted beyond what we are able and that He will protect us from catastrophe.</u> (1 Corinthians 10:13) It is critical that we believe this in all of our heart and especially in our spirit. If we do, we can face any fear knowing that we can overcome it with God's help.

8. <u>We must totally abandon our own pride and self-reliance, do our part to face our fears through faith and trust God to protect and deliver us from all of our fears.</u> As long as we try to provide even a small part of our own security and protection, we will fail.

9. <u>We must believe and expect that through faith, God will provide all we need, protect us from all evil and work everything for our good; so that we can possess the fantastic wonderful life of peace and happiness that He wants and has provided for each of us.</u> Insecurity and fear are the greatest hindrances to achieving God's abundant and eternal life; and finding our security through faith is one of the most important keys to obtaining this life. We must do everything we can to develop the faith to win this critical victory in our lives.

One of the most significant issues to be addressed in helping a Christian client feel more secure in life is to teach them the biblical principles of protection from catastrophe. Almost everyone will agree that God does not promise to remove all seemingly negative events from our lives at the moment that we are saved. However, most Christians do not have a clear understanding of what they can expect from God. We have three choices in life concerning protection from catastrophe. We can follow God's plan, the world's plan or the devil's plan. Each will lead to very different consequences for our lives. The chart at the end of this chapter can be used as an aid when summarizing these principles.

God's Plan for Our Security—Peace and Safety

1. <u>God's plan for us: only good.</u>

   Jer 29:11 For I know the thoughts that I think toward you, saith the LORD, thoughts of peace, and not of evil, to give you an expected end.

2. <u>Because God loves us and has our best interests in mind, He will work everything—even our mistakes—for our good if we love and yield to His plan for us.</u>

   Ro 8:28 And we know that all things work together for good to them that love God, to them who are the called according to his purpose.

   Ps 23:6 Surely goodness and mercy shall follow me all the days of my life: and I will dwell in the house of the LORD for ever.

3. <u>God promises to protect us if we will accept His love, rely on Him for protection and pray in faith.</u>

Ps 91:1 He that dwelleth in the secret place of the most High shall abide under the shadow of the Almighty.

14 Because he hath set his love upon me, therefore will I deliver him: I will set him on high, because he hath known my name.

15 He shall call upon me, and I will answer him: I will be with him in trouble; I will deliver him, and honour him.

Pr 18:10 The name of the LORD is a strong tower: the righteous runneth into it, and is safe.

2 Pe 1:4 Whereby are given unto us exceeding great and precious promises: that by these ye might be partakers of the divine nature, having escaped the corruption that is in the world through lust.

4. <u>When we accept Christ, we are accepted in Him. Because Christ perfectly fulfilled the law, we are free from the law that through sin leads to catastrophe.</u>

Ro 6:8 Now if we be dead with Christ, we believe that we shall also live with him:

9 Knowing that Christ being raised from the dead dieth no more; death hath no more dominion over him.

22 But now being made free from sin, and become servants to God, ye have your fruit unto holiness, and the end everlasting life.

5. <u>Although God allows the direct consequences of our choices so we can learn from our mistakes, He never allows us to be placed into a situation from which recovery is impossible or where we cannot, with His help, endure our circumstances.</u>

1 Co 10:13 There hath no temptation taken you but such as is common to man: but God is faithful, who will not suffer you to be tempted above that ye are able; but will with the temptation also make a way to escape, that ye may be able to bear it.

6. <u>God does not promise to protect us from all the struggles of this world, because they are tools for our growth, and when we overcome them He gets the glory.</u>

Ro 8:35 Who shall separate us from the love of Christ? shall tribulation, or distress, or persecution, or famine, or nakedness, or peril, or sword?

36 As it is written, For thy sake we are killed all the day long; we are accounted as sheep for the slaughter.

37 Nay, in all these things we are more than conquerors through him that loved us.

7. <u>God's protection is based on His eternal viewpoint of good knowing all things present and future, though it may not appear to be the obvious good from our temporal standpoint.</u>

Isa 55:8 For my thoughts are not your thoughts, neither are your ways my ways, saith the LORD.

9 For as the heavens are higher than the earth, so are my ways higher than your ways, and my thoughts than your thoughts.

12 For ye shall go out with joy, and be led forth with peace: the mountains and the hills shall break forth before you into singing, and all the trees of the field shall clap their hands.

Jo 9:2 And his disciples asked him, saying, Master, who did sin, this man, or his parents, that he was born blind?

3 Jesus answered, Neither hath this man sinned, nor his parents: but that the works of God should be made manifest in him.

 8.   When our perception of things seems to indicate that He has failed us, God asks that we have faith in Him and trust His infinite wisdom. He does not owe us an explanation.

Job 40:6 Then answered the LORD unto Job out of the whirlwind, and said,

7 Gird up thy loins now like a man: I will demand of thee, and declare thou unto me.

8 Wilt thou also disannul my judgment? wilt thou condemn me, that thou mayest be righteous?

9 Hast thou an arm like God? or canst thou thunder with a voice like him?

10 Deck thyself now with majesty and excellency; and array thyself with glory and beauty.

11 Cast abroad the rage of thy wrath: and behold every one that is proud, and abase him.

12 Look on every one that is proud, and bring him low; and tread down the wicked in their place.

13 Hide them in the dust together; and bind their faces in secret.

14 Then will I also confess unto thee that thine own right hand can save thee.

 9.   The result is peace and safety.

Php 4:7 And the peace of God, which passeth all understanding, shall keep your hearts and minds through Christ Jesus.

The World's Plan for Our Security Without God—Fear of Catastrophe

1.   The world without God: Chance.

Ec 9:11 I returned, and saw under the sun, that the race is not to the swift, nor the battle to the strong, neither yet bread to the wise, nor yet riches to men of understanding, nor yet favour to men of skill; but time and chance happeneth to them all.

2.   After God entrusted the world to us, we chose to be our own god and provide our own protection.

Ge 2:15 And the LORD God took the man, and put him into the garden of Eden to dress it and to keep it.

16 And the LORD God commanded the man, saying, Of every tree of the garden thou mayest freely eat:

17 But of the tree of the knowledge of good and evil, thou shalt not eat of it: for in the day that thou eatest thereof thou shalt surely die.

3:5 For God doth know that in the day ye eat thereof, then your eyes shall be opened, and ye shall be as gods, knowing good and evil.

6 And when the woman saw that the tree was good for food, and that it was pleasant to the eyes, and a tree to be desired to make one wise, she took of the fruit thereof, and did eat, and gave also unto her husband with her; and he did eat.

3. Our selfish choices bring evil consequences into the world and this can result in catastrophe in our lives.

   1 Co 10:6 Now these things were our examples, to the intent we should not lust after evil things, as they also lusted.

   7 Neither be ye idolaters, as were some of them; as it is written, The people sat down to eat and drink, and rose up to play.

   8 Neither let us commit fornication, as some of them committed, and fell in one day three and twenty thousand.

   9 Neither let us tempt Christ, as some of them also tempted, and were destroyed of serpents.

   10 Neither murmur ye, as some of them also murmured, and were destroyed of the destroyer.

   11 Now all these things happened unto them for ensamples: and they are written for our admonition, upon whom the ends of the world are come.

4. It is not "God's fault" for "allowing evil" because God is not responsible for our free choices. God does not do evil, neither can He be tempted to do evil.

   Ps 5:4 For thou art not a God that hath pleasure in wickedness: neither shall evil dwell with thee.

   Jas 1:13 Let no man say when he is tempted, I am tempted of God: for God cannot be tempted with evil, neither tempteth he any man:

5. Although a sinless person would be protected, all without Christ are vulnerable since we all sin.

   Job 4:7 Remember, I pray thee, who ever perished, being innocent? or where were the righteous cut off?

   Ro 3:23 For all have sinned, and come short of the glory of God;

6. The more we rely on ourselves for our protection the more fearful we become as we realize how limited we are.

   Job 3:25 For the thing which I greatly feared is come upon me, and that which I was afraid of is come unto me.

   26 I was not in safety, neither had I rest, neither was I quiet; yet trouble came.

7. God actively opposes those who are proud and want to be their own God so that they will eventually understand their need for Him.

   Job 33:17 That he may withdraw man from his purpose, and hide pride from man.

   Jas 4:6 But he giveth more grace. Wherefore he saith, God resisteth the proud, but giveth grace unto the humble.

8. Because we choose to rely on ourselves and we do not have enough information or capability, we can never guarantee our own protection.

   Job 4:6 Although affliction cometh not forth of the dust, neither doth trouble spring out of the ground;

7 Yet man is born unto trouble, as the sparks fly upward.

Lu 13:2 And Jesus answering said unto them, Suppose ye that these Galilaeans were sinners above all the Galilaeans, because they suffered such things?

3 I tell you, Nay: but, except ye repent, ye shall all likewise perish.

4 Or those eighteen, upon whom the tower in Siloam fell, and slew them, think ye that they were sinners above all men that dwelt in Jerusalem?

5 I tell you, Nay: but, except ye repent, ye shall all likewise perish.

9.   The result is fear of catastrophe.

Heb 2:15 And deliver them who through fear of death were all their lifetime subject to bondage.

The Devil's Plan for Our Security—Catastrophe

1.   The devil's Plan: Catastrophe

Jo 10:10 The thief cometh not, but for to steal, and to kill, and to destroy: I am come that they might have life, and that they might have it more abundantly.

2.   The devil introduced evil into the world when he tempted Adam and Eve and they sinned.

Ge 3:13 And the LORD God said unto the woman, What is this that thou hast done? And the woman said, The serpent beguiled me, and I did eat.

14 And the LORD God said unto the serpent, Because thou hast done this, thou art cursed above all cattle, and above every beast of the field; upon thy belly shalt thou go, and dust shalt thou eat all the days of thy life:

15 And I will put enmity between thee and the woman, and between thy seed and her seed; it shall bruise thy head, and thou shalt bruise his heel.

16 Unto the woman he said, I will greatly multiply thy sorrow and thy conception; in sorrow thou shalt bring forth children; and thy desire shall be to thy husband, and he shall rule over thee.

17 And unto Adam he said, Because thou hast hearkened unto the voice of thy wife, and hast eaten of the tree, of which I commanded thee, saying, Thou shalt not eat of it: cursed is the ground for thy sake; in sorrow shalt thou eat of it all the days of thy life;

18 Thorns also and thistles shall it bring forth to thee; and thou shalt eat the herb of the field;

19 In the sweat of thy face shalt thou eat bread, till thou return unto the ground; for out of it wast thou taken: for dust thou art, and unto dust shalt thou return.

3.   Evil continues in the world through lust–meeting needs through the flesh—and this leads to death.

Jas 1:14 But every man is tempted, when he is drawn away of his own lust, and enticed.

15 Then when lust hath conceived, it bringeth forth sin: and sin, when it is finished, bringeth forth death.

4.   The devil has power over us only when we sin, fail to rely on Christ or do not use the power given to us by Jesus.

Lu 10:19 Behold, I give unto you power to tread on serpents and scorpions, and over all the power of the enemy: and nothing shall by any means hurt you.

5. When we reject Christ, we become responsible for our own sin, and receive its consequences.

Ro 14:12 So then every one of us shall give account of himself to God.

6. Pride, which is self-reliance—telling God we want to do it ourselves—removes the protection of God and makes us vulnerable to attack.

Pr 16:18 Pride goeth before destruction, and an haughty spirit before a fall.

— Acting on something you don't have faith for

7. Presumption, tempting God or direct disobedience makes us vulnerable to attack because we do not rely on God for our protection.

Lu 4:9 And he brought him to Jerusalem, and set him on a pinnacle of the temple, and said unto him, If thou be the Son of God, cast thyself down from hence:

10 For it is written, He shall give his angels charge over thee, to keep thee:

11 And in their hands they shall bear thee up, lest at any time thou dash thy foot against a stone.

12 And Jesus answering said unto him, It is said, Thou shalt not tempt the Lord thy God.

13 And when the devil had ended all the temptation, he departed from him for a season.

Nu 14:41 And Moses said, Wherefore now do ye transgress the commandment of the LORD? but it shall not prosper.

42 Go not up, for the LORD is not among you; that ye be not smitten before your enemies.

43 For the Amalekites and the Canaanites are there before you, and ye shall fall by the sword: because ye are turned away from the LORD, therefore the LORD will not be with you.

44 But they presumed to go up unto the hill top: nevertheless the ark of the covenant of the LORD, and Moses, departed not out of the camp.

45 Then the Amalekites came down, and the Canaanites which dwelt in that hill, and smote them, and discomfited them, even unto Hormah.

Jo 5:14 Afterward Jesus findeth him in the temple, and said unto him, Behold, thou art made whole: sin no more, lest a worse thing come unto thee.

8. Not using the tools of faith, prayer or the armor of God to defeat the devil makes us vulnerable to being defeated.

Jas 4:2 Ye lust, and have not: ye kill, and desire to have, and cannot obtain: ye fight and war, yet ye have not, because ye ask not.

3 Ye ask, and receive not, because ye ask amiss, that ye may consume it upon your lusts.

Eph 6: 10 Finally, my brethren, be strong in the Lord, and in the power of his might.

11 Put on the whole armour of God, that ye may be able to stand against the wiles of the devil.

12 For we wrestle not against flesh and blood, but against principalities, against powers, against the rulers of the darkness of this world, against spiritual wickedness in high places.

13 Wherefore take unto you the whole armour of God, that ye may be able to withstand in the evil day, and having done all, to stand.

14 Stand therefore, having your loins girt about with truth, and having on the breastplate of righteousness;

15 And your feet shod with the preparation of the gospel of peace;

16 Above all, taking the shield of faith, wherewith ye shall be able to quench all the fiery darts of the wicked.

17 And take the helmet of salvation, and the sword of the Spirit, which is the word of God:

18 Praying always with all prayer and supplication in the Spirit, and watching thereunto with all perseverance and supplication for all saints;

9.   <u>The result is catastrophe</u>.

1 Th 5:3 For when they shall say, Peace and safety; then sudden destruction cometh upon them, as travail upon a woman with child; and they shall not escape.

How to Have a Happy Life

Protection from catastrophe is the foundation of having a happy life. According to Funk and Wagnall's Standard College Dictionary, happiness is "The state of quality of being pleased or content. Good fortune, prosperity, good luck." (1963) When we study the Word of God, we find that a number of areas of our life contribute to our happiness.

1.   <u>Protection from catastrophe</u>

De 33:29 Happy art thou, O Israel: who is like unto thee, O people saved by the LORD, the shield of thy help, and who is the sword of thy excellency! and thine enemies shall be found liars unto thee; and thou shalt tread upon their high places.

2.   <u>Prosperity</u>

Ps 128:2 For thou shalt eat the labour of thine hands: happy shalt thou be, and it shall be well with thee.

3.   <u>Trust and hope in God for the future</u>

Ps 144:15 Happy is that people, that is in such a case: yea, happy is that people, whose God is the LORD.

146:5 Happy is he that hath the God of Jacob for his help, whose hope is in the LORD his God:

4.   <u>Possessing and using wisdom</u>

Pr 3:13 Happy is the man that findeth wisdom, and the man that getteth understanding.

18 She is a tree of life to them that lay hold upon her: and happy is every one that retaineth her.

5.   <u>Living by God's principles</u>

Jo 13:17 If ye know these things, happy are ye if ye do them.

A common belief in this society is that if people are successful, they will be happy. This is not necessarily the case. The world's system fails in that it can never insure that anyone will be completely secure or that all their needs will be met in the future. Most people experience some moments of happiness in their lives, but are unable to maintain this state for significant periods of time. This is because they are basing their happiness on the current circumstances of their lives and circumstances. When they perceive that things are not going as they wish, their state of happiness vanishes. Because life will have its tribulations (John 16:33), happiness, to most people, is an elusive goal that easily slips out of their grasp. However, for those Christians who are willing to take God at His Word in faith, not only security, but also a life of continual happiness is possible. Both security and happiness are essential parts of the abundant life that God has provided for us. In order to achieve true happiness, we must do our part to:

1. Trust God for our protection. Avoid pride, tempting God, presumption, and direct disobedience. These are the requirements for remaining under His protection.

    Ps 91:1 He that dwelleth in the secret place of the most High shall abide under the shadow of the Almighty.

    2 I will say of the LORD, He is my refuge and my fortress: my God; in him will I trust.

    3 Surely he shall deliver thee from the snare of the fowler, and from the noisome pestilence.

2. Submit to God's plan for our life. His ways are better. God has a specific plan for our lives. He created us for this plan and gave us the talents to accomplish it as we trust and rely on Him. In order to be happy, we must fit within His perfect will for us.

    Jer 29:11 For I know the thoughts that I think toward you, saith the LORD, thoughts of peace, and not of evil, to give you an expected end.

    Isa 55:8 For my thoughts are not your thoughts, neither are your ways my ways, saith the LORD.

    9 For as the heavens are higher than the earth, so are my ways higher than your ways, and my thoughts than your thoughts.

3. Trust in His shield of faith. We must believe that we have absolute protection from evil as long as we rely on the shield of faith or the presence of God. He always has our best interests in mind from His standpoint of eternity. He knows the future outcome of everything. Only those things that are for our eternal good can pass through that shield of protection. In *The Christian's Secret of a Happy Life*, Hannah Whithall Smith (1983) explains a vision of this protection that helped her understand this all-important biblical truth.

    She thought she was in a perfectly dark place. A body of light came toward her from a distance, which gradually surrounded and enveloped her and everything around her. As it approached, a voice seemed to say, "This is the presence of God. This is the presence of God." While surrounded with this presence, all the great and awful things in life seemed to pass before her—fighting armies, wicked men, raging beasts, storms and pestilences, sin and suffering of every kind. At first she shrank back in terror. But she soon saw that the presence of God so surrounded and enveloped her and each one of these things, that not a lion could reach out a paw, nor a bullet fly through the air, except the presence of God moved out of the way to permit it. And she saw that if so thin a film of this glorious Presence of God were between her and the most terrible violence not a hair of her head could be ruffled, nor anything touch her, except the presence divided to let the evil through. Then all the smaller and annoying things of life passed before her. She also saw that she was so enveloped in this presence of God that not a cross look, nor a harsh word, not petty trial of any kind could affect her unless God's encircling presence moved out of the way to let it. (p. 134-135)

Eph 6:16 Above all, taking the shield of faith, wherewith ye shall be able to quench all the fiery darts of the wicked.

Job 1:10 Hast not thou made an hedge about him, and about his house, and about all that he hath on every side? thou hast blessed the work of his hands, and his substance is increased in the land.

4.   <u>Believe that God has met and will always meet all our needs, including our needs for worth, signifi-cance, security and love</u>. If we do not accept that our worth is based on God's love, our significance is based on our adoption as children of God, our security is complete in Christ, and we will never be separated from God's love, we cannot maintain a happy life because part of the concept of happiness requires that we know our needs have and will always be met. Without faith that our needs will be met, we will strive to meet those needs and again become entangled within the circumstances of our success or failures.

Php 4:19 But my God shall supply all your need according to his riches in glory by Christ Jesus.

5.   <u>Know that God will work everything, including our mistakes, for our good</u>. If we meet the criteria of this critical verse by loving God and submitting to God's plans for us, we can believe that every-thing, even our mistakes and failures, will be used by God for our good. If we do not believe this, our happiness will be constantly interrupted by events or the offenses of others that we interpret as negative. God is so great that even though He will not override the will of people, He is still able to control the events of our lives to turn them around for our long-term good.

Ro 8:28 And we know that all things work together for good to them that love God, to them who are the called according to his purpose.

6.   <u>Open our spiritual eyes to see the chariots of God</u>. If it is true that absolutely everything that happens to us will be used by God for our eternal good, then we must see all the events of our lives as good. In the book *A Christian's Secret of a Happy Life* (1983), the events of our lives are described as the chariots of God. But just like in the days of Elisha, we need our eyes to be opened so that we can see them as such. If we see them as enemies, they will run over us, but if we see them as friends, we can ride in them to victory over our circumstances.

They do not look like chariots. Instead they look like enemies, sufferings, trials, defeats, misun-derstandings, disappointments, unkindnesses. They look like misery and wretchedness waiting to roll over us and crush us into the earth. But if we could see them as they really are, we would recognize them as chariots of triumph in which we may ride to those heights of victory for which our souls have been longing and praying. The difficulty is the visible thing. The chariot of God is the invisible. ...Lord, open our eyes that we may see. ...And when our eyes are opened, we will see in all of the events of life, whether great or small; whether joyful or sad, a "chariot" for our souls. Everything that comes to us becomes a chariot the moment we treat it as such. And on the other hand, even the smallest trials may crush us into misery or despair if we let them. It does not matter what the events are, but how we take them. We can either lie down under them and let them roll over us and crush us, or we can view them as chariots of God and make them carry us triumphantly onward and upward. (1983, p. 216-217)

2 Ki 6:17 And Elisha prayed, and said, LORD, I pray thee, open his eyes, that he may see. And the LORD opened the eyes of the young man; and he saw: and, behold, the mountain was full of horses and chariots of fire round about Elisha.

7. <u>Abide in the vine</u>. We are always tempted to try to do the things of God in our own flesh. As we have seen in the previous chapters, this only increases our reliance on the flesh. We must learn to trust harder, instead of working harder. This is made very clear in the book of John.

Jo 15:4 Abide in me, and I in you. As the branch cannot bear fruit of itself, except it abide in the vine; no more can ye, except ye abide in me.

5 I am the vine, ye are the branches: He that abideth in me, and I in him, the same bringeth forth much fruit: for without me ye can do nothing.

6 If a man abide not in me, he is cast forth as a branch, and is withered; and men gather them, and cast them into the fire, and they are burned.

7 If ye abide in me, and my words abide in you, ye shall ask what ye will, and it shall be done unto you.

8 Herein is my Father glorified, that ye bear much fruit; so shall ye be my disciples.

9 As the Father hath loved me, so have I loved you: continue ye in my love.

10 If ye keep my commandments, ye shall abide in my love; even as I have kept my Father's commandments, and abide in his love.

11 These things have I spoken unto you, that my joy might remain in you, and that your joy might be full.

8. <u>Submit to the care of the good Shepherd knowing that, "surely goodness and mercy shall follow me all the days of my life…"</u> The 23rd Psalm is a perfect description of what God's abundant life is to be like. With an all-powerful Shepherd such as Christ, how could we not be happy sheep?

Ps 23:1 The LORD is my shepherd; I shall not want.

2 He maketh me to lie down in green pastures: he leadeth me beside the still waters.

3 He restoreth my soul: he leadeth me in the paths of righteousness for his name's sake.

4 Yea, though I walk through the valley of the shadow of death, I will fear no evil: for thou art with me; thy rod and thy staff they comfort me.

5 Thou preparest a table before me in the presence of mine enemies: thou anointest my head with oil; my cup runneth over.

6 Surely goodness and mercy shall follow me all the days of my life: and I will dwell in the house of the LORD for ever.

9. <u>Mount up on wings of eagles to see life from God's perspective</u>. Finally, the key to all of this is to see the events of our lives from the perspective of God. We need to mount up on the wings of eagles to look down on the vapor of our life from God's eternal perspective and see that everything is good. He has not failed us and He cannot fail us.

Isa 40:31 But they that wait upon the LORD shall renew their strength; they shall mount up with wings as eagles; they shall run, and not be weary; and they shall walk, and not faint.

THE PRINCIPLES OF PROTECTION FROM CATASTROPHE

God's plan for us: Good Jer 29:11	The world without God: Chance Ec 9:11	The devil's plan: Catastrophe Jo 10:10a
Because God loves and has our best interests in mind, He will work everything—even our mistakes—for good if we love and yield to His plans. Ro 8:28, Ps 23:6	After God entrusted the world to us, we chose to be our own God and provide our own protection. Ge 2:15-17, 3:5-6	The devil introduced evil into the world when he tempted Adam and Eve and they sinned. Ge 3:13-19
God promises to protect us if we will accept His love, rely on Him for protection and pray in faith. Ps 91, Pr 18:10, 2 Pe 1:4	Our selfish choices bring evil consequences into the world and this can result in catastrophe in our lives. 1 Co 10:6-11	Evil continues in the world through lust–meeting needs through the flesh–which leads to death. Jas 1:14-15
When we accept Christ, we are accepted in Him. Because Christ perfectly fulfilled the law, we are free from the law that through sin leads to catastrophe. Ro 6:8-9, 22	It is not "God's fault" for "allowing evil" because God is not responsible for our free choices. God does not do evil, neither can He be tempted to do evil. Ps 5:4, Jas 1:13	The devil has power over us only when we sin, fail to rely on Christ, or fail to use the power given to us by Jesus. Lu 10:19
Although God allows the direct consequences of our choices so we can learn from our mistakes, He never allows us to be tried beyond which we are able. 1 Co 10:13	Although a sinless person would be protected, all without Christ are vulnerable since we all sin. Job 4:7, Ro 3:23	When we reject Christ, we become responsible for our own sin, and receive its consequences. Ro 14:12
God does not promise to protect us from all struggles in this world because they are tools for growth, and when we overcome them He gets the glory. Ro 8:35-37	The more we rely on ourselves for our protection the more fearful we become as we realize how limited we are. Job 3:25-26	Pride which is self-reliance—telling God we want to do it ourselves—removes God's protection and makes us vulnerable to attack. Pr 16:18
God's protection is based on His eternal viewpoint of good knowing all things present and future, though it may not appear to be the obvious good from our temporal standpoint. Isa 55:8-12, Jo 9:2-3	God actively opposes those who are proud and want to be their own God so that they will eventually understand their need for Him. Job 33:17, Jas 4:6	Presumption, tempting God, or direct disobedience make us vulnerable to attack because we do not rely on God for our protection. Lu 4:9-13, Nu 14:41-45, Jo 15:14
When our perception of things seems to indicate that He has failed us, God asks that we rely on our faith in Him and trust His infinite wisdom. He does not owe us an explanation. Job 40:6-14	Because we choose to rely on ourselves and we do not have enough information or capability we can never guarantee our own protection. Job 5:6-7, Lu 13:2-5	Not using the tools of faith, prayer, or the armor of God to defeat the devil makes us vulnerable to be defeated. Jas 4:2-3, Eph 6:10-18
The result is peace and safety.	The result is fear of catastrophe.	The result is catastrophe.

Steps for Overcoming Insecurity

1. We learn to be insecure based on what we learn in our families of origin, what others tell us, and through the experiences of life.

2. Fear is a natural response to perceptions of threats to our well-being, prosperity or success. Fear manifests itself through anxiety, panic attacks, phobias, Post Traumatic Stress Disorder, obsessions and compulsions.

3. Because we are limited, the more we rely on ourselves the more we will be insecure.

4. Faith in God is the opposite of fear. We must establish a close, intimate relationship with God in order to trust Him more than our fears.

5. The more we concentrate on our problems and fears, the more they grow in strength; and the more we focus on God, the more our faith in Him grows to overcome our fears.

6. Facing our fears is the most effective way to overcome them. Facing them systematically a little at a time is a very effective method for overcoming all types of insecurity.

7. God promises that, if we will put our trust in Him, we will never be tempted beyond what we are able and that He will protect us from catastrophe.

8. Therefore, the answer for overcoming insecurity is to abandon our own pride and self-reliance, and to face our fears through faith that God will provide for all our needs and keep us safe in every situation.

9. Winning the victory over fear is key to achieving an abundant life filled with peace and happiness.

How to Have a Happy life

1. Trust in God for our protection avoiding: pride, tempting God, presumption and direct disobedience.

2. Submit to God's plan for our life. His ways are better. Jeremiah 29:11

3. Trust in His shield of faith. Only those things that are for our eternal good can pass through. Ephesians 6:16

4. Believe that God has and will always meet all our needs including our need for worth, significance, security, and love. Philipians 4:19

5. Know that God will work everything—even our mistakes—for our good. Romans 8:28

6. Open our spiritual eyes to see the chariots of God. Do not let them run over us but ride in them. 2 Kings 6:17

7. Abide in the vine. Not work harder but trust harder. John 15

8. Submit to the care of the good Shepherd knowing that, "surely goodness and mercy shall follow me all the days of my life…" Psalms 23:6

9. Mount up on wings of eagles to see life from God's perspective. Isaiah 40:31

Chapter 13

Faith and Love

Love provides the quality of life that makes living worthwhile. In the Bible, Christ summed up the total duty of man as loving God and others. The main quality of God Himself is love and Christians are to be known by their love. Our initial image of God is based on the love we receive from our parents. Without love, we will grow up feeling worthless and cynical about relationships. Love hunger leads to codependency and addictions.

But what is love? According to the dictionary it is, "A deep devotion or affection for another person or persons. A strong sexual passion for another person. A very great interest or enjoyment of something. The kindness and charitableness man should show toward one another." (Funk & Wagnalls, 1963) As an emotion, it motivates us to move toward a person and to have another's best interest in mind. It is the feeling that is associated with bonding, attachment and intimacy. The opposite of love is hate which motivates us to move away from others or to do them harm. When we do not feel loved, we may have feelings of fear of abandonment, rage, jealousy, despair, betrayal and loneliness.

Attachment

Integral to the concept of love is attachment. However, the emotion of love is actually just part of our attachment system that includes the biological components of attachment such as sexual and non-sexual touch as well as the emotions of love and the closeness of intimacy. Attachment adds strength to close or intimate relationships. However, it is possible to have an intimate relationship with someone without being attached to them; and it is possible to be attached to someone without being truly intimate with them.

Attachment is best understood in young children. It is absolutely essential that babies bond with their mothers through physical contact and have their physical and emotional needs met during the first days of their lives. If they do not, Reaction Attachment Disorder (RAD) can occur. Characteristics of unbonded children include a lack of empathy and emotional connectivity, extreme self-centeredness, distrust for others, acting out in extremely destructive and vicious ways, and a lack of regret for what they have done. RAD can be the precursor to Oppositional Defiant Disorder and Antisocial Personality Disorder.

If children are separated from attachment figures or attachment figures no longer meet their needs, experiments with children have shown that they go through three stages of detachment. First, they protest through crying or acting out. Second they go into despair where they withdraw, refusing to eat or interact with others; and finally, they detach and will even ignore the attachment figure when they are in need. (Clinton and Sibcy, 2002, pp 17-18)

Four basic attachment styles have been identified through observing the reactions of young children. Although the child's style can change due to new experiences and psychological development, they usually provide the general framework for relationships throughout the child's life.

1. The secure attachment style. These children view themselves as worthy of love and feel competent to obtain love when they need it. They view others as reliable, accessible and willing to respond to their needs. They seek out an attachment figure when they feel insecure and will act in ways that effectively meet their emotional needs.

2. The avoidant attachment style. These children view themselves as worthy of love and competent to obtain it, but view others as either unwilling, unavailable or untrustworthy of providing for their emotional needs. They tend to withdraw into themselves, discount their emotions and rely on themselves for nurturing. Many times, they will value accomplishing things over developing relationships.

3. The ambivalent attachment style. These children view themselves as unworthy of love or incompetent to get the caregiver's attention, but view the attachment figure as capable of comfort and protection. They tend to throw tantrums or act out in order to receive nurturing but have difficulty receiving it when the caregiver attempts to help them and, sometimes, become angry at the caregiver. They tend to perform for others in order to please them in the hope that if they do well enough their needs will be met. *Sometimes Overdo*

4. The disorganized attachment style. These children view themselves as unworthy of love or incompetent to obtain it; and they view others as unwilling, unavailable or untrustworthy to give it. Because they exhibit both negative viewpoints and because this style is many times the result of abusive behavior, these children are confused in their attachment attempts. Sometimes they will even run to a stranger for safety. This is because, at times, they have experienced the attachment figure meeting their needs; and at other times, they have experienced rejection or abuse from the same attachment figure. They tend to be overly emotional and cycle between wanting to be close and avoiding closeness. (Clinton and Sibcy, pp 24-28)

A person's overall attachment system operates similar to a thermostat. If the primary attachment figure becomes unavailable, refuses to meet his needs or is unreliable, he will protest in an effort to correct the perceived problem and to calm the anxiety that he feels. On the other hand, he may feel smothered by too much intervention or demands for closeness and take action to withdraw and get a little space. With insecure styles of attachment, an approach-avoidance dance can be initiated which will eventually damage the relationship. In some cases, when attachment wounds convince a person that the attachment figure is not safe, detachment may occur. Periods of protest and despair usually precede actual detachment. One of the most common signs of detachment is when the other person withdraws from non-sexual touch.

Because everyone emotionally needs someone who is trustworthy, always available and emotionally sensitive, God is the ultimate attachment figure. This is because God cannot lie, He is always available and, through the things that He suffered here on earth for us, He is very sensitive to our emotions. Because He does not change, He provides the ultimate safe haven that each and everyone needs and the safe base from which to venture out into the world. (Clinton and Sibcy, 2002, Hart, 2003)

How We Learn to Love   *Learns Attachment Style*

1. When a newborn child is born, he bonds to his primary caregiver. The child feels love through the facial expressions, the touch and the care he receives from his mother. These experiences provide the foundation required to express love later in his life. These experiences also provide for the child's perception of his value or worth. A child whose needs are met will feel worthy of another person's love. If the child's needs are neglected he feels that he must not be valuable enough to have his needs met and may begin the development of low self-worth.

2. As the child grows, from his experiences with his caregivers and others, he develops a sense of security (or insecurity) in the world and a sense of the reliability of others to meet his needs. During these early years the child also begins to develop ego defenses, the foundation of trust or faith, and the

child's initial perception of God. He asks, "Can others (including God) be trusted and relied upon to meet my needs or do I need to become self-sufficient, rely completely on myself, and become my own god?" The more he determines that he must rely on himself, the more insecure he will feel in this life, especially as he realizes his limitations to direct his own life and control the world around him. He needs to believe that God is his protector and that it is He that makes him secure in life.

3. <u>From these early experiences, the child determines if he is capable of obtaining love</u>. It may be possible that the child feels he is valuable and that his caregivers are reliable, but does not feel adequate in his attempts to ask for or obtain love. This is the area of significance and is usually based on his own or other's evaluation of his performance.

4. <u>From these experiences, we develop one of the four primary attachment styles that have already been discussed</u>. These attachment styles will greatly affect how we attempt to attach to others throughout our life. If we believe that we are valuable, that others are reliable and that we are capable of obtaining love from them, we will develop a secure style. If we believe that we are valuable but others are unreliable, we will develop an avoidant style and rely only on ourselves. If we do not feel worthwhile and see others as reliable, we will develop an ambivalent style, trying to make ourselves more acceptable to them. And if we see ourselves as worthless and others as unreliable, we will develop a disorganized attachment style and an emotionally confusing array of attempts to meet our needs.

Intimacy

Intimacy or being intimate is "characterized by pronounced closeness of friendship, relationship or association." (Funk & Wagnalls, 1963) In the Bible, Christ describes it as God's highest goal for people and the deep desire of God. It is to be known as we are and to know others as they truly are. It has a lot to do with openly revealing ourselves to another person without reservation or defensiveness. It is the ultimate in unity found in the Trintiy.

Jo 17:21 That they all may be one; as thou, Father, [art] in me, and I in thee, that they also may be one in us: that the world may believe that thou hast sent me.

22 And the glory which thou gavest me I have given them; that they may be one, even as we are one:

23 I in them, and thou in me, that they may be made perfect in one; and that the world may know that thou hast sent me, and hast loved them, as thou hast loved me.

Intimate or close relationships are characterized by five types of love. Of course, different types of relationships may or may not include any or all of these types. As an example, friendships will not include romantic love and romance can exist without commitment. Because these types of love are more easily differentiated in the Greek language than in the English language, I will provide the equivalent Greek word also.

1. <u>Unconditional commitment or acceptance</u>. In the Greek this is *agape* love or the type of love that is the main characteristic of God. It is the commitment that cements and stabilizes a relationship. It is best defined in the Bible in 1st Corinthians Chapter 13.

2. <u>Romantic attraction or desire</u>. The Greek the word is *eros*. This is the romance that attracts one lover to another. It is the chase, the attraction that initializes and sustains a romantic relationship.

3. <u>Friendship or companionship.</u> In the Greek this is *phileo*. It is also the root word for *philadelphia* which means, "brotherly love." It is the give and take in a relationship based on meeting each other's needs and enjoying the companionship of another.

4. <u>Spiritual or intuitive love.</u> The Greek word is *theleo*. This is the commonality of beliefs, having the same goals and outlook on life, having the same desires and wants, and feeling what the other feels. When "one cries the other tastes salt."

5. <u>Physical or sexual love.</u> In the Bible, the phrase "to know someone" is used, as when Adam "knew" his wife and she conceived." (Genesis 4:1) It is part of the attachment system that makes a couple one flesh. It is the cement of the marital relationship.

The World's System—Selfish Love

Because the natural man of this world is not saved, he is destined all of his life to be dominated by a desire to meet the needs of the self. This results in selfishness and sin. Consequently, it is not surprising that the world's system for love is the development and pursuit of selfish love. The world cannot go beyond this type of self-centered love because it has no capacity to overcome selfishness without faith and the Spirit of God. The closest it can come to the true unconditional love of God is motherly love. Unfortunately, in the world even motherly love has its selfish aspects. As a mother gives love to her child, she hopes that eventually the child will appreciate what she has done and love her back. This becomes clear when counseling a codependent mother who tries to live her life through her child or finds it impossible to allow her child to develop an independent life of his or her own.

In the world, selfish love is accepted as the norm. It is so subtle that we sometimes do not even know what we are missing. However, our actions make it all clear. I remember many years ago before I was married that a number of girls that I dated had the same poster. It said, "I love you because of who I am when I am with you." In other words, "I love you for what you do for me." The Love Bank Theory by Dr. Willard Harley Jr. (2001) makes this kind of love explicit. He says that each of us have a love back account for every other person in our lives. When we meet people and perceive that they meet our needs in some way, we give them points in their account. When they receive a certain number of points in their account, they become an acquaintance, friend, best friend, and, eventually, we love them. If they do things we perceive as against our best interests, we give them negative points. The more negative their account, the more they become someone we do not like, our enemy, our worst enemy, and finally someone we hate. Most divorces cite irreconcilable differences and many marriages fail due to marriage "deadlock." Marriage deadlock occurs when neither spouse is willing to do something for the other first because they no longer trust their mate to return the favor. Clearly selfish love is well established in our society and, unfortunately, in our churches.

The Consequences of the World's System—Insecure Love and Dysfunction

1. <u>Because selfish love can never provide the level of security required for a secure attachment, it easily leads to jealousy.</u> We desperately need others to be trustworthy, available and emotionally sensitive, so we can feel safe in our relationships. However, when the level of the other person's commitment in the relationship is dependent on meeting his needs, we can never feel completely safe. Another name for this type of selfish love is conditional love. We can count on being loved only to the extent that we meet certain conditions. If our relationship is based on conditional love, we must assume that if someone else met our spouse's needs better, she might leave us. This type of insecurity easily breeds jealousy.

2. <u>Selfish love looks out for itself first and will refuse to go beyond just being fair.</u> If necessary, a selfish lover will resort to manipulation and coercion to force the other person to meet his needs. Selfish love always wants the best for itself or at least to have its needs met equally in the relationship. To the extent it gives, it hopes to get at least as much in return. If there is not a mutual exchange, one of the persons in the relationship will feel used by the other person. In marriage, we call this level of fairness a win-win solution. This works only as long as each person is healthy, willing and able to give back as much as has been given. In the long run, this does not usually work perfectly because one spouse usually perceives that what he gives is of more value than what he has been given.

3. <u>Selfish love can never fully meet the giver's needs because he will reap what he has sown</u>. If a person sows only conditional love, that is what he will get back. Since conditional love is not capable of meeting a person's needs, his needs will never be fully met.

4. <u>Because selfish love violates the natural law called the paradox of love, it chases away rather than attracts the love of others</u>. The paradox of love states that those who pursue love in order to get their needs met repel the love of others, while those who give love unconditionally receive it back in abundance. Of course, most persons in a relationship initially try to show some measure of unconditional love, but the test of time will eventually expose selfish love for what it is.

5. <u>Selfish love has difficulty adapting to change</u>. It cannot easily weather the tests of psychological development or growth, because it is basically an agreement between two spouses to use each other to meet certain implied needs. If the dynamics of the relationship change, the implied agreement must also change. <u>Selfish love has difficulty adapting.</u> In some cases, this implied agreement is based on lust or taking advantage of each other's fears or inadequacies. As one person matures or changes, what they perceive as their needs and desires may also change and difficulties will arise. This is one of the reasons that so many teenage marriages eventually fail.

6. <u>Because a person primarily cares about his own feelings, he is easily provoked, blames the other person, strikes back when he feels hurt, and ends up in a deadlocked relationship filled with deep emotional pain</u>. When hurt, a person will almost automatically strike back and problems easily escalate when both people refuse to take responsibility for what has happened. Many people will try to get away with whatever they can in order to meet their own needs. Because the expectation of selfish love is that the person's needs, as they perceive them, will be met; their expectations can differ greatly, especially since males and females have significantly different emotional needs. In most relationships both partners eventually experience some level of disappointment. Because they expect that the other person should meet their needs, they blame the other person or refuse to meet the other person's needs until their needs are met first. When one or both mates are very insecure or desperately needy, attempts to force the other to meet all of a person's needs can eventually turn the relationship into an emotional hell on earth filled with angry accusations, deep hurt, and sometimes even domestic violence. If one perceives that the other does not have their best interest in mind, such relationships can easily become two enemies living in the same household.

7. <u>Selfish love and insecure attachment styles lead directly to codependency, addictions, domestic violence and other types of dysfunction</u>. Codependency underlies addictions, domestic violence and most other types of dysfunctional relationships. Codependency is typified by performance or approval self-worth. Performance self-worth is an attempt to be self-sufficient without attachment, and people pleasing is an attempt to make others like us so that we will feel loved. The avoidant attachment style leads to becoming a codependent independent worldly success if we would rather lead, or a codependent dependent rescuer if we would rather follow a good leader. This style can also lead a person to become a codependent worldly failure if the person does not feel adequate or a codependent responsibility avoidant if the person attempts to avoid failure by avoiding responsibility. The disorganized attachment style usually leads a person to become a codependent independent worldly failure or responsibility avoidant. The ambivalent attachment style many times results in a person becoming a codependent dependent passive or, if the person has been severely abused, a codependent relationship avoidant. (To understand these relationships better, see the chart at the end of this chapter. For a detailed understanding of codependency, codependent types, and biblical models for each, see my book *Transformation!*)

8. <u>Selfish love can motivate a person to protect themselves by avoiding deep attachments</u>. In our society most people do not even know their neighbor's names, eighty percent of men do not have a best friend, and a large majority of adults use some sort of diversion or false intimacy in an attempt to get their love needs met. These attempts by a person to artificially meet their needs for love can include almost

anything: drinking at bars, drugs, alcohol, karaoke, bowling, bingo, watching sports, pornography, "gentlemen's" clubs, sexual promiscuity, sexual and eating addictions, TV, soaps, romance novels, escape into fantasy, possessing things, maintaining a house or even vacations. Each can be used to make the person feel accepted and loved without the risk of deep emotional rejection.

9. <u>Selfish love easily fails due to superficial attachment</u>. Because people are afraid to become vulnerable out of fear of rejection, insecure attachment styles result in superficial attachments. Superficial attachment has its limit concerning how long or what a person is willing to do to maintain a relationship in which their needs are not completely met. Cohabitation is a clear example of this trend to avoid the commitment of a secure attachment. Lust, as a replacement for true love, is another example. Even in marriages, instead of being fully committed to a spouse, many people are tempted to escape into work, hobbies or relationship with children. Even work relationships are usually superficial where employers are not at all interested in anything more than the work they can extract from the employee, and few employees feel loyalty to their companies. Corporate raiders are not interested in the company, just in how much money they can make. For many, even their relationship to God is an external religion of obligation, and they easily shop for a church or pastor who will better meet their needs. Even most marriages are so superficially attached, that over fifty percent fail. Over eighty percent of cohabitations fail.

10. <u>Selfish love can never meet a person's deep need for unconditional love</u>. No matter how compatible the relationship, deep within each person is a need to be truly loved unconditionally without any strings attached. To some degree this kind of love is found in the parents of very healthy families, but even these parents are primarily motivated to meet their own needs. Jesus was willing to give His life to the slow, excruciating pain of the cross for even the worst sinner on earth. His life and sacrifice are the best examples of unselfish love.

God's System—Unconditional Love

The Bible is a book about love. It provides the basis for really understanding this very deep need.

1. <u>Unconditional love comes only from God and is a primary characteristic of God</u>

   1 Jo 4:7. Dear friends, let us love one another, for love comes from God. Everyone who loves has been born of God and knows God.

   8 Whoever does not love does not know God, because God is love.

2. <u>Jesus demonstrated love to us when He died for us.</u>

   1 Jo 3:16 This is how we know what love is: Jesus Christ laid down his life for us. And we ought to lay down our lives for our brothers.

3. <u>God's type of love is unconditional</u>. He loves and values us no matter what we have done or have not done. He is not a respecter of persons. He does not favor one over another based on their works or even their morals or obedience to Him.

   Ro 5:8 But God commendeth his love toward us, in that, while we were yet sinners, Christ died for us.

4. <u>Nothing can separate us from God's love.</u>

   Ro 8:35 Who shall separate us from the love of Christ? [shall] tribulation, or distress, or persecution, or famine, or nakedness, or peril, or sword?

39 Nor height, nor depth, nor any other creature, shall be able to separate us from the love of God, which is in Christ Jesus our Lord.

5.   <u>God's type of unconditional love fulfills the law</u>. This is because love is having another's best interests in mind and this is the purpose of all the law.

Ro 13:8 Owe no man any thing, but to love one another: for he that loveth another hath fulfilled the law.

10 Love worketh no ill to his neighbour: therefore love [is] the fulfilling of the law.

6.   <u>God values love above everything else</u>. It is even more important to Him than what we accomplish or do for Him.

Mr 12:33 And to love him with all the heart, and with all the understanding, and with all the soul, and with all the strength, and to love [his] neighbour as himself, is more than all whole burnt offerings and sacrifices.

7.   <u>It is through love that God draws people to Himself</u>.

Jer 31:3 The LORD hath appeared of old unto me, [saying], Yea, I have loved thee with an everlasting love: therefore with loving kindness have I drawn thee.

8.   <u>Because we have experienced God's love, we learn to love others</u>.

1 Jo 4:19 We love because he first loved us.

9.   <u>Our experience of God's love begins with our desire to know Him</u>. The more we seek Him, the more we will experience His love, and the more we experience His love the more we will develop the capacity to love God and others.

Pr 8:17 I love them that love me; and those that seek me early shall find me.

10. <u>Loving each other is crucial to the further development of God's type of love and is the basis of authentic spiritual life</u>.

1 Jo 3:14 We know that we have passed from death unto life, because we love the brethren. He that loveth not [his] brother abideth in death.

16 Hereby perceive we the love [of God], because he laid down his life for us: and we ought to lay down [our] lives for the brethren.

4:12 No man hath seen God at any time. If we love one another, God dwelleth in us, and his love is perfected in us.

11. <u>Love is the most valuable of all emotions and meets our deepest need</u>. The more we love, the more we are filled with the fullness of God. Without the motivation of love, all that we do is of little value.

So 8:7 Many waters cannot quench love, neither can the floods drown it: if [a] man would give all the substance of his house for love, it would utterly be contemned.

Eph 3:19 And to know the love of Christ, which passeth knowledge, that ye might be filled with all the fulness of God.

1 Co 13:1 If I speak in the tongues of men and of angels, but have not love, I am only a resounding gong or a clanging cymbal.

2 If I have the gift of prophecy and can fathom all mysteries and all knowledge, and if I have a faith that can move mountains, but have not love, I am nothing.

3 If I give all I possess to the poor and surrender my body to the flames, but have not love, I gain nothing.

12. The Bible clearly describes God's unconditional love. It is sometimes translated as charity since its prime characteristic is benevolence toward others. Unconditional love is clearly very different from selfish love.

1 Co 13:4 Charity suffereth long, and is kind; charity envieth not; charity vaunteth not itself, is not puffed up,

5 Doth not behave itself unseemly, seeketh not her own, is not easily provoked, thinketh no evil;

6 Rejoiceth not in iniquity, but rejoiceth in the truth;

7 Beareth all things, believeth all things, hopeth all things, endureth all things.

8 Charity never faileth:

13. Our human emotion of love is based on what others have done for us and how they have met our needs. This same emotion may accompany both selfish love and unconditional love. However, we must be careful not to base what we do on our emotions. Unconditional love transcends our emotions to do what is best even for others that we do not like and that do not meet our needs. Selfish love can and will never do this.

Lu 7:42 And when they had nothing to pay, he frankly forgave them both. Tell me therefore, which of them will love him most?

43 Simon answered and said, I suppose that he, to whom he forgave most. And he said unto him, Thou hast rightly judged.

Jo 10:17 Therefore doth my Father love me, because I lay down my life, that I might take it again.

14. Love is contagious. When our needs have been met by others, we feel love for them and want to meet their needs.

Jo 13:34 A new commandment I give unto you, That ye love one another; as I have loved you, that ye also love one another.

15. Love is the sign of true Christianity.

Jo 13:35 By this shall all [men] know that ye are my disciples, if ye have love one to another.

16. Love provides the motivation for our actions and our actions provide the basis of our attachment in loving relationships.

Jo 14:15 If ye love me, keep my commandments.

21 He that hath my commandments, and keepeth them, he it is that loveth me: and he that loveth me shall be loved of my Father, and I will love him, and will manifest myself to him.

23 Jesus answered and said unto him, If a man love me, he will keep my words: and my Father will love him, and we will come unto him, and make our abode with him.

17. <u>Great love can produce great sacrifice.</u>

Jo 15:12 This is my commandment, That ye love one another, as I have loved you.

13 Greater love hath no man than this, that a man lay down his life for his friends.

18. <u>The Holy Spirit within us draws us and produces love within us.</u>

Ro 5:5 And hope maketh not ashamed; because the love of God is shed abroad in our hearts by the Holy Ghost which is given unto us.

Ga 5:22 But the fruit of the Spirit is love, joy, peace, longsuffering, gentleness, goodness, faith,

23 Meekness, temperance: against such there is no law.

19. <u>Love should be our primary motivation in everything that we do.</u>

2 Co 5:14 For the love of Christ constraineth us; because we thus judge, that if one died for all, then were all dead:

20. <u>Fear is defeated through love.</u> <u>The basis of fear is that there will be no one available to meet our needs when we need them. For the child held lovingly in his mother's arms, there is no fear.</u> For the Christian in the arms of God, there is nothing for us to fear.

1 Jo 4:18 There is no fear in love; but perfect love casteth out fear: because fear hath torment. He that feareth is not made perfect in love.

2 Ti 1:7 For God hath not given us the spirit of fear; but of power, and of love, and of a sound mind.

21. <u>When we feel loved, it is easy to forgive the wrongs others have done to us.</u>

1 Pe 4:8 And above all things have fervent charity among yourselves: for charity shall cover the multitude of sins.

22. <u>Love is the end result of spiritual and psychological development and is the ultimate sign of Christian maturity.</u> (See *Revelations That Will Set You Free* for a detailed explanation of spiritual growth.)

2 Pe 1:5 And beside this, giving all diligence, add to your faith virtue; and to virtue knowledge;

6 And to knowledge temperance; and to temperance patience; and to patience godliness;

7 And to godliness brotherly kindness; and to brotherly kindness charity (Agape love).

The Consequences of God's System—True Love and Satisfaction

1. <u>The type of unconditional love that God provides meets our deepest needs and provides the safe attachment relationships that we desperately need</u>. Below I have provided my paraphrase of the description of unconditional love in 1st Corinthians 13:4-8. Who would not want to have a relationship with someone that loves us like this:

    Love puts up with a lot, is calmly nice, is not competitive, is more concerned about others, humbly serves others, is not offensive in any way, is not demanding, is not irritating or easily exasperated, does not hold the past against you, loves the truth and hates evil, is always on your side trying to make you look good, always believes in you, always expects the best in every situation, never quits or abandons you no matter what happens, and is always and will always be totally committed to you.

2. <u>Because God's love is not based on what we do, we can always be assured that His love will never fail us</u>. Divorce could not and would not ever exist if both persons in the relationship had been practicing unconditional love, since they would always have the other person's best interest in mind no matter what happened.

3. <u>Unconditional love provides the basis for secure attachments</u>. A secure attachment style requires that we view ourselves as worthy of love and others as safe. With unconditional love we no longer have to live up to the other's expectations, and they do not have to be perfect because our total focus is on meeting the needs of the other person. Even if our needs are not met, we can trust God to meet those unmet needs.

4. <u>Unconditional love eliminates irrational jealousy because it focuses on the needs of the other person, not on our fear of losing someone to meet our needs</u>. In fact, if it is best for the other person, the unconditional lover will give up the relationship in order to ensure that the other's needs are met.

5. <u>Since unconditional love goes beyond fairness and primarily has the other person's best interest in mind, it eliminates relationship deadlock</u>. Relationship deadlock is not an issue since the unconditional lover will act based on what is best for the other person; not what the other person will do for him.

6. <u>Sowing unconditional love will result in reaping the unconditional love that we so desperately need in our lives</u>. This does not mean that in each and every case the person we attempt to love unconditionally will love us back in the same way; but that God will use that person, or others to ensure that our needs are met.

7. <u>Unconditional love fulfills the paradox of love since it does not **attempt** to get love from others but to give it liberally to all that will receive it</u>. According to the **paradox** of love, it is not those who pursue, manipulate, or demand that others meet their needs, but **those** who unconditionally love others who, in return, have their needs met.

8. <u>Unconditional love easily adapts to change because it is not **dependent** on any needs or actions of the other person</u>. In fact, it does not change at all no matter **what the other** person does or needs. The unconditional lover will always have the best interests of **those that** are loved, whatever they may be, as the basis for his love.

9. <u>Unconditional love is not easily provoked and stands strong even in the face of the most vicious attacks and rejection</u>. At the most, the unconditional lover will simply set boundaries and become more concerned for the welfare of the one who is attacking or rejecting him. Therefore, unconditional love provides one of the strongest healing agents for dysfunctional relationships. The Apostle Peter suggests that simply doing what is right can bring healing to relationship problems even if the other person refuses to follow the Word of God.

1 Pe 3:1 Likewise, ye wives, be in subjection to your own husbands; that, if any obey not the word, they also may without the word be won by the conversation (or actions) of the wives;

2 While they behold your chaste conversation coupled with fear.

7 Likewise, ye husbands, dwell with them according to knowledge, giving honour unto the wife, as unto the weaker vessel, and as being heirs together of the grace of life; that your prayers be not hindered.

8 Finally, be ye all of one mind, having compassion one of another, love as brethren, be pitiful, be courteous:

9 Not rendering evil for evil, or railing for railing: but contrariwise blessing; knowing that ye are thereunto called, that ye should inherit a blessing.

 10. <u>Unconditional love is also the answer for codependency, addictions, domestic violence and dysfunctional relationships.</u> These types of problems result from deep insecurity within the person. Unconditional love provides that immovable wall of security in life, because it will love the dysfunctional person no matter what they do. It will also not enable them since protecting them from their own consequences will not be in their long-term interest. (See my book *Transformation!* for biblical counseling models for each of these problems.)

 11. <u>In order to have unconditional love, we must have been delivered from our selfishness through faith.</u> To the degree selfishness prevails in our lives, unconditional love cannot exist since it is focused on others, not on meeting our own needs. Because most Christians have not yet completely overcome the selfishness in their lives, selfish love is still predominant in most of our churches. This is not God's will. It is His will that we should all be transformed through the process of salvation by faith until the entire expression of our lives is God's type of unconditional love. Unconditional love is the full expression of God Himself in our lives.

The Process of Transformation to Develop Unconditional Love

The process of moving from insecure attachment styles to a secure style and developing God's type of unconditional love is somewhat complex. Consequently, I have developed a flow diagram presented at the end of this chapter describing this process. Please refer to it as you read the steps in this process described in more detail below. (Also see the biblical attachment models of Jonathan, David, Michal, and Saul in Chapter 20 of this book.)

 1. <u>The change to God's type of love begins with the process of salvation by faith.</u> In order to be delivered from our selfishness we must believe that God has and will meet all our needs. Until this has happened, all of our expressions of love will be selfish and when we love this way, we will receive the consequences of selfish love just like everyone else who bases their relationships on it.

Php 4:19 But my God shall supply all your need according to his riches in glory by Christ Jesus.

 2. <u>We must experience God as our ultimate attachment figure.</u> He loves us unconditionally, will never abandon us, can never fail us, is always available and is emotionally sensitive to us; because, in the form of Jesus, He experienced what we feel. Consequently, having a deep trusting relationship with God is the key ingredient to rebuilding the trust required to have a secure attachment style. We need to just crawl up into His arms and let Him love us until we feel secure in His unconditional love.

Ro 5:8 But God commendeth his love toward us, in that, while we were yet sinners, Christ died for us.

Heb 4:15 For we have not an high priest which cannot be touched with the feeling of our infirmities; but was in all points tempted like as we are, yet without sin.

13:5 Let your conversation be without covetousness; and be content with such things as ye have: for he hath said, I will never leave thee, nor forsake thee.

 3. <u>We need to see ourselves as God sees us—One of His dear children who He loves without any regard to our works or even our failures.</u> We are loved by God and nothing can separate us from that love. His love must be the foundation for our self-worth or value.

Ro 8:38 For I am persuaded, that neither death, nor life, nor angels, nor principalities, nor powers, nor things present, nor things to come,

39 Nor height, nor depth, nor any other creature, shall be able to separate us from the love of God, which is in Christ Jesus our Lord.

 4. <u>We need to see others as God sees them. They are also His children through faith and He loves them even with all their mistakes and failures.</u> We should trust others only as far as they are trustworthy and rely primarily on God to make up the difference. Jesus did not overly commit Himself or put too much of His trust in men. Because David and Jonathan trusted God, they were able to maintain a healthy relationship even though neither was perfect. (See the model of Jonathan for developing healthy attachments later in this book.)

Ga 3:26 For ye are all the children of God by faith in Christ Jesus.

Jo 2:24 But Jesus did not commit himself unto them, because he knew all men,

25 And needed not that any should testify of man: for he knew what was in man.

 5. <u>Insecure attachment styles are changed through the experiences of healthy earthly and heavenly attachments.</u> Support groups can be very effective in helping build our trust in others. David was greatly influenced through his healthy attachment with Jonathan and God. Our experiences with trustworthy, available and emotionally sensitive people provide an experiential basis for developing our own secure attachment style:

2 Sa 9:7 And David said unto him, Fear not: for I will surely shew thee kindness for Jonathan thy father's sake, and will restore thee all the land of Saul thy father; and thou shalt eat bread at my table continually.

1 Chr 22:7 And David said to Solomon, My son, as for me, it was in my mind to build an house unto the name of the LORD my God:

 6. <u>We have finally achieved a secure attachment style when we are able to deeply attach and yet maintain good boundaries.</u> When Jonathan and Saul were killed, David greatly mourned over them. Even after Absalom rebelled against him and was killed by Joab, David was so attached that "he wished he could have died instead of him." From all this we see that through the healthy relationships with Jonathan and God, David was finally able to change his insecure ambivalent style into a secure attachment style.

2 Sa 1:26 I am distressed for thee, my brother Jonathan: very pleasant hast thou been unto me: thy love to me was wonderful, passing the love of women.

18:33 And the king was much moved, and went up to the chamber over the gate, and wept: and as he went, thus he said, O my son Absalom, my son, my son Absalom! would God I had died for thee, O Absalom, my son, my son!

7. <u>The more secure we are that our needs will be met and the more love we feel, the more motivated we are to meet the needs of others and show love to them</u>. Fortunately, even if our father abandoned us or our mother did not show us the nurturing that we needed, if we have failed over and over again, or if we have had such negative experiences in life that we have a hard time trusting anyone, God invites us to experience His love. He will make us feel secure in this world through an intimate relationship with Him. He cannot fail us, will not leave us and is perfectly sensitive to us since He, in the form of Jesus, walked among us and has experienced life with us.

8. <u>Even before we have fully developed a secure attachment style and unconditional love, we must begin using and exercising it</u>. As we start giving unconditional love, we will start getting it back. Receiving unconditional love will help us feel more secure and trusting of others and strengthen our faith in God. We must repent of our defenses and efforts at self-protection. God will take care of us. We must learn to set others free to make their own decisions and learn from their own consequences. Finally, whatever we sow is what we will reap.

Ga 6:7 Be not deceived; God is not mocked: for whatsoever a man soweth, that shall he also reap.

9. <u>Faith is the key that holds this entire process of the development of love together</u>. Ideally, we begin by believing that we are of value to others, that others are trustworthy, and that we are capable of obtaining love from others. When our life experiences contradict these feelings, our experience and faith in God Who can never fail, Who makes us completely secure, and Who makes us significant without works, makes us feel worthwhile, secure, and significant. With a secure attachment style, the experience of God's love, and the belief that God can be trusted to meet all our needs, we experience the feelings of being loved unconditionally, which motivate us to love others in the same way.

10. <u>We must realize that God is love and that we must attach fully and unconditionally to Him through faith</u>. In the verses that I have paraphrased below, we should realize that since God is love, these verses are actually a description of God (as suggested one day on the Worship Channel). Can you, the reader, imagine a safer person to trust with your emotions and attach to than God Himself?

1 Co 13:4-8 God puts up with a lot, is calmly nice, is not competitive, is more concerned about others, humbly serves others, is not offensive in any way, is not demanding, is not irritating or easily exasperated, does not hold the past against you, loves the truth and hates evil, is always on your side trying to make you look good, always believes in you, always expects the best in every situation, never quits or abandons you no matter what happens, and is always and will always be totally committed to you.

I would like to conclude this chapter with a story told by Harry C. Mabry. A man, who had just arrived in heaven, asked for a glimpse of hell so that he could better appreciate the fact that he had made it to heaven. In his glimpse of hell, he saw a long table filled with the most delicious food imaginable. The problem with hell was that those in hell had to abide by a single rule: They could only eat food with four-foot chopsticks. Because the four-foot chopsticks were too long, no one was able to pick up any of the food and turn the chopsticks around in order to feed himself. Consequently, everyone in hell was starving to death in the midst of plenty. When the man finally arrived in heaven, he was shocked to find an identical table filled with the same delicious food and the same rule; that they could only eat with four-foot chopsticks. However, in heaven they were having a great time feeding each other! (Tan, p. 758) That is the difference between those who love selfishly and those who liberally give unconditional love to others. It makes the difference between living in heaven and hell.

At this point, we have seen the role that faith plays in meeting all four of our basic needs: self-worth, significance, security and love. If you have not yet done so, please review the chart on the following page that integrates this entire process of the development of unconditional love in our lives through faith. (For a detailed explanation of the different types of codependency, see my book *Transformation!*) In the next chapters, models will be developed for using faith to resolve some of the common problems that result from attempting to meet our needs without God.

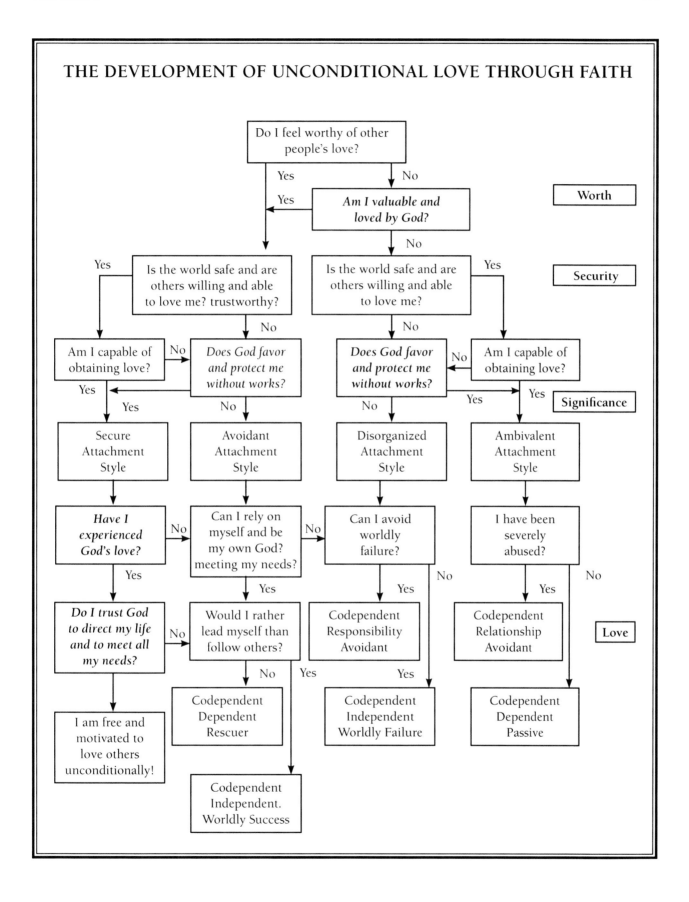

THE DEVELOPMENT OF UNCONDITIONAL LOVE THROUGH FAITH

Steps for Developing Unconditional Love

1. Love is an emotion that motivates us to draw close to and have the best interest of another person or God in mind.

2. Intimacy in close relationships consists of commitment, companionship, common goals and beliefs, romantic love, and physical love. These are all part of our attachment system.

3. In order to develop the ability to love, we must experience love from our parents and/or God.

4. Based on our perceptions of our experiences we develop either secure or insecure attachment styles depending on whether we view ourselves worthy and able to obtain love, and others as willing and reliable to give love.

5. Insecure attachment styles usually lead to selfish love relationships and codependency.

6. God is the ultimate secure attachment figure because He is absolutely trustworthy, always available and sensitive to our emotional needs.

7. Insecure attachment styles can be overcome through the experience of secure attachment with God and others.

8. In addition to a secure attachment style, the development of unconditional love requires faith to believe that all our needs are and will be met, and an intimate experience of the love of God.

PART V

Models for Resolving Problems with Self-worth

Chapter 14

Overcoming
Low Self-image through Faith
(Barak)

One of the ways to clearly understand how faith is used to resolve root problems is to examine the solutions to these problems as they are presented in the Bible. As I established in my book, *Transformation!*, the Bible is full of solutions for psychological problems hidden in the types and shadows interpretation of well-known biblical narrative stories. If everything that has been suggested so far in this book is true, then the application of Faith Therapy to each of these situations should clearly identify the root cause of the problem and present a solution based on faith.

During my initial interview, Charles was constantly looking down and almost never made eye contact. He was an extreme example of what low self-image can do. He had never been good enough to meet the expectations of his parents and had been constantly made fun of in school. Although he was in his late thirties, he still worked as a stock boy at a local grocery store. Most of the other employees avoided or ridiculed him. He was a definite loner although a couple of the girls at work would talk to him out of sympathy. Even though he tried to act as if everything was normal within his extremely limited world, in actuality, he lived in the constant emotional turmoil of self-condemnation and fear of rejection. Although he was a Christian, he had a hard time fitting into any church and, therefore, attended only occasionally. If anyone paid genuine attention to him, he initially felt great, but soon began to anticipate the rejection that he knew would come as soon as they really got to know him. He believed that there was something fundamentally wrong with him. Charles was convinced that anything he did would eventually lead to failure and rejection and, as a consequence, he was immobilized within his safe but very lonely world.

The Model of Barak

As we search the scriptures for a biblical model for overcoming low self-image, we come to the story of Barak's defeat of the Canaanites who were under the command of Sisera. The name Canaan means, "lowland" and it stands for low self-image. Their defeat by Barak is described in Judges Chapters 4 and 5.

1. The problem of low self-image is an intellectual one. It is based on the principles that we believe concerning the worth of man. The problem is something that is within us. Jabin, the name of the king of the Canaanites, means, "intellect." He is the King of Hazor, which means, "enclosure or castle." Putting this together, I believe this clearly indicates that the problem of low self-image resides in our mental faculty.

2. Overcoming low self-image will be a very difficult battle because our ways of thinking are strong and have been established over a long period of time. The Canaanite army had 900 chariots of iron. Chariots stand for capability and iron stands for strength, but nine stands for insufficiency. This was a very formidable fighting force, but there was something insufficient about it. It was led by a commander named Sisera. His name means, "meditation or battle array." The worldly lies about self-image have been repeated and meditated on to such an extent that they have become so strongly fortified that they are even imbedded in the sub-conscious mind.

3. It takes both revelation and dedication to defeat low-self image. Deborah, whose name means, "Bee" (which suggests hard work or dedication) called for Barak. Barak means, "lightening flash," which in this context, I believe, means revelation. This revelation comes from God. I believe that this is revealed in Barak's father's name, which means, "father of delight or pleasantness" who came from the "holy place." Although Deborah gave him directions from God for the battle, he refused to go without her. Because of his refusal, she accompanied him to the battle, but the glory was given to a woman. I believe this is saying that revelation alone would be enough to deliver us, but most of us require perseverance to convince ourselves that the revelation is true. Women are known for favoring their intuition over their intellect. The truth of a Godly self-image may already be established in our mind, but we must believe it in our heart. This will take perseverance.

4. The lies about self-image are to be defeated by drawing them out and showing them to be inconsistent, which will result in a transformation in the client's thinking. Barak was to go to Mount Tabor, the mount of transfiguration. He was to draw Sisera to the river Kishon, which means, "winding or crooked." When the lies of the world system of self-image are drawn out and challenged, they are found to be inconsistent and erroneous. They are not straight and true. We find later that because of the rain (Word of God), the river overflowed and washed the chariots away. God will get involved using his "water of the Word" to stop the thoughts of low self-image in their tracks. In chapter five we find that the "mountains melted before the Lord" possibly suggesting the chariots became mired in the mud or were swept away in a flash flood.

5. Even the universe itself proves that our concepts about self-image are wrong. We are told in Judges 5:20 that "the stars fought against Sisera." If we compare ourselves and our accomplishments to the magnitude and splendor of the universe, we must understand that we, and everything we do, are absolutely nothing without God.

6. Deciding to willingly challenge our preconceived ideas is the key to beginning the road to victory. In Judges 5:9, we are told that it was the nobles (those in charge, our will) that gave themselves willingly to the task of defeating the Canaanites.

7. The actions required are a matter of wrestling with the lies and dwelling on the truth of the Word. Barak was told to call 10,000 men of Naphtali (wrestling) and Zebulun (dwelling) as his army. Ten thousand usually stands for human infirmity and failure. Without God's help, there was no way that they could win.

8. We must accept that the lie has become a part of us, refuse to deny its existence, challenge it with the simple truth we have learned, and "nail it" with the Word of God. Jael invited Sisera (meditations or thoughts) into her tent (acceptance). She gave him milk (simple truth) to drink. She did not agree to follow his request to say he was not in the tent. She then took a tent stake (truth is the mooring of our intellectual life) and drove it through his temple (which would pass through the brain or the location of the lie) with a hammer (one of the types of the Word of God).

9. Changing self-image takes persistence and perseverance in removing the old lies and embracing the truth. The heroine of this story was Jael. Her name means, "mountain goat," which, I believe, is characterized by persistence and perseverance in difficult situations. She was married to a man named Heber (companion) who was a Kenite (possession), a descendent of Hobob (cherished), the father-in-law of Moses (who stands for the law or truth), who pitched his tent at Zaanaim (removings) near Kedesh (holy place).

10. When we have totally overcome the lies concerning self-image with the truth of God in an experiential way (that includes our emotions), we will have total victory. After driving the tent stake through Sisera's temple, she "smote off his head." (Judges 5:26) We are told that Barak was to "lead captivity captive" (Judges 5:12), a term that was later used to describe Christ's complete victory over the devil. (Ephesians 4:8) In Judges 4:24 the war continued until King Jabin himself was defeated. The final

result was that the land had rest 40 years. Four represents God's government in the affairs of men and 40 is the biblical length of the complete, successful reign of a ruler.

Clearly, what I have been describing is a lifelong process, but I have found that dramatic changes are possible for clients who will seriously take on the challenge of developing a truly biblical self-image through faith.

Steps for Overcoming Low Self-image

1. We must realize that the problem of low self-image is an intellectual one based on the strongly established lies of the world's system for evaluating self-worth and significance.

2. We must be willing to challenge our preconceived ideas concerning worth and significance with God's truth.

3. The lies of self-image are defeated by drawing them out and showing them to be crooked and inconsistent until our thinking is transformed.

4. We must accept that the lie has become part of us, offer it the simple truth, and "nail it" with the Word of God, trusting the Word of God more than the word of men.

5. We must completely accept and act on the fact that we are worthwhile without regard to our successes or failures, and treat all men as they are—of great and equal value.

6. We must fight pride in our lives by being careful not to accept credit for anything we do, since without Christ we cannot do anything of eternal value.

7. We must accept the significance that God has provided for us when He adopted us as His sons and daughters and made us joint heirs with Jesus Christ.

8. Changing our self-image takes persistence and perseverance until our new image in Christ becomes a revelation to our spirit.

Chapter 15

Overcoming Pride through Faith
(King Nebuchadnezzar)

Pride is a self-defense mechanism to compensate for feelings of inferiority or worthlessness. In one ditch on the side of the road to health are feelings of inferiority and on the other side is the ditch of pride. King Nebuchadnezzar was the greatest of the Babylonian kings. His name means, "Nebo is the protector from misfortune." It is the job of our self to protect us and insure that our needs are met. Because pride extols the self over God and takes credit for what God has done, God resists it and gives grace to the humble. A humble person is one that rightly evaluates himself and sees that God made him, has given him what he has, has promoted him; and therefore, he is completely dependent on God.

Jeff considered himself successful in life. He was very driven to accomplish things and make himself successful. However, he seemed to oscillate between feeling worthless and being full of pride. He seemed to have a pattern. When he started a new job, he was humble and hard working. As he became more competent, he began to feel that only he could do the job right. This led to pride. Soon something would happen, and he would either fail, be fired, or something he was responsible for would go wrong. After feeling like a failure, he would again become humble and hardworking in an attempt to recover his reputation. In fact, he said, almost everything that had gone wrong in his life was associated with times he allowed himself to be proud. He determined never to let that happen to him again, since he was not fond of failure.

1. <u>The temptation to be proud comes when we think things are going good for us or when we are feeling insecure.</u> As we have seen, Nebuchadnezzar stands for the self. He was at rest and flourishing.

    Da 4:4 I Nebuchadnezzar was at rest in mine house, and flourishing in my palace:

2. <u>God warns us against pride.</u> People of the world (the wisemen of Babylon) cannot understand the warnings against pride (the dream), since they also rely totally on themselves and are proud of what they accomplish.

    Da 4:5 I saw a dream which made me afraid, and the thoughts upon my bed and the visions of my head troubled me.

    6 Therefore made I a decree to bring in all the wise men of Babylon before me, that they might make known unto me the interpretation of the dream.

    7 Then came in the magicians, the astrologers, the Chaldeans, and the soothsayers: and I told the dream before them; but they did not make known unto me the interpretation thereof.

3. <u>The spirit, which includes our conscience, will warn us against pride.</u> Here Daniel stands for our spirit as indicated in the verses below. We will have conviction in our spirit when we begin to brag or act arrogantly.

Da 4:9 O Belteshazzar, master of the magicians, because I know that the spirit of the holy gods is in thee, and no secret troubleth thee, tell me the visions of my dream that I have seen, and the interpretation thereof.

4. <u>The temptation to be proud begins with a false evaluation of our importance to ourselves and others</u>.

Da 4:10 Thus were the visions of mine head in my bed; I saw, and behold a tree in the midst of the earth, and the height thereof was great.

11 The tree grew, and was strong, and the height thereof reached unto heaven, and the sight thereof to the end of all the earth:

12 The leaves thereof were fair, and the fruit thereof much, and in it was meat for all: the beasts of the field had shadow under it, and the fowls of the heaven dwelt in the boughs thereof, and all flesh was fed of it.

5. <u>God watches for pride and will make sure that it does not continue for long</u>. The very things that we have pride in will be taken from us.

Da 4:13 I saw in the visions of my head upon my bed, and, behold, a watcher and an holy one came down from heaven;

14 He cried aloud, and said thus, Hew down the tree, and cut off his branches, shake off his leaves, and scatter his fruit: let the beasts get away from under it, and the fowls from his branches:

6. <u>Because God still cares for us, He will give us a chance to recover if we will repent and turn from our pride</u>. Iron usually stands for irresistible power and brass stands for shame. Grass stands for weakness and instability. Dew stands for gracious refreshing blessings. Therefore, these verses are telling us that God's power to put down pride is irresistible and ends in our shame. He makes the proud person feel weak and unstable, but showers him with gracious refreshing when he repents. Instead of being brilliant, he will find himself acting more like an animal just meeting the basest of needs. Seven stands for completeness. God's judgment of pride will end when it has been completely eradicated.

Da 4:15 Nevertheless leave the stump of his roots in the earth, even with a band of iron and brass, in the tender grass of the field; and let it be wet with the dew of heaven, and let his portion be with the beasts in the grass of the earth:

16 Let his heart be changed from man's, and let a beast's heart be given unto him; and let seven times pass over him.

7. <u>God resists pride so that we realize that we cannot be our own God; and that promotion comes from God, not from our own intelligence or efforts</u>. God can accomplish His wishes even through the basest of men if He chooses to do so. As we know, at one point God even used a donkey to speak for Him. (Numbers 22:28)

Da 4:17 This matter is by the decree of the watchers, and the demand by the word of the holy ones: to the intent that the living may know that the most High ruleth in the kingdom of men, and giveth it to whomsoever he will, and setteth up over it the basest of men.

8. <u>When the human spirit realizes that the self is about to be humbled because of pride, it is distraught</u>. This humbling seems to the spirit (Daniel) as a negative event to be wished on one's enemies.

Da 4:18 This dream I king Nebuchadnezzar have seen. Now thou, O Belteshazzar, declare the interpretation thereof, forasmuch as all the wise men of my kingdom are not able to make known unto me the interpretation: but thou art able; for the spirit of the holy gods is in thee.

19 Then Daniel, whose name was Belteshazzar, was astonied for one hour, and his thoughts troubled him. The king spake, and said, Belteshazzar, let not the dream, or the interpretation thereof, trouble thee. Belteshazzar answered and said, My lord, the dream be to them that hate thee, and the interpretation thereof to thine enemies.

9. <u>If we fall into pride, we will be humbled</u>. Complete recovery requires that we realize that we are weak as grass "that passeth away," we exist only by the grace of God (dew), we grow our faith in God (hair), and we become strong in Him (claws).

Da 4:33 The same hour was the thing fulfilled upon Nebuchadnezzar: and he was driven from men, and did eat grass as oxen, and his body was wet with the dew of heaven, till his hairs were grown like eagles' feathers, and his nails like birds' claws.

10. <u>We have real understanding only when we realize who we are in God's sight and thank God for all that He has done for us</u>. We must realize that all of us are really nothing without God and that we do not have a right to question anything He does.

Da 4:34 And at the end of the days I Nebuchadnezzar lifted up mine eyes unto heaven, and mine understanding returned unto me, and I blessed the most High, and I praised and honoured him that liveth for ever, whose dominion is an everlasting dominion, and his kingdom is from generation to generation:

35 And all the inhabitants of the earth are reputed as nothing: and he doeth according to his will in the army of heaven, and among the inhabitants of the earth: and none can stay his hand, or say unto him, What doest thou?

11. <u>When we confront our pride and repent, God will restore and uplift us (our self) again, since we are now willing to obey God and rely on Him in faith</u>.

Da 4:36 At the same time my reason returned unto me; and for the glory of my kingdom, mine honour and brightness returned unto me; and my counsellors and my lords sought unto me; and I was established in my kingdom, and excellent majesty was added unto me.

Overcoming Pride

1. We must understand that pride is a self-defense mechanism against low self-worth, and an attempt of the self to meet its need to feel valuable. We are tempted to be prideful when things are going well or when we are feeling insecure.

2. We must realize that pride is a statement to God that we can handle life on our own without His help. Therefore, God will withdraw His help and protection, and will let us live our life without His help until we repent.

3. God sees pride as a very serious sin, because it is the sin of rebellion which was authored by Satan when he led a third of the angels to rebel against God.

4. Therefore, God actively resists proud people and gives unmerited favor to those who humble themselves. Humility is not putting ourselves down but an honest evaluation of ourselves from God's point of view.

5. Prideful people believe the lie of the world that their worth is based on their performance, and they are deluding themselves that who they are and what they do on this earth is of great value without God. The Bible states that those who compare themselves with others are not wise.

6. If we do not repent and humble ourselves immediately, we will bring disaster upon ourselves and will be brought low with shame, experience how weak we really are, and may even feel and act like a brute beast.

7. Until we realize that our very existence, everything we have, and even our promotion comes from God, and give the glory to God, our way of thinking and viewing life will be distorted.

8. We must repent, ask for forgiveness, give all the glory to God, and deal with our underlying problem of self-worth. When we humble ourselves, God will uplift us and restore us to our rightful place.

PART VI

Models for Resolving Problems with Significance

Chapter 16

Overcoming
Selfish Desires through Faith
(Jephthah)

Selfish desire is the motivation we have to obtain or accomplish things to meet our needs. It is usually an issue of significance since we want what we want to make life better for us. Lot's son, through incest with his younger daughter, was Ammon. One authority suggests that this name might mean, "desire." (Smith's Bible Dictionary, 1999) I suggest it stands for "selfish desires." The Bible warns us about selfish or evil desires:

> Jas 1:13 When tempted, no one should say, "God is tempting me." For God cannot be tempted by evil, nor does he tempt anyone;
>
> 14 but each one is tempted when, by his own evil desire, he is dragged away and enticed.
>
> 15 Then, after desire has conceived, it gives birth to sin; and sin, when it is full-grown, gives birth to death. (NIV)

It is our selfish or evil desires that dominate our lives and lead us into a sinful lifestyle. Many clients do not recognize the influence of these desires as a pattern of failure, since they are readily justified in our society.

Doug had a desire to be a millionaire by the time he was thirty. In order to accomplish this he had started a business on the side, while he worked at a government job. Because he did not see his government job as important to meeting his needs, he did only what he had to do on the job and would find excuses to leave his place of employment. Numerous times his boss found him at his business during work hours. Of course, he had no time for his family at all. His entire life was consumed seeking success in his business venture. The things of God meant nothing to him. He saw nothing wrong with what he was doing. Finally, his boss took action for termination and filed charges concerning the fraudulent use of government property. Doug still defended himself as the victim of an overly ambitious boss.

The Bible gives us a model for dealing with evil or selfish desires in the story of Jepthah beginning in Judges Chapter 11.

1. <u>The battle with selfish desires is rooted in the struggle within us between the flesh and the spirit</u>. Jephthah means, "he opens." I believe he represents our will or choices, which determine whether we are open, or closed to our desires. He was born of Gilead (grandson of Manasseh, the eldest son of Joseph, the son of Israel) and a harlot. The children of Israel usually represent those born of the Spirit. Each Christian is born of the flesh and of the Spirit. Consequently, it is clear that Jephthah symbolizes the struggles of a Christian.

2. <u>We must win the battle over selfish desires, or we will lose our inheritance</u>. Jephthah's brothers drove him out of his inheritance, since the flesh has no inheritance with the sons of promise and faith. This is the same as the type of Ishmael (also the flesh) being sent away from Isaac (the Spirit). (Genesis 21:10) We all have been rejected and denied our inheritance, because of the sin that results from our flesh.

Jud 11:2 And Gilead's wife bare him sons; and his wife's sons grew up, and they thrust out Jephthah, and said unto him, Thou shalt not inherit in our father's house; for thou [art] the son of a strange woman.

3. <u>We want to run from our problems to gather with others with similar desires, so that we will have "the good life."</u> The land of Tob where Jephthah fled means, "Good."

Jud 11:3 Then Jephthah fled from his brethren, and dwelt in the land of Tob: and there were gathered vain men to Jephthah, and went out with him.

4. <u>When we try to find the "good life" for ourselves, our selfish desires will eventually try to take over our soul.</u> As I have said, I believe that Ammon stands for selfish desires.

Jud 11:4 And it came to pass in process of time, that the children of Ammon made war against Israel.

5. <u>Our spirit wants us (our will) to leave the good life in order to fight our selfish desires.</u> Gilead stands for the spirit. Our will (Jepththah) does not want to fight the selfish desires unless it can be in charge.

Jud 11:5 And it was so, that when the children of Ammon made war against Israel, the elders of Gilead went to fetch Jephthah out of the land of Tob:

6 And they said unto Jephthah, Come, and be our captain, that we may fight with the children of Ammon.

7 And Jephthah said unto the elders of Gilead, Did not ye hate me, and expel me out of my father's house? and why are ye come unto me now when ye are in distress?

6. <u>He who overcomes selfish desires qualifies himself to lead God's people.</u> When our will becomes totally submitted to God, it is qualified to lead our entire being. In fact, it is God's desire that our life be directed by a sanctified will.

Jud 11:9 And Jephthah said unto the elders of Gilead, If ye bring me home again to fight against the children of Ammon, and the LORD deliver them before me, shall I be your head?

10 And the elders of Gilead said unto Jephthah, The LORD be witness between us, if we do not so according to thy words.

7. <u>We must dedicate ourselves to God in order to lead the fight against our selfish desires and always be watchful against them.</u> Mizpeh means, "watchtower."

Jud 11:11 Then Jephthah went with the elders of Gilead, and the people made him head and captain over them: and Jephthah uttered all his words before the LORD in Mizpeh.

8. <u>We need to try to determine why our flesh and selfish desires are rising up.</u> Many times the answer is because we have feelings of insignificance or envy.

Jud 11:12. And Jephthah sent messengers unto the king of the children of Ammon, saying, What hast thou to do with me, that thou art come against me to fight in my land?

9. <u>When we were saved, God took away the territory from our selfish desires, but they want the territory back</u>.

Jud 11:13 And the king of the children of Ammon answered unto the messengers of Jephthah, Because Israel took away my land, when they came up out of Egypt, from Arnon and the Amorites even unto Jabbok, and unto Jordan: now therefore restore those [lands] again peaceably.

10. <u>The strongholds of selfish desires in our lives have their basis in our being trodden down or deprived in the past</u>. The Amorites stand for the flesh, which looks to meet its unmet needs through various worldly desires. Jahaz means, "trodden down." Sihon means, "warrior." Our selfish desires will fight to stay alive, but they must be defeated, or they will again attempt to retake the land (soul).

Jud 11:20 But Sihon trusted not Israel to pass through his coast: but Sihon gathered all his people together, and pitched in Jahaz, and fought against Israel.

21 And the LORD God of Israel delivered Sihon and all his people into the hand of Israel, and they smote them: so Israel possessed all the land of the Amorites, the inhabitants of that country.

11. <u>We cannot reason with selfish desires</u>

Jud 11:28 Howbeit the king of the children of Ammon hearkened not unto the words of Jephthah which he sent him.

12. <u>God's Spirit must empower us to want to be delivered from these desires and to do something about them</u>. Our spirit (Gilead), our mind (Manasseh means, "causing forgetfulness") and our conscience (Mizpeh means, "watchtower of Gilead" or "the spirit") must be enlisted to defeat our selfish desires.

Jud 11:29. Then the Spirit of the LORD came upon Jephthah, and he passed over Gilead, and Manasseh, and passed over Mizpeh of Gilead, and from Mizpeh of Gilead he passed over [unto] the children of Ammon.

13. <u>We must make a vow to give to God whatever God chooses in order to be delivered</u>. Many of our desires are very dear to us, and we do not want to give them up. To be victorious we must be willing to give up anything that God asks of us. Jephthah vowed to sacrifice anything that was in his house. We must be willing to sacrifice any of the desires within us for the Kingdom of God's sake.

Jud 11:30 And Jephthah vowed a vow unto the LORD, and said, If thou shalt without fail deliver the children of Ammon into mine hands,

31 Then it shall be, that whatsoever cometh forth of the doors of my house to meet me, when I return in peace from the children of Ammon, shall surely be the LORD'S, and I will offer it up for a burnt offering.

14. <u>With God's help, we can overcome selfish desires that are based on shame and covetousness</u>. Aroer means, "ruins or shame," and Minnith means, "distribution or covetousness." Our selfish desires are an expression of a covetous spirit, and we are ashamed of them. Once these underlying factors are confronted and defeated, selfish desires will experience "a great slaughter."

Jud 11:32 So Jephthah passed over unto the children of Ammon to fight against them; and the LORD delivered them into his hands.

33 And he smote them from Aroer, even till thou come to Minnith, [even] twenty cities, and unto the plain of the vineyards, with a very great slaughter. Thus the children of Ammon were subdued before the children of Israel.

15. <u>In the battle to overcome selfish desires, we may have to sacrifice things that are very dear to us</u>. We all have a favorite selfish desire that we do not want to sacrifice. I believe that Jephthah's daughter represents those desires that are our pride and joy. He had to be willing to sacrifice her just as Abraham was called upon by God to sacrifice Isaac.

Jud 11:34 And Jephthah came to Mizpeh (watchtower) unto his house, and, behold, his daughter came out to meet him with timbrels and with dances: and she [was his] only child; beside her he had neither son nor daughter.

35 And it came to pass, when he saw her, that he rent his clothes, and said, Alas, my daughter! thou hast brought me very low, and thou art one of them that trouble me: for I have opened my mouth unto the LORD, and I cannot go back.

36 And she said unto him, My father, [if] thou hast opened thy mouth unto the LORD, do to me according to that which hath proceeded out of thy mouth; forasmuch as the LORD hath taken vengeance for thee of thine enemies, [even] of the children of Ammon.

16. <u>Our emotions will fight to defend our selfish desires</u>. Ephraim means, "double ash-heap" and usually stands for shame, an emotion. Our emotions will not be happy that we have defeated our selfish desires.

Jud 12:1 And the men of Ephraim gathered themselves together, and went northward, and said unto Jephthah, Wherefore passedst thou over to fight against the children of Ammon, and didst not call us to go with thee? we will burn thine house upon thee with fire.

17. <u>Our emotions will not help deliver us out of the hands of our selfish desires, because they are too closely attached</u>. Many of our selfish desires meet our emotional needs.

Jud 12:2 And Jephthah said unto them, I and my people were at great strife with the children of Ammon; and when I called you, ye delivered me not out of their hands.

18. <u>Our emotions must be brought under control in order to have complete victory over our selfish desires</u>. Again, it is the spirit (Gilead) that teams up the will (Jepththah) to bring our emotions into line with our will. The accusation in this verse, that the Gileadites were fugitives of Ephraim, suggests that our emotions (Ephraim) want the spirit to be under its control. The spirit, however, needs to act independently to bring the emotion under its control.

Jud 12:4 Then Jephthah gathered together all the men of Gilead, and fought with Ephraim: and the men of Gilead smote Ephraim, because they said, Ye Gileadites [are] fugitives of Ephraim among the Ephraimites, [and] among the Manassites.

19. <u>None of our unruly emotions can be allowed to escape</u>.

Jud 12:5 And the Gileadites took the passages of Jordan before the Ephraimites: and it was [so], that when those Ephraimites which were escaped said, Let me go over; that the men of Gilead said unto him, [Art] thou an Ephraimite? If he said, Nay;

20. <u>You can tell the allies of selfish desires by the results they bring</u>. Do our desires truly bring life? The Ephraimites (emotions) wanted to escape, but could not say Shibboleth which means, "flowing stream of life." Our emotions are supposed to be a reflection of our will and perceptions, but can easily get out of control. They cannot bring life themselves, but are to reflect the life in us. In this analogy, they could not "say" or produce life in the same way that the spirit does.

Jud 12:6 Then said they unto him, Say now Shibboleth: and he said Sibboleth: for he could not frame to pronounce [it] right. Then they took him, and slew him at the passages of Jordan: and there fell at that time of the Ephraimites forty and two thousand.

21. <u>Victory over selfish desires is usually not long-lasting and will have to be fought again and again, but those who continue to fight will find a place among the saints of God</u>. The number six stands for man's sufficiency. Gilead means, "rocky region or hill" and here stands for the spiritual people of God, possibly those whose lives are founded upon a rock (Jesus).

Jud 12:7 And Jephthah judged Israel six years. Then died Jephthah the Gileadite, and was buried in [one of] the cities of Gilead.

Overcoming Selfish Desires

1. We must realize that our selfish desires keep us from inheriting the abundant life in Christ.

2. We must enlist our will and our spirit to fight against our selfish desires when they attempt to take over our soul.

3. We must be willing to pay the price and actually sacrifice whatever it takes to win the victory.

4. It is God who will give us the victory over our selfish desires.

5. Our emotions of shame and neediness, which underlie our selfish desires, must also be overcome.

6. We can tell which desires must be eliminated by the consequences they bring into our lives. Only the Spirit can bring us life.

7. All desires that do not bring forth the life of God must be eliminated.

8. We should be prepared to fight off selfish desires periodically throughout our lifetime.

Chapter 17

Overcoming Strife through Faith
(Gideon)

Strife and contention destroy many marriages and relationships. They usually result from envy and competition, which stem from our attempts to meet our needs for significance through the flesh.

Julianna was single again after her third divorce. Her life was a constant series of conflicts. Any injustice at work resulted in an ongoing feud that most of the time ended up in her supervisor's office. If accused of anything, she had to prove that she was right. She would go to any means to prove that she was right, and things usually escalated until they were out of control. When offended, she felt she had a right to address the wrong as she saw fit. The result was a constant list of location and job changes. She was also in constant conflict with the pastor of the church she attended. Her fourth marriage resulted in a series of explosive arguments, which threatened to end the marriage. Fortunately, Julianna began to trust God to deal with the strife in her life, took responsibility for her own actions and decided to get help.

The Bible provides an answer for this all-too-common problem. We find our model for overcoming strife and contention in the story of Gideon. Midian, the tribe of people who are the ancestors of today's Arabs, literally means, "strife."

1. <u>When strife and contentions come, everyone wants to hide</u>. They are usually the result of the evil that occurs when people attempt to get their needs met at the expense of others.

   Jud 6:1 And the children of Israel did evil in the sight of the LORD: and the LORD delivered them into the hand of Midian seven years.

   2 And the hand of Midian prevailed against Israel: [and] because of the Midianites the children of Israel made them the dens which [are] in the mountains, and caves, and strong holds.

2. <u>Strife and contention will destroy our increase and the sustenance of life</u>.

   Jud 6:3 And [so] it was, when Israel had sown, that the Midianites (Strife) came up, and the Amalekites (the flesh), and the children of the east, even they came up against them;

   4 And they encamped against them, and destroyed the increase of the earth, till thou come unto Gaza, and left no sustenance for Israel, neither sheep, nor ox, nor ass. *Strife destroys*

   People around you.

3. <u>When strife comes, it multiplies and brings many other problems with it</u>. It eventually impoverishes all that it touches.

   Jud 6:5 For they came up with their cattle and their tents, and they came as grasshoppers for multitude; [for] both they and their camels were without number: and they entered into the land to destroy it.

6 And Israel was greatly impoverished because of the Midianites; and the children of Israel cried unto the LORD.

Jas 3:16 For where envying and strife is, there is confusion and every evil work.

 4.   Strife results from struggles for prominence and from disobeying God. The Israelites were worshipping the gods of the Amorites, which stand for prominence.

Jud 6:10 And I said unto you, I [am] the LORD your God; fear not the gods of the Amorites, in whose land ye dwell: but ye have not obeyed my voice.

5.   Many times we give up, blame God for not helping and just try to hide from the strife in our lives. Oak trees stand for bitterness of death. Ophrah means, "fawn." Joash means, "given by God." Abinezer means, "my father is help" or "will meet my needs." Gideon means "feller, hewer or warrior." Consequently, I believe this verse is trying to tell us that where there should have been new life (fawn) given by God to provide for his needs, even Gideon, the warrior, was hiding to avoid the destruction that strife brings.

Jud 6:11. And there came an angel of the LORD, and sat under an oak which [was] in Ophrah, that [pertained] unto Joash the Abiezrite: and his son Gideon threshed wheat by the winepress, to hide [it] from the Midianites.

6.   God sees us as capable of beating strife and contention in our lives with His help.

Jud 6:12 And the angel of the LORD appeared unto him, and said unto him, The LORD [is] with thee, thou mighty man of valour.

7.   God wants us to do something about it.

Jud 6:14 And the LORD looked upon him, and said, Go in this thy might, and thou shalt save Israel from the hand of the Midianites: have not I sent thee?

8.   Winning over strife will require a sacrifice on our part that is acceptable to God.

Jud 6:19 And Gideon went in, and made ready a kid, and unleavened cakes of an ephah of flour: the flesh he put in a basket, and he put the broth in a pot, and brought [it] out unto him under the oak, and presented [it].

9.   Trusting Jesus to meet our needs is the answer to peace in our lives.

Jud 6:23 And the LORD said unto him, Peace [be] unto thee; fear not: thou shalt not die.
24 Then Gideon built an altar there unto the LORD, and called it Jehovahshalom (God is my peace): unto this day it [is] yet in Ophrah of the Abiezrites.

10.   The first step to overcome strife is that we must tear down the idols in our lives that have been passed down to us. Most of us have fallen into the trap of competing with others to get our needs met. It is this whole set of premises concerning the "rat race" of life that must be thrown down.

Jud 6:25 And it came to pass the same night, that the LORD said unto him, Take thy father's young bullock, even the second bullock of seven years old, and throw down the altar of Baal that thy father hath, and cut down the grove that [is] by it:

26 And build an altar unto the LORD thy God upon the top of this rock, in the ordered place, and take the second bullock, and offer a burnt sacrifice with the wood of the grove which thou shalt cut down.

11. When we believe that everything we need is given by God, our idols lose their power.

Jud 6:31 And Joash (Gideon's father) said unto all that stood against him, Will ye plead for Baal? will ye save him? he that will plead for him, let him be put to death whilst [it is yet] morning: if he [be] a god, let him plead for himself, because [one] hath cast down his altar.

32 Therefore on that day he called him Jerubbaal, saying, Let Baal plead against him, because he hath thrown down his altar.

12. Strife and the flesh are allies.

Jud 6:33. Then all the Midianites and the Amalekites (the flesh) and the children of the east were gathered together, and went over, and pitched in the valley of Jezreel.

13. We must declare, according to God's Word, that we can overcome strife in our lives. When we decide to do God's will and put an end to strife, we will find allies in all those who truly want peace.

Jud 6:34 But the Spirit of the LORD came upon Gideon, and he blew a trumpet (usually stands for declaring God's word); and Abiezer (my father is help –those who have faith) was gathered after him.

35 And he sent messengers throughout all Manasseh (causing to forget – those who want to put strife behind them); who also was gathered after him: and he sent messengers unto Asher (those who want to be happy), and unto Zebulun (those who want to be exalted of God), and unto Naphtali (those who are willing to wrestle things out and win); and they came up to meet them.

14. To win, we must be convinced that God will bless what He calls us to do with or without regard to what others do. God's methods for overcoming strife require us to do what is right unilaterally. We must know that He will bless what we do to stop strife, with or without the cooperation of others. We must also know that even if we fail, God will still bring an end to strife through what other people do. Consequently, we are assured of victory because it is God Who will help us either way.

Jud 6:36 And Gideon said unto God, If thou wilt save Israel by mine hand, as thou hast said,

37 Behold, I will put a fleece of wool (God's work through Gideon) in the floor (real world); [and] if the dew (grace) be on the fleece only, and [it be] dry upon all the earth (human efforts of others) [beside], then shall I know that thou wilt save Israel by mine hand, as thou hast said.

38 And it was so: for he rose up early on the morrow, and thrust the fleece together, and wringed the dew out of the fleece, a bowl full of water (life).

39 And Gideon said unto God, Let not thine anger be hot against me, and I will speak but this once: let me prove, I pray thee, but this once with the fleece; let it now be dry only upon the fleece (if his works for God failed), and upon all the ground (human efforts of others) let there be dew (grace).

40 And God did so that night: for it was dry upon the fleece only, and there was dew on all the ground.

15. <u>Fearful people cannot overcome strife. Fear is the opposite of faith</u>.

Jud 7:3 Now therefore go to, proclaim in the ears of the people, saying, Whosoever [is] fearful and afraid, let him return and depart early from mount Gilead. And there returned of the people twenty and two thousand; and there remained ten thousand.

16. <u>Those who desperately seek to meet their needs cannot overcome strife</u>. We must believe that God will meet our needs in order to love others, in spite of what they do.

Jug 7:5 So he brought down the people unto the water: and the LORD said unto Gideon, Every one that lappeth of the water with his tongue, as a dog lappeth, him shalt thou set by himself; likewise every one that boweth down upon his knees to drink.

6 And the number of them that lapped, [putting] their hand to their mouth, were three hundred men: (not desperate to drink water) but all the rest of the people bowed down upon their knees to drink water.

7 And the LORD said unto Gideon, <u>By the three hundred men that lapped</u> will I save you, and deliver the Midianites into thine hand: and let all the [other] people go every man unto his place.

17. <u>We need to speak what God says—that He has and will meet all our needs in all circumstances</u>. The sword stands for the Word of God. We need to declare to ourselves what God says about strife. Confession reflects and strengthens our faith.

Jud 7:16. And he divided the three hundred men [into] three companies, and he put a trumpet in every man's hand, with empty pitchers, and lamps within the pitchers.

17 And he said unto them, Look on me, and do likewise: and, behold, when I come to the outside of the camp, it shall be [that], as I do, so shall ye do.

18 When I blow with a trumpet (speak God's truth), I and all that [are] with me, then blow ye the trumpets also on every side of all the camp, and say, [The sword] of the LORD, and of Gideon.

18. <u>The best time for intervention is after a crisis, when things are darkest (the middle watch) and when circumstances are changing</u>.

Jud 7:19 So Gideon, and the hundred men that [were] with him, came unto the outside of the camp in the beginning of the middle watch; and they had but newly set the watch: and they blew the trumpets, and brake the pitchers that [were] in their hands.

19. <u>We must break our pattern of actions, not take what others do personally and let the light of the Spirit show forth</u>.

Jud 7:20 And the three companies blew the trumpets (spoke God's truth), and brake the pitchers (died to our way of doing things and taking things personally), and held the lamps in their left (a new way of doing things) hands, and the trumpets in their right hands to blow [withal]: and they cried, The sword of the LORD, and of Gideon.

20. <u>We do not overcome strife by fighting, but only by doing what is right and standing our ground in faith.</u>

Jud 7:20 And they stood every man in his place round about the camp: and all the host ran, and cried, and fled.

21 And the three hundred blew the trumpets, and the LORD set every man's sword against his fellow, even throughout all the host: and the host fled to Bethshittah in Zererath, [and] to the border of Abelmeholah, unto Tabbath.

23 And the men of Israel gathered themselves together out of Naphtali, and out of Asher, and out of all Manasseh, and pursued after the Midianites.

21. <u>We can use our past failures and negative emotions to set our resolve to never again give in to the temptation to live in strife.</u> Ephraim again stands for the emotions of shame from our past life of strife. This shame can be used to overcome the temptation to have strife even with evil people and the devil himself.

Jud 7:24 And Gideon sent messengers throughout all mount Ephraim (double ash heap or shame of the past), saying, Come down against the Midianites, and take before them the waters unto Bethbarah and Jordan. Then all the men of Ephraim gathered themselves together, and took the waters unto Bethbarah and Jordan.

25 And they took two princes of the Midianites, Oreb and Zeeb; and they slew Oreb (raven - evil people) upon the rock Oreb, and Zeeb (wolf - the devil) they slew at the winepress of Zeeb, and pursued Midian, and brought the heads of Oreb and Zeeb to Gideon on the other side Jordan.

Overcoming Strife

1. We need to tear down our idols—the things we depend on instead of God. It is our attempts to meet our own needs that lead to strife.

2. Be absolutely convinced God will meet every need.

3. We need to enlist a small number of dedicated, Christian people of courage to stand with us (a support group).

4. Decide to take a stand, even when others are fearful after a crisis.

5. Declare what God says—that He will meet all our needs and will give us peace.

6. Change how we act (break the vessel of the flesh). Use quiet, loving boundaries, not conflict.

7. Live it! (Show our light) Use love, kindness and assertiveness.

8. Stand our ground. If we do what is right without regard to what others do, God will give us peace.

9. We can use our past failures to strengthen our resolve to never again give in to the temptation to live in strife.

PART VII

Models for Resolving Problems with Security

Chapter 18

Overcoming Fear through Faith
(The Fiery Furnace)

Fear confronts all of us. In *Hinds Feet on High Places* (1986) Hannah Hurnard suggests that we are all "fearlings." Fear is the emotion of unbelief. It is the opposite of faith. Either we believe that God will protect us and take care of us, or we will be afraid. Fear mobilizes us to run from a perceived threat. Fear is an emotion and, therefore, is controlled by how we perceive the threats in our lives. The ultimate answer for fear is to face it with our faith in God.

Phil was a very successful engineer. Even though the economy was bad, he had no fear of ever being laid off. He was the type of person who met his deadlines, and his products were successful. He had just identified the correct formula to get production rolling on his latest design, but he was having such anxiety attacks that he had skipped work. Although Phil did not realize it, he was in the rat race of life, had performance self-worth and his anxiety was justified. When he was working on a new project, he was stressed to meet the deadlines and uphold his stellar reputation. When he had completed one, he knew he would be given an even more difficult project the next time around. Consequently, there would never be an end to his stress until he failed. Until then he would continue to be promoted to a larger fish bowl with bigger sharks. Before he could face his fears, he had to face the lies in his life that he believed. He had to learn that his "great accomplishments" were truly of little value and, especially in the field of technology, would soon pass into history. When Phil realized that in Christ he was already so significant that he could not make himself any more significant, that true success was finding the will of God and doing it, and that God was his true boss; he was able to exit the rat race, and his anxiety disappeared. He could now do his best for God, give credit to God for what he did, and nothing else mattered.

In the book of Daniel, we find three Hebrew slaves facing the fear of their lives. Either Shadrach, Meshach, and Abednego must renounce their faith in God by worshipping the golden statue of the king; or they must face being thrown into a furnace of fire. This story deals with the fear of the soul. In our lives, we each face the same quandary. Either we face the fears of our lives that, to us, seem like certain death, or we bow down to the self, become dominated by the flesh and admit that God is not able to save us. This story begins in the first chapter of Daniel.

1. The self wishes to enslave us to do its bidding and make us be its servant though fear. The children of Israel were conquered by King Nebuchadnezzar of Babylon. Nebuchadnezzar was the greatest of the Babylonian kings. His name means "Nebo is the protector from misfortune," and he is a type of the self. Our self believes that it can be its own God and protect itself from misfortune. It tries to conquer and control us through fear. Babylon symbolizes confusion and antagonism against God. I, therefore, suggest that Babylon stands for our world. Jehoiakim means "he who Jehovah has set up."

    Da 1:1 In the third year of the reign of Jehoiakim king of Judah came Nebuchadnezzar king of Babylon unto Jerusalem, and besieged it.

2 And the Lord gave Jehoiakim (He who Jehovah has set up) king of Judah into his hand, with part of the vessels of the house of God: which he carried into the land of Shinar to the house of his god; and he brought the vessels into the treasure house of his god.

2.   <u>The self wants to dominate what is good in us and conform us to its will</u>. In life, we are all enslaved by our physical and psychological needs of the self. We feel fear that these needs will not be met, unless we protect our selves and meet our needs through the flesh. Our self wants us to learn the language or lies of the world to meet our needs through it, instead of God. It wants us to learn to speak the world's language of pride. Ashpenaz means, "I will make prominent the sprinkled." Later, he is called Melzar, which means, "the master of the wine." He controlled what they ate and was responsible for their mental and physical development. Possibly, he stands for our desires that are concerned about meeting our physical and psychological needs. We must have the agreement of our desires in order to restrict what we eat and guide our future. Our desires usually focus on what they think is the best for our flesh.

Da 1:3 And the king spake unto Ashpenaz the master of his eunuchs, that he should bring certain of the children of Israel, and of the king's seed, and of the princes;

4 Children in whom was no blemish, but well favoured, and skilful in all wisdom, and cunning in knowledge, and understanding science, and such as had ability in them to stand in the king's palace, and whom they might teach the learning and the tongue of the Chaldeans.

3.   <u>The self wants to feed us the lies of the world, because it wants to do things in its own way</u>. The result is that by over-relying on ourselves, we are filled with fear instead of faith. Unfortunately, even most Christians are greatly influenced to believe the world's message by what we are taught in school, what we read and what we see on television and in the movies. This provides the foundation for how we interpret our world and this provides the basis for our fears. Unfortunately, small children have no other reference point for interpreting their world than what they are taught and experience. We are supposed to eat of the flesh of the Word of Christ and drink of the wine of His Spirit, instead of the lies and doctrines of this world, or we will be consumed by the fears of this world.

Da 1:5 And the king appointed them a daily provision of the king's meat, and of the wine which he drank: so nourishing them three years, that at the end thereof they might stand before the king.

4.   <u>God has given us, through faith, all we need in life for our protection and to meet our needs</u>. Jesus told his disciples over and over, "fear not." Daniel means, "God is my judge or judge of God." I suggest that this stands for our conscience or spirit. God wants us to let Him be the judge of all things. Hananiah means, "Jehovah is gracious, God has favored, or given." As a Christians, we know that God favors us even when we are without merit, or if we fail. If we truly believe this, it provides an emotional foundation for fighting our fears. Mishael means, "who is like God." It is our will that determines if we will be conformed to be like God, or if we will become our own God. Azariah means, "Jehovah has helped." We can count on God to meet all of our needs according to His riches in glory (Philipians 4:19). We must remember all that God has done for us when fear tries to overcome us.

Da 1:6 Now among these were of the children of Judah, Daniel, Hananiah, Mishael, and Azariah:

5.   <u>The self wishes to change our character (name) and make us see ourselves as self-reliant and, yet, a slave to this world</u>. The eunuch (desires) changed the names of the Hebrew children. Our desires

cannot be fruitful in themselves, but must work through our soul to make us what we are. We will act according to how we see ourselves. Daniel was renamed Belteshazzar which means, "protect his life" or "the god Bel protects the king." Our self wants our spirit to focus on self-protection instead of what God wants us to do. Hananiah was renamed Shadrack which means, "a royal scribe." Our self wants our emotions simply to reflect whatever it wants and desires in the world. Mishael was renamed Meshach which means, "a guest of a king or a shadow of a prince." The self wants our mind to see ourselves as his guest on this earth and become like the world, full of pride. Azariah was renamed Abednego which means, "a servant of Nebo or Ishtar," which was the goddess of love and fertility. The self wants our will to follow whatever feels good and brings it pleasure. Consequently, these three names approximate the desires for the lust of the flesh, the lust of the eyes, and the pride of life. They represent an attempt to meet the basic needs of the self for worth and significance, security, and love. The self wants us to accept our slave names. He wants us to believe that if we will simply rely on our self and do things as the world does, our needs will be met. It wants us to be secure in our own accomplishments, and suggests that if we will worship the God of pleasure, everything will be wonderful. Conformity to the world can be and is a strong temptation for all of us.

Da 1:7 Unto whom the prince of the eunuchs gave names: for he gave unto Daniel the name of Belteshazzar; and to Hananiah, of Shadrach; and to Mishael, of Meshach; and to Azariah, of Abednego.

6. <u>We must not eat from the world's table, or we will not accomplish what God wants for our lives</u>. It is fear that "we will lose our head" i.e. not get our needs met, that tries to keep us from avoiding the world's "food."

Da 1:8 But Daniel purposed in his heart that he would not defile himself with the portion of the king's meat, nor with the wine which he drank: therefore he requested of the prince of the eunuchs that he might not defile himself.

9 Now God had brought Daniel into favour and tender love with the prince of the eunuchs.

10 And the prince of the eunuchs said unto Daniel, I fear my lord the king, who hath appointed your meat and your drink: for why should he see your faces worse liking than the children which are of your sort? then shall ye make me endanger my head to the king.

7. <u>The first step in overcoming fear is to face our fears, obey God and test what happens. We must act on our faith</u>. Ten stands for human infirmity and failure. We are afraid we might fail if we do things God's way. But if we will face our fear, we will find that God's ways work best.

Da 1:11 Then said Daniel to Melzar, whom the prince of the eunuchs had set over Daniel, Hananiah, Mishael, and Azariah,

12 Prove thy servants, I beseech thee, ten days; and let them give us pulse to eat, and water to drink.

13 Then let our countenances be looked upon before thee, and the countenance of the children that eat of the portion of the king's meat: and as thou seest, deal with thy servants.

14 So he consented to them in this matter, and proved them ten days.

8. <u>Experience is the strongest evidence for our faith</u>. When the world attempts to make us worship it, we must be ready to face our fiery trials with faith. The things of God are ten times better than anything that the world has to offer us, especially when we receive God's wisdom and understanding. Melzer means, "master of the wine," which possibly represents our soul. Even the flesh and the self have to admit that the things that God gives us result in a better life.

Da 1:15 And at the end of ten days their countenances appeared fairer and fatter in flesh than all the children which did eat the portion of the king's meat.

16 Thus Melzar took away the portion of their meat, and the wine that they should drink; and gave them pulse.

17 As for these four children, God gave them knowledge and skill in all learning and wisdom: and Daniel had understanding in all visions and dreams.

18 Now at the end of the days that the king had said he should bring them in, then the prince of the eunuchs brought them in before Nebuchadnezzar.

19 And the king commmuned with them; and among them all was found none like Daniel, Hananiah, Mishael, and Azariah: therefore stood they before the king.

20 And in all matters of wisdom and understanding, that the king enquired of them, he found them ten times better than all the magicians and astrologers that were in all his realm.

9.   The self wants to be worshipped and will set itself up to be worshipped as god, if it gets the chance. Dura means, "dwelling," and the number six stands for man's sufficiency. Gold stands for deity. Our self will submit to no one and wants our mind, emotions and will to come into conformity with its wishes. The fact that the image was huge suggests that this is a significant temptation for all of us. We all are tempted to want to be our own God and to worship ourselves. Possibly, Daniel (our spirit) is not in this story, since our spirit cannot be coerced by fear. The self loves to make itself seem important.

Da 3:1 Nebuchadnezzar the king made an image of gold, whose height was threescore cubits, and the breadth thereof six cubits: he set it up in the plain of Dura, in the province of Babylon.

3 Then the princes, the governors, and captains, the judges, the treasurers, the counsellors, the sheriffs, and all the rulers of the provinces, were gathered together unto the dedication of the image that Nebuchadnezzar the king had set up; and they stood before the image that Nebuchadnezzar had set up.

10.   The self threatens that if we refuse to worship and rely totally on it, our needs will not be met and we will be consumed by the fire of our fears. It is the fear that our needs will not be met that motivates us to worship the self.

Dn 3:5 That at what time ye hear the sound of the cornet, flute, harp, sackbut, psaltery, dulcimer, and all kinds of musick, ye fall down and worship the golden image that Nebuchadnezzar the king hath set up:
6 And whoso falleth not down and worshippeth shall the same hour be cast into the midst of a burning fiery furnace.

7 Therefore at that time, when all the people heard the sound of the cornet, flute, harp, sackbut, psaltery, and all kinds of musick, all the people, the nations, and the languages, fell down and worshipped the golden image that Nebuchadnezzar the king had set up.

11.   Others, especially those of the world, will say to us (our self) that we are not doing enough to meet our needs (or worship the self). They will suggest that we are missing out on life by not fully pursuing our desires and making something out of ourselves.

Da 3:8 Wherefore at that time certain Chaldeans came near, and accused the Jews.

10 Thou, O king, hast made a decree, that every man that shall hear the sound of the cornet, flute, harp, sackbut, psaltery, and dulcimer, and all kinds of musick, shall fall down and worship the golden image:

12 There are certain Jews whom thou hast set over the affairs of the province of Babylon, Shadrach, Meshach, and Abednego; these men, O king, have not regarded thee: they serve not thy gods, nor worship the golden image which thou hast set up.

12. <u>The self rages against us by saying that we are not trying hard enough to focus on its needs and demanding that we increase our efforts to meet its lusts.</u> It wants to give us another chance to conform to this world, or it threatens to destroy our soul with fear.

Da 3:13 Then Nebuchadnezzar in his rage and fury commanded to bring Shadrach, Meshach, and Abednego. Then they brought these men before the king.

15 Now if ye be ready that at what time ye hear the sound of the cornet, flute, harp, sackbut, psaltery, and dulcimer, and all kinds of musick, ye fall down and worship the image which I have made; well: but if ye worship not, ye shall be cast the same hour into the midst of a burning fiery furnace; and who is that God that shall deliver you out of my hands?

13. <u>The only answer to overcoming the self is to face the fear with faith that our needs may go unmet.</u> Our mind, emotions and will must declare that even if we are consumed by fear and God does not meet our needs, we still will not worship the self. Self, of course, will be extremely unhappy, because the only thing it has to hold on to the throne of our life with is fear. Seven stands for completeness and fear can be completely overwhelming at times. This is especially true of panic attacks and phobias. Fear is so powerful, we are sure we will be destroyed by it.

Da 3:16 Shadrach, Meshach, and Abednego, answered and said to the king, O Nebuchadnezzar, we are not careful to answer thee in this matter.

17 If it be so, our God whom we serve is able to deliver us from the burning fiery furnace, and he will deliver us out of thine hand, O king.

18 But if not, be it known unto thee, O king, that we will not serve thy gods, nor worship the golden image which thou hast set up.

19 Then was Nebuchadnezzar full of fury, and the form of his visage was changed against Shadrach, Meshach, and Abednego: therefore he spake, and commanded that they should heat the furnace one seven times more than it was wont to be heated.

14. <u>Fear binds us so that we feel helpless and powerless over our circumstances.</u> However, it will be our circumstances and fear, itself, that will be consumed in the fire. The very basis of fear is our reliance on ourselves, knowing that we are limited and incapable of directing and doing everything necessary to always protect ourselves and meet all our needs. The soldiers who attempted to throw them into the fire (use fear to control them) were themselves consumed by it. People who try to force others to meet their needs (abusers) through fear will eventually be consumed by the fear when others resist their advances.

Da 3:20 And he commanded the most mighty men that were in his army to bind Shadrach, Meshach, and Abednego, and to cast them into the burning fiery furnace.

21 Then these men were bound in their coats, their hosen, and their hats, and their other garments, and were cast into the midst of the burning fiery furnace.

22 Therefore because the king's commandment was urgent, and the furnace exceeding hot, the flame of the fire slew those men that took up Shadrach, Meshach, and Abednego.

15. <u>Even if we do not do everything perfectly (fall down), if we face our fears, God will personally meet us in our fears and lift us up.</u> Our self will be amazed, when we trust God and face our fears, because we are delivered from our fears.

Da 3:23 And these three men, Shadrach, Meshach, and Abednego, fell down bound into the midst of the burning fiery furnace.

24 Then Nebuchadnezzar the king was astonied, and rose up in haste, and spake, and said unto his counsellors, Did not we cast three men bound into the midst of the fire? They answered and said unto the king, True, O king.

25 He answered and said, Lo, I see four men loose, walking in the midst of the fire, and they have no hurt; and the form of the fourth is like the Son of God.

16. <u>When we act on our faith to face our fears, we will not be harmed in any way.</u> Their hair (faith) was not hurt, their clothing (character) was not burned, and they did not even have the smell of smoke (emotional consequences) on them.

Da 3:26 Then Nebuchadnezzar came near to the mouth of the burning fiery furnace, and spake, and said, Shadrach, Meshach, and Abednego, ye servants of the most high God, come forth, and come hither. Then Shadrach, Meshach, and Abednego, came forth of the midst of the fire.

27 And the princes, governors, and captains, and the king's counsellors, being gathered together, saw these men, upon whose bodies the fire had no power, nor was an hair of their head singed, neither were their coats changed, nor the smell of fire had passed on them.

17. <u>When we have successfully faced our fears with faith, even our self will give God the glory and agree that we should not worship ourselves rather than God.</u> Even the king's words—the threats that caused the fear—were negated and turned to nothing. <u>When faced with faith, panic attacks, phobias and anxiety simply</u> cannot overcome us.

Da 3:28 Then Nebuchadnezzar spake, and said, Blessed be the God of Shadrach, Meshach, and Abednego, who hath sent his angel, and delivered his servants that trusted in him, and have changed the king's word, and yielded their bodies, that they might not serve nor worship any god, except their own God.

18. <u>People who speak against faith and run from their fears or rely on themselves will end up cut into emotional pieces, and their lives become a pile of refuse.</u> In this story, self (Nebuchadnezzar) finally realized the power of faith, and made a declaration that speaking against faith (which diminishes it) is a crime, which leads to death and destruction in their lives.

Da 3:29 Therefore I make a decree, That every people, nation, and language, which speak any thing amiss against the God of Shadrach, Meshach, and Abednego, shall be cut in pieces, and their houses shall be made a dunghill: because there is no other God that can deliver after this sort.

19. <u>Facing our fears in faith leads to a better life and promotion in this world.</u>

Da 3:30 Then the king promoted Shadrach, Meshach, and Abednego, in the province of Babylon.

Overcoming Fear

1. Fear is an emotion of insecurity that occurs when our security is threatened or when we are not sure that our basic needs will be met. It is energy to avoid whatever threatens us.

2. Satan uses fear to keep us in bondage and prevent us from fulfilling what God has called us to do. He does this by getting us to rely on ourselves and make ourselves our own god instead of trusting God to meet our needs.

3. Our fear is based on our perception of our world and ourselves. Satan attempts to get us to believe what the world says, have our emotions reflect our worldly circumstances, and convince us that we must be conformed to this world in order to get our needs met.

4. Because we are so limited in what we can do, we can never guarantee our own safety in this world or fully meet our needs. Our attempts to become self-reliant result in even more fear. Those that set themselves up as their own god and rely on themselves fall into the trap of fear.

5. The first step in overcoming fear is to not obey or rely on ourselves and to have faith in God, no matter how difficult or threatening the circumstances might be.

6. We must not bow down to the self, but face our fear, trusting in God. If we rely on ourselves, we are doomed to a life of insecurity without God. If we run from our fear, our problem seems more threatening and our fear will grow.

7. If we face our fears, trusting in faith that God will protect us and meet all our needs, He will be there for us, go through our fears with us, and help us conquer the insecurity in our lives. Every time we overcome fear our faith grows. He has promised that we will never be tempted beyond that which we are able and will always have a way of escape. (1 Corinthians 10:13)

Chapter 19

Overcoming
Spiritual Oppression through Faith
(Daniel and the Lions)

When we are dealing with fear in the spiritual realm, we are usually dealing with the oppression of the devil and the fear of death. Satan does not want us to serve and worship God and will do anything to restrain us. In the world, the devil has two strategies. Either he tries to make us think he does not exist, or he tries to scare us into not obeying God's will for our lives. The answer again is to face our fears with our faith in God. Daniel had to do just that.

William had been diagnosed with schizophrenia and obsessive-compulsive disorder. He had been hospitalized and now was taking psychoactive medication. He came to counseling concerned that he had committed the unpardonable sin and that he was doomed, no matter what he did, to go to hell. This type of oppression and belief system is not unusual for those who are on the verge of relapsing into psychosis. Psychosis usually develops when a person is no longer able to meet even the need to feel safe. The person simply yields to spiritual pressure to lapse into unreality. This is an attempt to feel that everything is okay in an unreal world. If the client believes that they have committed the unpardonable sin, that repentance is useless, and that, no matter what they do, they will go to hell anyway, life is hopeless. If life is hopeless, then one way to cope with life is to slip into unreality. William had to learn that Satan lost all of his power 2000 years ago at the cross and that he was being deceived. The unpardonable sin is blasphemy against the Holy Spirit. The result of blasphemy against the Holy Spirit is that the person rejects the drawing of the Holy Spirit and drives Him away. This is an unpardonable sin, because, without the drawing of the Holy Spirit, we cannot be saved. If we reject the drawing of the Holy Spirit throughout our lifetime and are not saved, our sins are not forgiven. Over and over again, William had to restudy the Word of God on this subject, face the lies of Satan (in the den of lions), and rebuke them. When he did, he walked away from the temptation to escape into unreality and did not relapse.

1. For the Christian, the self or our will has ordained that our spirit is to be in control of our lives. The number 12 (and 120) stands for the government of God. In this case, Darius, whose name means, "holder, restrainer or he that informs himself again," stands for the self or our will. Daniel, which means, "to judge for God" again stands for our spirit. The goal of spiritual warfare is that the self should not suffer damage. The three presidents possibly stand for our spirit, our soul and our flesh, since all make decisions concerning our welfare.

   Da 6:1 It pleased Darius to set over the kingdom an hundred and twenty princes, which should be over the whole kingdom;

   2 And over these three presidents; of whom Daniel (spirit) was first: that the princes might give accounts unto them, and the king should have no damage.

   3 Then this Daniel was preferred above the presidents and princes, because an excellent spirit was in him; and the king thought to set him over the whole realm.

2. <u>Our flesh and soul do not want to be under the control of our spirit, but they can find nothing against our spirit except that it wants to obey God and do His will.</u>

    Da 6:4 Then the presidents and princes sought to find occasion against Daniel concerning the kingdom; but they could find none occasion nor fault (the spirit is without fault); forasmuch as he was faithful, neither was there any error or fault found in him.

3. <u>In order to overthrow the dominion of the spirit, the flesh and soul try to bring the spirit again under the law of the self.</u> The law required that everyone rely only on the self for thirty days. This symbolizes the Jewish law that had to be obeyed and fulfilled in human strength, relying on the self. The law cannot be changed; because this is, in fact, the Old Testament law. It must be fulfilled.

    Da 6:7 All the presidents of the kingdom, the governors, and the princes, the counsellors, and the captains, have consulted together to establish a royal statute, and to make a firm decree, that whosoever shall ask a petition of any God or man for thirty days, save of thee, O king, he shall be cast into the den of lions.

4. <u>The spirit cannot and will not rely on the self to try to obey the law, since it relies only on God.</u> If we attempt to fulfill the law in the strength of our self, we would have to rely on the flesh and, therefore, supplant the spirit.

    Da 6:10 Now when Daniel knew that the writing was signed, he went into his house; and his windows being open in his chamber toward Jerusalem, he kneeled upon his knees three times a day, and prayed, and gave thanks before his God, as he did aforetime.

5. <u>When we walk according to the spirit, the flesh accuses us of not obeying the law.</u>

    Da 6:12 Then they came near, and spake before the king concerning the king's decree; Hast thou not signed a decree, that every man that shall ask a petition of any God or man within thirty days, save of thee, O king, shall be cast into the den of lions? The king answered and said, The thing is true, according to the law of the Medes and Persians, which altereth not.

    13 Then answered they and said before the king, That Daniel, which is of the children of the captivity of Judah, regardeth not thee, O king, nor the decree that thou hast signed, but maketh his petition three times a day.

6. <u>The penalty for sin (breaking the law) is death which results in being sent to hell, symbolized by the den of lions (devils).</u> It is the self's hope that God will deliver us from hell. If the spirit is indeed overcome by the devil, the self will be dominated by the flesh; so it is greatly troubled by this possibility. But the self can do nothing about it, but be concerned. It has no power to change the law or deliver the spirit from Satan.

    Da 6:16 Then the king commanded, and they brought Daniel, and cast him into the den of lions. Now the king spake and said unto Daniel, Thy God whom thou servest continually, he will deliver thee. — *This Prophesied Danial Outcome unknown to King*

7. <u>The lions (devils) can have no power over the spirit because of what Jesus did on the cross.</u> Jesus took our place, fulfilled the law and took the power of death from Satan. The angel, here, is Jesus who delivered us all that are led by the spirit (saved) from the power of the lions (devils) and made us innocent in the sight of God. Because of the sacrifice of Jesus, our sins are forgiven, and we are

delivered from the law and the fear of death. When we realize what Jesus has done for us, we no longer have to fear spiritual oppression by Satan or fear death.

Da 6:19 Then the king arose very early in the morning, and went in haste unto the den of lions.

20 And when he came to the den, he cried with a lamentable voice unto Daniel: and the king spake and said to Daniel, O Daniel, servant of the living God, is thy God, whom thou servest continually, able to deliver thee from the lions?

21 Then said Daniel unto the king, O king, live for ever.

22 My God hath sent his angel, and hath shut the lions' mouths, that they have not hurt me: forasmuch as before him innocency was found in me; and also before thee, O king, have I done no hurt.

8. <u>Because the accusers (the flesh) are under the law (not saved), they have no protection from what the lions (devils) choose to do to them.</u> They are bound by spiritual oppression and the fear of death and were therefore, devoured by the lions.

Da 6:24 And the king commanded, and they brought those men which had accused Daniel, and they cast them into the den of lions, them, their children, and their wives; and the lions had the mastery of them, and brake all their bones in pieces or ever they came at the bottom of the den.

9. <u>When the self (King Darius) realizes the power of the spirit (Daniel) and that devils (the lions) have no power against him, he decrees that everyone must fear God and makes the spirit the ruler of all that the self controls.</u> Thus, the flesh has been "crucified," and the believer continues to walk according to the control of the spirit.

Da 6:26 I make a decree, That in every dominion of my kingdom men tremble and fear before the God of Daniel: for he is the living God, and stedfast for ever, and his kingdom that which shall not be destroyed, and his dominion shall be even unto the end.

28 So this Daniel prospered in the reign of Darius, and in the reign of Cyrus the Persian.

Overcoming Spiritual Oppression

1. Spiritual oppression is an attempt by Satan to make us live in fear of him and what he can do to us.

2. Spiritual oppression has its basis in the law because without sin, Satan has no basis for attacking us.

3. We must understand that Satan lost all his rights and power when Jesus won the victory over him at the cross. The only right to power he has today is through deception. As long as we believe he can attack us, he will be able to use fear to keep us from fulfilling the will of God for us.

4. Satan's strategy is to get us to believe that we must rely on ourselves to get our needs met. If he succeeds, we will feel insecure, be afraid of what he can do, and make ourselves vulnerable to his attack, because we have become our own God and are responsible for protecting ourselves. Satan only has power to the degree we believe his lies.

5. The first step in overcoming spiritual oppression is to maintain our faith in God, no matter what Satan may threaten to do.

6. We must realize that Jesus has fulfilled the law for us, that He is in us and we are in Christ, and that all of our sins have been forgiven. Therefore, because we are innocent in the sight of God, Satan has no right or power to harm us.

7. The client must face his fears of Satan and death, trust in the finished works of Christ and continue to do the will of God no matter what others may say or do. God will protect us and meet all our needs, He will be there for us, go through our fears with us, and help us conquer the insecurity in our lives. Every time we overcome fear, our faith grows. He has promised that we will never be tempted beyond that which we are able and will always have a way of escape. (1 Corinthians 10:13)

PART VIII

Models for Resolving Problems with Love

Chapter 20

Developing
Healthy Attachments through Faith
(Jonathan, David, Saul, and Michal)

As we have already discussed, one of our deepest needs is to be loved. Most of our conflicts in our attempts to be loved are problems with attachment, and the answer to our attachment problems is faith. To understand this from a biblical perspective, let us examine the lives of some of the best-known figures of the Old Testament: Jonathan, David, Saul and Michal. (A review of attachment theory presented in the chapter on meeting our need for love would be helpful for those who are not familiar with this subject.)

Almost immediately after the wedding, their marriage was in trouble. After only a matter of days, Julie let Matt know what she thought of him—"He was a selfish, insensitive, inconsiderate, low-life." He had never been able to live up to the expectations of his father, and now it was happening again. He responded by withdrawing and just put up with her ravings. The more he withdrew, the more she felt abandoned and reacted to the lack of attachment. Even when he did everything he could to plan a wonderful vacation, she focused on the few things he did not do. He could never be good enough for her, so he just quit trying. He had an avoidant attachment style and she had a disorganized attachment style. Her constantly changing attachment attempts confused him. Sometimes, she desperately wanted him to be sensitive to her strong emotions and other times she would give him the cold shoulder for almost anything he did. He admitted that he was probably not the most sensitive guy in the world, but things got worse when he quit trying. All he really wanted was peace, and there was no way to have it with her around. They needed to understand that each of them was simply reacting to the attachment alarms of their spouse. Both just wanted to be loved, but by now, they saw each other as extremely unsafe attachment figures. Both were going to have to take responsibility for their attachment styles and change them into a secure style, deal with the bitterness between them, and make themselves safe for the other to re-attach. This would be a long process.

The Secure Attachment Style

1. The first requirement for a secure attachment style is that we view ourselves as worthy of love and capable of obtaining love. Jonathan, whose name means, "Jehovah has given," is a biblical example of a secure attacher. The fact that his father, King Saul, gave him this particular name indicates that his father valued him as a gift from God, especially, since he would be in line to be the next king and carry on Saul's heritage after he died. Perhaps, because he was the crown prince, he was highly valued and received exceptional treatment as a child from all around him. The fact that he was trusted and favored by his father is clear from the fact that he asked Jonathan to lead the remainder of the Israelite army. Anyone who has met one will agree that secure attachers are a definite gift from God.

1 Sa 13:2 Saul chose him three thousand men of Israel; whereof two thousand were with Saul in Michmash and in mount Bethel, and a thousand were with Jonathan in Gibeah of Benjamin: and the rest of the people he sent every man to his tent.

14:49 Now the sons of Saul were Jonathan, and Ishui, and Melchishua: and the names of his two daughters were these; the name of the firstborn Merab, and the name of the younger Michal:

2. <u>The second requirement of secure attachment is that we view others as trustworthy to provide a safe haven for us</u>. Although it might be hard for us to believe that anyone, even Saul's son, could view Saul as reliable, Jonathan did trust his father. In turn, Jonathan was the closest person to Saul and was so trusted by him that when there were only two swords in all of Israel, Jonathan was given the second one.

1 Sa 13:16 And Saul, and Jonathan his son, and the people that were present with them, abode in Gibeah of Benjamin: but the Philistines encamped in Michmash.

22 So it came to pass in the day of battle, that there was neither sword nor spear found in the hand of any of the people that were with Saul and Jonathan: but with Saul and with Jonathan his son was there found.

 3. <u>Since no one on earth can ever be totally relied upon in all circumstances, truly secure attachers place their ultimate reliance on God</u>. Jonathan trusted God so much that he was willing to go against the entire Philistine army with only his armor bearer at his side. Johnathan's armor bearer trusted him so much that he was willing to follow Jonathan wherever he went. However, Jonathan was not presumptuous. He first sought a sign from God that what he was about to do was the will of God.

1 Sa 14:6 And Jonathan said to the young man that bare his armour, Come, and let us go over unto the garrison of these uncircumcised: it may be that the LORD will work for us: for there is no restraint to the LORD to save by many or by few.

7 And his armourbearer said unto him, Do all that is in thine heart: turn thee; behold, I am with thee according to thy heart.

8 Then said Jonathan, Behold, we will pass over unto these men, and we will discover ourselves unto them.

9 If they say thus unto us, Tarry until we come to you; then we will stand still in our place, and will not go up unto them.

10 But if they say thus, Come up unto us; then we will go up: for the LORD hath delivered them into our hand: and this shall be a sign unto us.

 4. <u>Those with secure attachment styles are able to freely give of themselves without requiring anything in return</u>. They are able to attach closely with others at the deepest level without fear of losing their own identity. Love is the emotion that results from attachment.

1 Sa 18:1 And it came to pass, when he had made an end of speaking unto Saul, that the soul of Jonathan was knit with the soul of David, and Jonathan loved him as his own soul.

5. <u>Commitment, which is a sign of unconditional attachment, may be expressed through the making of a covenant</u>. Today, the ultimate in attachment is marriage, and it is signified by the covenant of marriage. True attachment can be so close that the "two become one flesh." Although Jonathan and David were just friends, Jonathan loved David "as he loved his own soul."

1 Sa 18:3 Then Jonathan and David made a covenant, because he loved him as his own soul.

 6. <u>In attachment, we make our heart so vulnerable to the other person that we trust them with our reputation, share our inner-most thoughts and words, sharpen each other's character, and offer our strength and power to make the other person feel safe</u>. Hart sums this up in the words trust, availability and sensitivity. (2003) A feeling of safety must exist before we will be willing to truly

attach to another person. Insecure people fear and avoid attachment due to the vulnerability that it requires.

✗ 1 Sa 18:4 And Jonathan stripped himself of the robe (reputation) that was upon him, and gave it to David, and his garments (character), even to his sword (words), and to his bow (strength and power), and to his girdle (heart).

✗ 7. <u>We can trust a secure attacher even with our life</u>. David trusted Jonathan with his life again and again when King Saul sought to kill him. King Saul trusted Jonathan so much that Jonathan was one of the few people who could change Saul's mind. Secure attachers make excellent mediators.

1 Sa 19:1 And Saul spake to Jonathan his son, and to all his servants, that they should kill David.

2 But Jonathan Saul's son delighted much in David: and Jonathan told David, saying, Saul my father seeketh to kill thee: now therefore, I pray thee, take heed to thyself until the morning, and abide in a secret place, and hide thyself:

3 And I will go out and stand beside my father in the field where thou art, and I will commune with my father of thee; and what I see, that I will tell thee.

4 And Jonathan spake good of David unto Saul his father, and said unto him, Let not the king sin against his servant, against David; because he hath not sinned against thee, and because his works have been to thee-ward very good:

5 For he did put his life in his hand, and slew the Philistine, and the LORD wrought a great salvation for all Israel: thou sawest it, and didst rejoice: wherefore then wilt thou sin against innocent blood, to slay David without a cause?

6 And Saul hearkened unto the voice of Jonathan: and Saul sware, As the LORD liveth, he shall not be slain.

7 And Jonathan called David, and Jonathan shewed him all those things. And Jonathan brought David to Saul, and he was in his presence, as in times past.

8. <u>Those with secure attachment styles will never leave or abandon us no matter what happens</u>. Jonathan never abandoned Saul even after Saul accused him of violating an order that he had not even heard, and sentenced him to death. Saul even threw his javelin at Jonathan because he supported David. Yet, in the end, Jonathan died in battle at Saul's side.

1 Sa 14: 43 Then Saul said to Jonathan, Tell me what thou hast done. And Jonathan told him, and said, I did but taste a little honey with the end of the rod that was in mine hand, and, lo, I must die.

44 And Saul answered, God do so and more also: for thou shalt surely die, Jonathan.

45 And the people said unto Saul, Shall Jonathan die, who hath wrought this great salvation in Israel? God forbid: as the LORD liveth, there shall not one hair of his head fall to the ground; for he hath wrought with God this day. So the people rescued Jonathan, that he died not.

20:30 Then Saul's anger was kindled against Jonathan, and he said unto him, Thou son of the perverse rebellious woman, do not I know that thou hast chosen the son of Jesse to thine own confusion, and unto the confusion of thy mother's nakedness?

32 And Jonathan answered Saul his father, and said unto him, Wherefore shall he be slain? what hath he done?

33 And Saul cast a javelin at him to smite him: whereby Jonathan knew that it was determined of his father to slay David.

34 So Jonathan arose from the table in fierce anger, and did eat no meat the second day of the month: for he was grieved for David, because his father had done him shame.

 9.   However, because secure attachers are secure, they can be counted on to do what is right in the long term best interests of everyone involved. Even though King Saul, Jonathan's father, wanted David killed, Jonathan supported David when he was hiding from Saul. Attachment, at its very heart, is a covenant of mutual support to do what is right and have the long-term best interest of other people in mind.

1 Sa 20:42 And Jonathan said to David, Go in peace, forasmuch as we have sworn both of us in the name of the LORD, saying, The LORD be between me and thee, and between my seed and thy seed for ever. And he arose and departed: and Jonathan went into the city.

23:16 And Jonathan Saul's son arose, and went to David into the wood, and strengthened his hand in God.

 10. Secure attachers will even sacrifice their own interests for the sake of another. This is the clearest sign of true love. Jonathan was willing to give up his rightful claim to be the next king and take a supporting position out of his love for David and what he believed was God's plan for their lives.

1 Sa 23:17 And he said unto him, Fear not: for the hand of Saul my father shall not find thee; and thou shalt be king over Israel, and I shall be next unto thee; and that also Saul my father knoweth.

18 And they two made a covenant before the LORD: and David abode in the wood, and Jonathan went to his house.

The Ambivalent Attachment Style

In this story, David is our example of a person who typifies an ambivalent attachment style. As our story continues, please note how this style is significantly different from a secure style and how insecurity leads to dysfunction.

 1.   Those with ambivalent attachment styles do not believe they are worthy of the love and the support of others unless they perform adequately to deserve that love. David was the youngest in his family and so looked down on that he was given the lowly job of sheep herder (many times a chore given to children or slaves), he was not even invited to the meal when Samuel came to anoint one of the brothers as king, and his older brothers saw him as a prideful upstart when he asked questions concerning the possibility of fighting the giant Goliath. Even after he killed Goliath, King Saul had to ask who he was, even though he had been playing the harp for him in the palace for a considerable time. How others view us is generally the basis of how we view ourselves. When David was asked to be the king's son-in-law, he saw himself as so unworthy that King Saul gave his older daughter, who was supposed to be David's wife, to another man.

1 Sa 17:28 And Eliab his eldest brother heard when he spake unto the men; and Eliab's anger was kindled against David, and he said, Why camest thou down hither? and with whom hast thou left those few sheep in the wilderness? I know thy pride, and the naughtiness of thine heart; for thou art come down that thou mightest see the battle.

29 And David said, What have I now done? Is there not a cause?

57 And as David returned from the slaughter of the Philistine, Abner took him, and brought him before Saul with the head of the Philistine in his hand.

58 And Saul said to him, Whose son art thou, thou young man? And David answered, I am the son of thy servant Jesse the Bethlehemite.

1 Sa 18:18 And David said unto Saul, Who am I? and what is my life, or my father's family in Israel, that I should be son in law to the king?

19 But it came to pass at the time when Merab Saul's daughter should have been given to David, that she was given unto Adriel the Meholathite to wife.

23 And Saul's servants spake those words in the ears of David. And David said, Seemeth it to you a light thing to be a king's son in law, seeing that I am a poor man, and lightly esteemed?

2. <u>Ambivalent attachers view others as safe and trustworthy to provide a safe haven for them</u>. With the treatment David received in his family, it is hard to believe that he had learned to trust others. However, because David was a man after God's own heart; he may have trusted God to make up for other people's failures. David's mother and father or other relatives may have provided strong nurturing when he was a child. The fact that, under these circumstances, he was able to develop such a deep trust in God suggests that this must have been the case. Jesse means, "Jehovah exists, to possess something, or to be wealthy." At the very least, he grew up in a good family. He demonstrated that he was naively trusting throughout his life by relying on men like Saul, Joab, Ahithophel, Amnon, and Absalom, all of whom eventually betrayed him in some way.

3. <u>Those with ambivalent attachment styles try to please others since they believe that this will make them acceptable to be loved by them</u>. David was never able to please his brothers and it frustrated him. He was such a great performer for King Saul that all the people loved him. Saul felt threatened by him when the women sang that David had killed his ten thousands and Saul only his thousands.

1 Sa 18:7 And the women answered one another as they played, and said, Saul hath slain his thousands, and David his ten thousands.

8 And Saul was very wroth, and the saying displeased him; and he said, They have ascribed unto David ten thousands, and to me they have ascribed but thousands: and what can he have more but the kingdom?

9 And Saul eyed David from that day and forward.

4. <u>The ambivalent attacher will continue to pursue unreliable attachment figures even after they prove themselves unsafe hoping to perform well enough to be accepted by them</u>. Even when King Saul was trying to kill David, David continued to try to be reconciled to Saul through Jonathan. David even spared King Saul's life twice trying to prove that he was not Saul's enemy. He was still not able to please Saul. After Saul died, he lamented him on an equal basis with Jonathan. *People please*

1 Sa 24:10 Behold, this day thine eyes have seen how that the LORD had delivered thee to day into mine hand in the cave: and some bade me kill thee: but mine eye spared thee; and I said, I will not put forth mine hand against my lord; for he is the LORD'S anointed.

11 Moreover, my father, see, yea, see the skirt of thy robe in my hand: for in that I cut off the skirt of thy robe, and killed thee not, know thou and see that there is neither evil nor transgression in mine hand, and I have not sinned against thee; yet thou huntest my soul to take it.

12 The LORD judge between me and thee, and the LORD avenge me of thee: but mine hand shall not be upon thee.

26:23 The LORD render to every man his righteousness and his faithfulness: for the LORD delivered thee into my hand to day, but I would not stretch forth mine hand against the LORD'S anointed.

24 And, behold, as thy life was much set by this day in mine eyes, so let my life be much set by in the eyes of the LORD, and let him deliver me out of all tribulation.

25 Then Saul said to David, Blessed be thou, my son David: thou shalt both do great things, and also shalt still prevail. So David went on his way, and Saul returned to his place.

2 Sa 1:17 And David lamented with this lamentation over Saul and over Jonathan his son:

The Avoidant Attachment Style

As we continue our story, we are introduced to Michal. She is a clear example of an avoidant attachment style.

1. <u>Those with avoidant attachment styles believe that they are worthy of love and able to obtain it</u>. Michal, Saul's second daughter is an example of this. Her name means, "who is like God." Probably being brought up as a daughter of a king made her feel that she was worthy of love. However, her name makes it clear that she had a tendency to want to be like God or be her own god, relying only on herself.

2. <u>Avoidant attachers do not view others as safe attachment figures</u>. Michal was definitely not viewed by King Saul as important, since he offered her to David as a wife in an attempt to have David killed while he was trying to obtain the dowry and "to be a snare for him." It appears King Saul was shocked when she fell in love with David, possibly because he was never able to connect with her himself.

1 Sa 18:20 And Michal Saul's daughter loved David: and they told Saul, and the thing pleased him.

21 And Saul said, I will give him her, that she may be a snare to him, and that the hand of the Philistines may be against him. Wherefore Saul said to David, Thou shalt this day be my son in law in the one of the twain.

28 And Saul saw and knew that the LORD was with David, and that Michal Saul's daughter loved him.

29 And Saul was yet the more afraid of David; and Saul became David's enemy continually.

3. <u>Avoidants trust only themselves, get their needs met though performance, and attach superficially</u>. They also value performance in others. Michal fell in love with David, the ultimate performer in Israel. She even risked her life to help him escape from her father, but afterward easily changed attachments to her new husband Phalti (my deliverance) the son of Laish (lion), which was of Gallim (springs). From Phalti's name and heritage, he also seems to have been quite a performer and deeply in love with Michal. This is clear from the fact that he followed her crying, when King David had her brought back to him. He also may have been a secure attacher, like Jonathan.

1 Sa 19:11 Saul also sent messengers unto David's house, to watch him, and to slay him in the morning: and Michal David's wife told him, saying, If thou save not thy life to night, to morrow thou shalt be slain.

12 So Michal let David down through a window: and he went, and fled, and escaped.

13 And Michal took an image, and laid it in the bed, and put a pillow of goats' hair for his bolster, and covered it with a cloth.

17 And Saul said unto Michal, Why hast thou deceived me so, and sent away mine enemy, that he is escaped? And Michal answered Saul, He said unto me, Let me go; why should I kill thee?

25:44 But Saul had given Michal his daughter, David's wife, to Phalti the son of Laish, which was of Gallim.

2 Sa 3:14 And David sent messengers to Ishbosheth Saul's son, saying, Deliver me my wife Michal, which I espoused to me for an hundred foreskins of the Philistines.

15 And Ishbosheth sent, and took her from her husband, even from Phaltiel the son of Laish.

16 And her husband went with her along weeping behind her to Bahurim. Then said Abner unto him, Go, return. And he returned.

4. <u>Because those with an avoidant attachment style strongly believe that others are not safe, it is extremely difficult for anyone to convince them otherwise.</u> David acted insensitively when he required Abner to bring Michal back to him as part of a peace treaty. He did not even ask Michal if she wanted to come back to him. As a result, after David danced before the Ark, Michal quickly reached the conclusion that David could not be trusted and was showing off to the other women.

 2 Sa 6:20 Then David returned to bless his household. And Michal the daughter of Saul came out to meet David, and said, How glorious was the king of Israel to day, who uncovered himself to day in the eyes of the handmaids of his servants, as one of the vain fellows shamelessly uncovereth himself! *This is an Attachment Alarm*

21 And David said unto Michal, It was before the LORD, which chose me before thy father, and before all his house, to appoint me ruler over the people of the LORD, over Israel: therefore will I play before the LORD.

5. <u>When confronted with someone they see as untrustworthy, unavailable, or insensitive, the avoidant easily detaches emotionally, but may remain in the relationship.</u> David's reaction to Michael was clearly insensitive and, since he now had a number of other wives, he was not as available as he had been before. Although it is not clear which one detached, we are told that "Therefore" Michal had no more children, suggesting that as a consequence of this attachment wound, they no longer had sex (or for some other reason she was unable to have children.)

2 Sa 6:23 Therefore Michal the daughter of Saul had no child unto the day of her death.

21:8 But the king took the two sons of Rizpah the daughter of Aiah, whom she bare unto Saul, Armoni and Mephibosheth; and the five sons of Michal the daughter of Saul, whom she brought up for Adriel the son of Barzillai the Meholathite:

9 And he delivered them into the hands of the Gibeonites, and they hanged them in the hill before the LORD: and they fell all seven together, and were put to death in the days of harvest, in the first days, in the beginning of barley harvest.

The Disorganized Attachment Style

King Saul is a clear example of a person with a disorganized attachment style.

1. <u>Those with a disorganized attachment style do not believe that they are worthy of love or capable of obtaining love from others.</u> King Saul was so insecure that he hid in the baggage when he was to be crowned king. When David was successful in battle, Saul became jealous of him. Jealousy is a clear

sign of feelings of inferiority. Twice, when David spared his life, he said to David that David was a better man than he was.

1 Sa 10:20 And when Samuel had caused all the tribes of Israel to come near, the tribe of Benjamin was taken.

21 When he had caused the tribe of Benjamin to come near by their families, the family of Matri was taken, and Saul the son of Kish was taken: and when they sought him, he could not be found.

22 Therefore they enquired of the LORD further, if the man should yet come thither. And the LORD answered, Behold, he hath hid himself among the stuff.

23 And they ran and fetched him thence: and when he stood among the people, he was higher than any of the people from his shoulders and upward.

24:17 And he (Saul) said to David, Thou art more righteous than I: for thou hast rewarded me good, whereas I have rewarded thee evil.

26:21 Then said Saul, I have sinned: return, my son David: for I will no more do thee harm, because my soul was precious in thine eyes this day: behold, I have played the fool, and have erred exceedingly.

 2. <u>Disorganized attachers do not believe that they can trust others to be safe as attachment figures</u>. Saul was suspicious of everyone. He viewed all that were not with him as enemies. When tormented, he did not go to his advisers to be comforted, but to David. But as David played the harp, he threw a javelin at him. He tried to kill David because he was afraid David would replace him as king. He killed all of the priests of Nob simply because they helped David, even though they had no idea that King Saul was hunting him.

1 Sa 22:17 And the king said unto the footmen that stood about him, Turn, and slay the priests of the LORD; because their hand also is with David, and because they knew when he fled, and did not shew it to me. But the servants of the king would not put forth their hand to fall upon the priests of the LORD.

18 And the king said to Doeg, Turn thou, and fall upon the priests. And Doeg the Edomite turned, and he fell upon the priests, and slew on that day fourscore and five persons that did wear a linen ephod.

19 And Nob, the city of the priests, smote he with the edge of the sword, both men And women, children and sucklings, and oxen, and asses, and sheep, with the edge of the sword.

 3. <u>Many disorganized attachers have histories of being abused, abusing others or failing to meet the expectations of others</u>. Consequently, they seem to be confused as to what they really want. A child, who sometimes is comforted and sometimes rejected and treated roughly, will not know whether to seek out or run from their attachment figure when they need comfort. They may even run to a stranger who they see as a safer risk. Saul had unsuccessfully tried to find his father's donkeys. Donkeys stand for capabilities suggesting that Saul could never be good enough for his father.

1 Sa 9:3 And the asses of Kish Saul's father were lost. And Kish said to Saul his son, Take now one of the servants with thee, and arise, go seek the asses.

5 And when they were come to the land of Zuph, Saul said to his servant that was with him, Come, and let us return; lest my father leave caring for the asses, and take thought for us.

4. <u>The disorganized attachment style exhibits the characteristics of both the ambivalent and the avoidant styles</u>. This is because they see themselves as unworthy of love and others as unreliable to show them love. King Saul wavered between trying to please Samuel and God and trying to please the people. He both admired David and wanted to kill him.

1 Sa 15:20 And Saul said unto Samuel, Yea, I have obeyed the voice of the LORD, and have gone the way which the LORD sent me, and have brought Agag the king of Amalek, and have utterly destroyed the Amalekites.

24 And Saul said unto Samuel, I have sinned: for I have transgressed the commandment of the LORD, and thy words: because I feared the people, and obeyed their voice.

30 Then he said, I have sinned: yet honour me now, I pray thee, before the elders of my people, and before Israel, and turn again with me, that I may worship the LORD thy God.

31 So Samuel turned again after Saul; and Saul worshipped the LORD.

 5. <u>Disorganized attachers many times are emotionally distraught. Because they see their attachment needs as catastrophic, they overreact to attachment issues in order to force others to attach to them</u>. Saul expressed his attachment distress by throwing javelins and was tormented emotionally.

1 Sa 18:10 And it came to pass on the morrow, that the evil spirit from God came upon Saul, and he prophesied in the midst of the house: and David played with his hand, as at other times: and there was a javelin in Saul's hand.

11 And Saul cast the javelin; for he said, I will smite David even to the wall with it. And David avoided out of his presence twice.

12 And Saul was afraid of David, because the LORD was with him, and was departed from Saul.

 6. <u>Those with a disorganized attachment style will sometimes become so emotionally distraught that they will threaten to or even commit suicide</u>. When he was defeated and wounded in battle, Saul chose to kill himself rather than face his failure or try to escape from the enemy forces.

1 Sa 31:3 And the battle went sore against Saul, and the archers hit him; and he was sore wounded of the archers.

4 Then said Saul unto his armourbearer, Draw thy sword, and thrust me through therewith; lest these uncircumcised come and thrust me through, and abuse me. But his armourbearer would not; for he was sore afraid. Therefore Saul took a sword, and fell upon it.

Changing Attachment Styles

Because attachments styles are developed through our experiences, they can be difficult to change. However, through developing healthy faith in God and associating with others who do have secure attachment styles, it is possible to turn an insecure style of attachment into a secure one. Let us examine the steps required to do this.

1. <u>We must be saved and believe that God will meet all our needs in order to feel secure and overcome our selfishness</u>. Do you remember the process of salvation by faith discussed earlier in this book? Without committing our lives to God and believing that He will meet all of our needs, we will never be secure and will never be able to overcome the selfishness in our lives. Therefore, salvation by faith is the first essential step to overcoming insecure attachment problems.

Php 4:19 But my God shall supply all your need according to his riches in glory by Christ Jesus.

2. <u>God is the ultimate attachment figure because He loves us unconditionally, will never abandon us, can never fail us, is always available, and is emotionally sensitive to us.</u> When He was here on earth, He experienced what we feel. Consequently, having a deep trusting relationship with God is a key ingredient to rebuilding the trust required to have a secure attachment style.

Ro 5:8 But God commendeth his love toward us, in that, while we were yet sinners, Christ died for us.

Heb 13:5 Let your conversation be without covetousness; and be content with such things as ye have: for he hath said, I will never leave thee, nor forsake thee.

Ro 8:31 What shall we then say to these things? If God be for us, who can be against us?

Heb 4:14 Seeing then that we have a great high priest, that is passed into the heavens, Jesus the Son of God, let us hold fast our profession.

15 For we have not an high priest which cannot be touched with the feeling of our infirmities; but was in all points tempted like as we are, yet without sin.

3. <u>We need to see ourselves as God sees us—one of His dear children whom He loves without any regard to our works or even our failures.</u> We are loved by God and nothing can separate us from that love. Even after David committed adultery with Bathsheba and murdered Uriah, David learned to accept himself as God did and went on with his life trusting in the forgiveness of God. However, it took David a significant period of time to overcome his insecure attachment style.

Ro 8:38 For I am persuaded, that neither death, nor life, nor angels, nor principalities, nor powers, nor things present, nor things to come,

39 Nor height, nor depth, nor any other creature, shall be able to separate us from the love of God, which is in Christ Jesus our Lord.

Ps 51:1 Have mercy upon me, O God, according to thy lovingkindness: according unto the multitude of thy tender mercies blot out my transgressions.

2 Wash me throughly from mine iniquity, and cleanse me from my sin.

3 For I acknowledge my transgressions: and my sin is ever before me. 10 Create in me a clean heart, O God; and renew a right spirit within me.

11 Cast me not away from thy presence; and take not thy holy spirit from me.

12 Restore unto me the joy of thy salvation; and uphold me with thy free spirit.

4. <u>We need to see others as God sees them. They are also His children through faith and He loves them even with all their mistakes and failures.</u> We should trust others only as far as they are trustworthy and rely primarily on God to make up the difference. Although Jonathan was not perfect, David was able to trust him as long as he lived. However, both David and Jonathan primarily put their trust in God.

Ga 3:26 For ye are all the children of God by faith in Christ Jesus.

Ps 118:8 It is better to trust in the LORD than to put confidence in man.

Jo 2:23 Now when he was in Jerusalem at the passover, in the feast day, many believed in his name, when they saw the miracles which he did.

24 But Jesus did not commit himself unto them, because he knew all **men**,

26 And needed not that any should testify of man: for he knew what was in man.

6. <u>Insecure attachment styles are changed through the experiences of healthy earthly and heavenly attachments</u>. David was greatly influenced through his healthy attachment with Jonathan. He even honored Jonathan by sparing Jonathan's son's life, treating him as one of his own sons and having Jonathan's son eat at his own table. David was a man after God's own heart, and his level of attachment to God is clear from his desire to build a wonderful temple for God.

    2 Sa 9:7 And David said unto him, Fear not: for I will surely shew thee kindness for Jonathan thy father's sake, and will restore thee all the land of Saul thy father; and thou shalt eat bread at my table continually.

    21:7 But the king spared Mephibosheth, the son of Jonathan the son of Saul, because of the LORD'S oath that was between them, between David and Jonathan the son of Saul.

    1 Chr 22:7 And David said to Solomon, My son, as for me, it was in my mind to build an house unto the name of the LORD my God:

    8 But the word of the LORD came to me, saying, Thou hast shed blood abundantly, and hast made great wars: thou shalt not build an house unto my name, because thou hast shed much blood upon the earth in my sight.

7. <u>We must start giving unconditional love and securely attach ourselves to others in order to receive unconditional love in return</u>. According to the paradox of love, we can receive unconditional love only when we sow or give unconditional love to others with no strings attached.

    Ga 6:7 Be not deceived; God is not mocked: for whatsoever a man soweth, that shall he also reap.

8. <u>Without the experience of secure attachments, most people will continue in their insecure attachment styles for the remainder of their lives and lose out on loving and feeling loved</u>. King Saul went to his death feeling deserted by God and dishonored in battle. Michal lost out on having a loving relationship with David. He even had her five adopted children executed. We can only guess what a bitter existence she lived until her death, especially as she watched while Bathsheba eventually took Michal's place in David's heart.

    2 Sa 12:24 And David comforted Bathsheba his wife, and went in unto her, and lay with her: and she bare a son, and he called his name Solomon: and the LORD loved him

    1 Sa 28:15 And Samuel said to Saul, Why hast thou disquieted me, to bring me up? And Saul answered, I am sore distressed; for the Philistines make war against me, and God is departed from me, and answereth me no more, neither by prophets, nor by dreams: therefore I have called thee, that thou mayest make known unto me what I shall do.

    16 Then said Samuel, Wherefore then dost thou ask of me, seeing the LORD is departed from thee, and is become thine enemy?

9. <u>We have finally achieved a secure attachment style when we are able to deeply and unconditionally attach and love others</u>. When Jonathan and Saul were killed, David greatly mourned over them. Even after Absalom rebelled against him and was killed by Joab, David was so attached that "he wished he could have died instead of him." From all this, we see that through the healthy relationships with Jonathan and God, David was finally able to change his insecure ambivalent style into a secure attachment style.

2 Sa 1:23 Saul and Jonathan were lovely and pleasant in their lives, and in their death they were not divided: they were swifter than eagles, they were stronger than lions.

25 How are the mighty fallen in the midst of the battle! O Jonathan, thou wast slain in thine high places.

26 I am distressed for thee, my brother Jonathan: very pleasant hast thou been unto me: thy love to me was wonderful, passing the love of women.

2 Sa 18:33 And the king was much moved, and went up to the chamber over the gate, and wept: and as he went, thus he said, O my son Absalom, my son, my son Absalom! would God I had died for thee, O Absalom, my son, my son!

Developing Healthy Attachments

1. Healthy or secure attachments lead to love, and love is the very essence of God. We learn to love others by experiencing love.

2. Those with insecure attachments perceive themselves as undeserving or incapable of obtaining love or view others as unsafe, untrustworthy, unavailable, or insensitive. They lead to conflict and almost every type of evil. Avoidant attachers see themselves as okay and others as unreliable. Ambivalent attachers question their own worth, but see others as safe. Those with a disorganized style question their own worth and the reliability of others to meet their emotional needs.

3. The first step in overcoming insecure attachment styles is to see ourselves and others as God does—made in His image, very good, but in the process of being delivered from sin.

4. We must see ourselves as valuable simply because God made us in His image and loves us, and we must trust God to make up for the weaknesses of others. We must never over-rely on other's opinions or let them take the place of God in our lives.

5. We must make God our primary attachment figure since He cannot fail, will not leave us, and is sensitive to all our needs because He walked on this earth with us as Jesus.

6. We should seek out and attach to secure attachment figures, as well as God, in order to experience healthy attachments.

7. We are to do what is right in all circumstances and love others, having their best interest in mind. In order to do this, we must experience His unconditional love for us, appreciate all that He has done for us, and know that He has and will always meet our needs.

Chapter 21

Overcoming Lust through Faith
(Ehud)

The word lust means, "a strong craving or desire, or an intense sexual appetite." (The New Webster's Concise Dictionary of the English Language, 1997, edited by Sidney Landau) Lust is the flesh's counterfeit for love. It is a strong selfish desire that leads to addiction, takes a man captive or is the basis for besetting sins. It is usually associated with sexual sin, which is an attempt to meet needs for love through the flesh. Lot's first-born son, through incest with his eldest daughter, was Moab. The Moabites were those who lead the Israelites into fornication. Therefore, I believe that Moab represents lust.

Love and lust are very different. Love is personal, lust is impersonal. Love is focused on a particular object; lust is unfocused and capable of fixing on almost any object. Love tends toward faithfulness, lust is a wanderer. Love seeks stability, lust is short-lived and mercurial. Love is an affair of the mind and heart, lust is an affair of the emotions and hormones. Love is a matter of giving, lust is a matter of taking. Lust is increased in strength by a lack in other areas. Lust is not the same feeling or drive as love and, therefore, is not satisfied or resolved by married love. Lust depletes our drive, makes married sex less stimulating, and relationships less needed. Lust is like a drug and requires more to meet its need. In lust, evil provides more stimulation because it is really false intimacy. Lust destroys true intimacy. (Smalley, 1988)

Leroy had graduated from seminary, pastored several churches and currently had a good job with a major corporation. He knew the Bible well, and from his legalistic point of view, he could quote large parts of the Scripture. He also used the Scripture to dominate his wife and family. After a brief Internet affair, he became infatuated with a married woman at work. Although he was confronted, he refused to end the affair and felt abused when his wife filed for separation. Numerous times, he claimed that he had ended the affair, but the log of his cell phone clearly indicated otherwise. Although his wife was careful to keep the matter confidential, he was eventually removed from the part-time pastorate. Eventually, when the affair resulted in the divorce of both couples, his new girlfriend quickly discovered that he had had another Internet affair while he was going with her. He eventually took early retirement, alienated his entire family and moved from church to church, wherever he could find a place to minister. As far as I know, he was never able or willing to deal with his problem with lust.

The model for deliverance from lust is found in the story of Ehud. It begins in Judges Chapter 3.

1. Entertaining evil opens a door to lust.

    Jud 3:12 And the children of Israel did evil (wickedness; to do hurt) again in the sight of the LORD: and the LORD strengthened Eglon (calf-like or idol of food and profit) the king of Moab (lust) against Israel, because they had done evil in the sight of the LORD.

2. No matter how long we have been controlled by lust, we can have a new beginning. The number eighteen is a combination of ten and eight. Ten stands for human infirmity and failure and eight stands for a new beginning. It is our choice.

Jud 3:14 So the children of Israel served Eglon the king of Moab eighteen years

3. <u>The key to deliverance from lust comes through believing that we are so favored of God that He will meet all of our needs, thanking Him for what He has done and being willing to die to our immediate gratification in order to be fruitful.</u> In order to win the victory over lust we will have to have an unusual approach. Ehud means, "I will give thanks or strong." He was a Benjamite which means, "son of the right hand or favored of God" from Gera which means, "a grain," (which must be willing to die to produce fruit). Ehud was left-handed which suggests he had an unusual approach or outlook on life.

I will give thanks to

Jud 3:15 But when the children of Israel cried unto the LORD, the LORD raised them up a deliverer, Ehud the son of Gera a Benjamite a man left-handed: and by him the children of Israel sent a present unto Eglon the king of Moab.

4. <u>We must make the truth of God's Word a part of our character and strength</u>. I believe that the two-edged dagger stands for the Word of God. It was an arm's length (cubit) long suggesting that victory is within his grasp and hidden under his clothing (character) on his right thigh which stands for strength.

Jud 3:16 But Ehud made him a dagger which had two edges (God's Word), of a cubit length and he did gird it under his raiment upon his right thigh (strength).

5. <u>We cannot win the battle over lust by directly confronting it in our own strength and saying that we will not do its bidding any more.</u> Doing this only makes it worse. Lust must be dealt with by trusting God for deliverance. Ehud did not confront Eglon, but acted as if he was accepting Eglon's domination by presenting him a present.

Jud 3:17 And he brought the present unto Eglon king of Moab: and Eglon [was] a very fat man. (the character of lust)

18 And when he had made an end to offer the present, he sent away the people that bare the present.

6. <u>We must turn back from our secret idols or the objects of our lust.</u> Lust itself can be an idol if we see it as a means to make our lives more exciting and fulfilled.

Jud 3:19 But he himself turned again from the quarries that [were] by Gilgal (where idols were made), and said, I have a secret errand unto thee, O king: who said, Keep silence (lust desires secrecy). And all that stood by him went out from him. (Lust wants it all for itself.)

7. <u>Lust must be killed with the truth of the Word of God directed to the seat of the hunger.</u> Ehud stabbed Eglon in the stomach with the dagger of the Word of God. Lust is based on inordinate desire. We must use God's Word to convince ourselves that we do not have to have the things of this world to be happy.

Jud 3:20 And Ehud came unto him; and he was sitting in a summer parlour, which he had for himself alone. And Ehud said, I have a message from God unto thee. And he arose out of [his] seat.

21 And Ehud put forth his left hand, and took the dagger (God's Word) from his right thigh, and thrust it into his belly (seat of hunger):

22 And the haft also went in after the blade; and the fat closed upon the blade, so that he could not draw the dagger out of his belly; and the dirt came out.

8. <u>We must close forever the door to lust and lock it with accountability.</u> When we realize the filth we encounter through lust, we will never want to go back to it. In the Hebrew, the word for "parlour" is better-interpreted "latrine." To escape Ehud had to climb through and experience the filth of the latrine. This is much clearer in the New Living Translation (NLT) below.

Jud 3:23 Then Ehud went forth through the porch, and shut the doors of the parlour upon him, and locked them. (AV)

Jud 3:23 Then Ehud closed and locked the doors and climbed down the latrine and escaped through the sewage access. (NLT)

9. <u>We can use the shame of the past as motivation to help us make a final end to lust and its allies.</u> We can tell others that we have decided to remove lust completely from our lives.

Jud 3:27 And it came to pass, when he was come, that he blew a trumpet in the mountain of Ephraim, and the children of Israel went down with him from the mount, and he before them.

10. <u>We need to block lust's access and not allow any of it into our lives.</u>

Jud 3:28 And he said unto them, Follow after me: for the LORD hath delivered your enemies the Moabites into your hand. And they went down after him, and took the fords of Jordan toward Moab, and suffered not a man to pass over.

11. <u>Lust can be completely defeated.</u>

Jud 3:29 And they slew of Moab at that time about ten thousand (the infirmity of man) men, all lusty (fat), and all men of valour (strength); and there escaped not a man.

12. <u>We can have victory for a lifetime. Without lust we can have rest.</u>

Jud 3:30 So Moab was subdued that day under the hand of Israel. And the land had rest fourscore years.

Overcoming Lust

1. We must believe and thank God that He will meet our needs and we must be willing to die to our lust. It is our enemy.

2. We must realize that God favors us no matter what we may have done.

3. We must understand that lust meets only the temporary desires of the flesh and never really satisfies our deepest needs.

4. We must make the truth of God a part of our character.

5. Victory is within our grasp, but we must use our sword (God's Word) to get the victory.

7. We cannot defeat lust by trying to stop it in our own strength.

8. We must use the Word of God to attack the seat of the hunger (the belly) by trusting God to meet our deepest needs.

9. We must close and lock the door to lust. Accountability is necessary for long-term victory.

10. We must escape from our idols of lust and put as much distance between them and us as possible.

11. We can use the shame of our past as motivation to completely defeat lust in our lives.

PART IX

Application

Chapter 22

A Case Study

Before concluding this book, I would like to present a case study of the application of Faith Therapy to resolve a deeply rooted problem. These kinds of problems do not usually manifest themselves suddenly in the life of the client, but have their roots early in the family of origin. I am not blaming current problems on the client's parents or the child's environment, but recognizing that early childhood experiences do have a significant effect on how he views himself and how he learned to cope with life. I have chosen a complex and difficult case as my example in order to encourage those that face severe problems in their lives, that, with God, nothing is impossible. Because of the nature of this case, the names and details presented have been altered in order to protect the identity of the client.

Robert, or Bob, as his parents called him, was the second of three children. He had an older brother and younger sister. Although Bob's family seemed pretty normal and went to church regularly, as a child, Bob viewed himself as sort of an "ugly duckling" and tried to compete with his older brother to prove he was worth something. Very early, he sought acceptance with older neighborhood children. One time, he and his brother were caught "playing doctor." Bob did not know it at that time, but the shame he felt would lead to a lifetime struggle to find sexual acceptance. At night, when the boys would camp out, they would tell sexual stories, look at Playboy magazines, take their clothes off and "mess around." They would dare each other to take chances running around naked and exposing themselves for the rush of possibly "getting caught." One time on the way home from the swimming pool the other kids dared Bob to take his clothes off behind a train car and expose himself. As he did, some people came out of the train station, and he almost got caught. This daring game was very exciting, but underneath was Bob's need to be accepted unconditionally; especially in the area of his sexual desires. Another time, his older brother talked one of the neighborhood girls into taking all her clothes off and they took turns pretending they were having sex with her. He was so young at the time that he did not really even know what to do, but the chance of getting caught made it all very exciting and just being involved made him feel sexually accepted. Fortunately, because his sister was so much younger than the boys were; she was never included in these "activities."

As Bob grew up he was very shy but desperately wanted to "be somebody," so he tried out for sports. He would put out in effort what he lacked in talent, but never felt fully accepted as part of the team. He was devastated anytime he failed at something. At other times, he had struggles with pride, lying, and stealing in order to get what he wanted. Because he always viewed himself as inadequate, all of his attempts to be somebody stressed him out. He got into the habit of coping with his stress by looking at Playboy magazines, playing with himself, and periodically daring himself to take chances sexually. Afterward he felt frightened and ashamed and, of course, this all increased his problems with low-self worth, which led to more acting out.

Somehow Bob never got caught, even though he had many close calls. He made it through high school and got his college degree in business. He settled into a secure corporate job, but all the time he continued to give in to temptation especially when he felt stressed. He was desperately afraid that someday he would get caught, become disgraced, and be fired, but the temptation of the adrenaline rush and his need for sexual acceptance would eventually overpower his will. In an effort to deal with his problem, he married a good Christian woman and accepted Christ as his savior. His salvation experience seemed temporarily to alleviate his problem with lust when he totally focused his life on Christ, but eventually his old problem returned. When things became very stressful in his life, the old temptations returned; and he periodically returned to medicating his stress through acting out sexually. However, now that he was saved, he felt even guiltier for what he was doing, and his feelings of worthlessness increased. As he continued to take chances in order to get the adrenaline rush, his problem with lust began to get more and more out of control, and he finally decided to get help for his problem.

Bob's deeply rooted problem was based on his feelings of worthlessness and his need to find sexual acceptance. When people feel worthless, they fear rejection, develop an insecure attachment style and therefore, do not closely attach to others. This lack of attachment and Bob's early childhood sexual experiences led him to try to meet his sexual needs through the false intimacy of pornography, masturbation and fantasy, instead of through a deep loving relationship with his wife. His daring game was simply a way of enhancing his sexual excitement through an adrenaline rush. The shame he had felt as a child continued to drive him to want to be accepted sexually. In fact, an analysis of his sexual fantasies clearly showed that all of his sexual acting out was designed to meet this desire. As an example, the majority of Bob's fantasies included undressing and being exposed to groups of other people who accepted or desired sexual activity with him. One of his fantasies was to be part of a group playing "strip poker" or going to a club where public sexual activity was accepted. Another included going to a "clothing optional beach" where he could be naked and yet be accepted by others. Of course, he did not actually act out on any of these fantasies, but when he thought about them, he became sexually excited.

Because he had not yet grown spiritually out of his legalistic view of life, instead of trusting God, he was trying to overcome his growing sexual addiction through his own efforts. The flesh will never succeed in overcoming the flesh. Because he felt worthless and believed that no one could possibly love him, he could not imagine how God could really care for him or do anything but detest him as a loser and a sexual pervert. In fact, to Bob, God was a combination of a harsh judge who would eventually expose and punish him, and a genie that he wanted to bless his efforts to run his own life.

A faith assessment of Bob's life showed that, although he trusted God for eternal life, he was not relying on God to meet his deepest needs. According to the Faith Ladder he had hope that God would eventually deliver him in twenty or thirty years, but not now. He had faith in his mind (mental ascent), but not in his emotions, will, or spirit. His need deficits were primarily for love, acceptance and self-worth. He was trying to meet these needs through his accomplishments, and sometimes, through his sexual acting out. His efforts to climb the corporate ladder in his own strength provided the stress that fueled his addiction.

Finally, Bob came to an end in himself and recognized that he could not be his own god and successfully overcome the problems in his life through his own efforts. This was the first step to his recovery. It was critical that Bob recognize that he did not have enough information to direct his own life and that he needed to yield the control of his life to God. Most of us do not experientially do this until we have run out of alternatives. This is especially true if we have not yet realized that God does love us and will always have our best interests in mind. God cannot help us until we are willing to do what he tells us to do. When Bob became convinced that he could not successfully run his own life, he exited the rat race of life and made Jesus Lord and director of his life.

Next, Bob had to be convinced that his method of evaluating himself according to his works, the approval of others, and his moral failures was invalid. God loved him, made him in His image and said that he was very good. His worth had nothing to do with his performance and everything to do with what Jesus had done for him on the cross. He was crucified with Christ, his old man was dead, he was forgiven, and was now risen with Christ. Therefore, he could now choose to do right. God valued him and everyone else equally. He loved each of them enough to send his Son to die for them while they were yet sinners. However, he had to convince himself, build his faith in what the Bible says about his worth, and start acting like it was true before the jury of his heart would agree and it would become a reality in his life. For Bob, changing how he viewed himself came slowly over many months.

Fortunately, after Bob's salvation experience, he had spent many hours studying the Bible and reading numerous helpful books. Part of this was his attempt to discover the key to resolving his problem. Unfortunately, most of what Bob knew about God was head knowledge, and head knowledge is just mental ascent and will not, by itself, change how a person views God. Bob needed a new faith that God loved and accepted him just like he was and that he could trust God always to have his best interest in mind. He needed to be taught concerning the grace of God and that God had unmerited favor for him without his works. In fact, God did not evaluate him based on what he did, but on what Christ had done for him. God answered his prayers, not based on his merit, but on the merit of Christ. Therefore, he could have faith that God would give him anything he asked for that would be good for his life. As Bob saw more answers to prayer, his faith was strengthened to ask and receive more. Bob began to view God as someone on his side, not against him.

As Bob began experiencing a personal relationship with God, the only truly safe attachment figure, he also began to attach emotionally with God. His well-established insecure attachment style and his fear of rejection were slowly transformed into a more secure style. He no longer took so many things personally that others did, and he was able to care more for others as his faith increased that God would meet all his needs, even when others failed him. In fact, his entire outlook on life became more positive.

Bob had a major breakthrough when his counselor loaned him a series of audio tapes by evangelist Duncan Fillmore on the subject of God's unmerited favor. He listened to these tapes over and over again, presenting evidence to his heart that God loved him as he was, until it got into his spirit. Bob received the revelation that God actually liked him and that he had the absolute favor of God. If God promised that he would work everything, even Bob's mistakes, for Bob's good, how could Bob lose? Bob's outlook on life changed to one where his future would only be better than his past. Along with this revelation came a freedom that he had never experienced before. Because Jesus fulfilled the law, he was free from the law and could now do anything that would be good for him. There was no condemnation to those who were in Christ (Romans 8:1). However, this new liberty did not mean that he would not get the consequences of his choices, but that God would still love and favor him even if he failed. This new way of looking at life helped remove much of the stress and shame from his life.

Since Bob was still struggling with his lust, this new revelation had both positive and negative effects. Initially, Bob sometimes used God's grace as an "occasion for the flesh," but when he failed, he no longer degraded himself, but saw his failure as an unfortunate occurrence from which he could learn. He knew he was still okay and that, even though God hated sin, God still loved and favored him. The experience of this newfound freedom from the law was so exhilarating that out of appreciation for what Christ had done for him, he did not want to act out sexually. In fact, over a period of time, he seldom was tempted to view Internet pornography, and his problem with masturbation greatly decreased.

As Bob's faith grew, he felt that because of what Jesus did, he was now acceptable both to God and to himself. As his fear of rejection subsided and he continued to develop a more secure attachment style, he more boldly and deeply attached to his wife. As their sexual relationship improved, he was not as tempted to seek the false intimacy that he had previously used to medicate his emotions. In fact, his emotions were now much more stable since he quit trying to please people; and by faith, he had entered more into the rest of God. Since he knew that God would work all things for his good, he no longer feared failure to the degree he once had and the stress that he had experienced was further reduced. He was okay with God's help, he could trust others since God was the one meeting all his needs, and he looked forward to a great and wonderful future.

The last vestige of this problem, which needed to be overcome, was his temptation to get an adrenaline rush from sexually acting out to medicate his emotions when he felt stressed, depressed or bored. Although this problem had become much less frequent, he would still be tempted sometimes when all of his family was gone, and he was alone. Possibly, this was due to the loneliness he felt when they were not around.

During a session of Theophostic Ministry (Smith, 1996) Bob was taken back to the time that he and his brother were caught playing "doctor." He felt the shame and identified with the lie that he was somehow "bad" because of what they had done. This shame had been accentuated by the fact that in his family sex was never talked about and was repeatedly denounced in the church he attended. In this session, Jesus told him that in the Garden of Eden, Adam and Eve were naked and not ashamed. It was okay for him to have sexual desire and be sexual. In fact, God had created sex for pleasure and enjoyment in marriage; and he was to find the sexual acceptance that he had always longed for from his wife with God's complete approval. God would and had provided everything he desired to fulfill him in this area. It was not wrong to be sexual, but as the Apostle Paul made it clear, his sexually acting out "was not expedient" (1 Corinthians 6:12). His relationship with his wife could and should be far more fulfilling than the "false intimacy' that he had previously relied on.

Through the model for overcoming lust presented in the last chapter, Bob finally saw lust as his enemy, something that he did not need in his life, and poison to his soul. He found that if he refused to entertain lust even for a moment and focused his life completely on God, he could overcome this temptation. In fact, the more he focused his life on God, the stronger he seemed to become in overcoming the problem of lust in his life. Eventually, his faith reached the point on the Faith Ladder where he knew he was free of his sexual addiction, and that he will always be free. Of course, he would need to be on guard against the tricks of Satan and continue to regard lust in his life as the poison that it is. He would have to rely on Christ for his continued deliverance and growth in the things of God.

Today, Bob is enjoying the abundant life that God always intended for him to have. He has a good Christian marriage, is involved in a ministry in his church and has stated on a number of occasions that he is forever grateful for what Christ, through faith, has done in his life. It is just amazing to him how God has taken him from a kid who, at one point in his life, did not feel he would ever be delivered from his addiction, to being totally free from both it, the emotional turmoil, and the stress that was so predominant in his life. He feels he is now entering into "the rest of the people of God." (Hebrews Chapter 4) According to Bob, he is the happiest he has ever been in his life. He goes around just wanting to praise God. He is looking forward to what God is going to do with his life knowing that, no matter what happens, everything will work out for his good (Romans 8:28), and that surely goodness and mercy will follow him all the days of his life: and he will dwell in the house of the LORD for ever. (Psalms 23:6)

Conclusion

In this book, I have attempted to explain how the process of salvation works through the development of our faith. I explained that the Greek word for salvation in the Bible means more than God's gift of eternal life. It also includes healing and complete wholeness in the mind, emotions, will and spirit, during this lifetime. Consequently, every Christian has a right to expect that through this process, he will be healed and made completely whole in every way. Unfortunately the reality of this truth has not been experienced by the majority of our church members.

Although we, as pastors, have proven somewhat effective in helping people deal with their simpler and superficial problems, we have usually failed to help those with the more complex and deeply rooted problems. The core issue to these problems is our sin nature, which is manifested in our attempts to be our own God and meet our own needs without God in our lives. Unless the root problems caused by unmet needs are met through faith, the problem will simply manifest itself again in other ways.

In this book, I have also attempted to address psychological healing at its deepest level—the basic needs of the person. I have provided a biblical understanding of the process of salvation or wholeness by faith and a foundation for the application of faith in therapy. I have presented a discussion of faith, steps for increasing faith and the tools for the assessment of faith. I suggested methods for identifying and analyzing root causes, and biblical solutions for resolving unmet needs. Finally, I suggested a number of counseling models for dealing with common, deeply rooted problems.

At the very heart of Faith Therapy is the fact that faith in Jesus Christ is the answer for all of the problems that we face in life today. Although additional biblical principles and techniques are required to clear away the debris and chaos caused by these problems, at the very core of each problem is a lack of faith or trust that God wants to and will meet all of our needs. This lack of faith results in our desire and our attempts to be our own God and meet our own needs through the flesh. I believe that it has been a lack of this understanding of the process of salvation by faith and a lack of emphasis on faith in our counseling that has hindered our attempts to bring dramatic and lasting results.

This book is the first of the four books in "The Just Shall Live by Faith" series of books. It provides the overall foundation for Faith Therapy and the tools and methods for applying faith to address deeply rooted problems. The second book, *Transformation!,* provides "The Biblical Plan for Christian Counseling" and biblical models for dealing with many of the most complex and difficult problems. The third book, *Revelations That Will Set You Free,* gives a detailed, step-by-step roadmap for the process of salvation as it leads to spiritual maturity and psychological wholeness. Finally, *Principles for Life,* provides a basic understanding of a large number of biblical principles and a biblical method for building counseling plans from biblical principles. All four of these books work hand-in-hand to provide everything that is needed for implementing a Faith Therapy program in a church, providing the information needed to apply Faith Therapy as a new counseling modality or to integrate current counseling practices within the framework of salvation by faith. Consequently, if you have been intrigued by this process of salvation that God has provided for us as it is described in this book and want to learn more about it, I suggest that you read the remainder of the books in this series.

Even if you, the reader, are not yet fully convinced of the validity of some of the specific concepts and methods that I have suggested, I challenge you to continue your study of Faith Therapy and to test these ideas by applying them in pastoral ministry, Christian counseling and support groups. I do not claim to have the final answers or revelations on any of the subjects presented, but believe that they provide the basis for a more effective, simple, biblical, faith-based methodology for Christian counseling in the church.

At Word of Life Church, Word of life Counseling Center and Word of Life Institute, we are continuing to develop and to apply Faith Therapy. I take no credit for what we are doing, because God has led me and others step by step, revelation by revelation, in understanding these concepts. However, I do take total responsibility for all mistakes, errors, misconceptions, and lack of insight contained in this book. We have only just begun to understand the impact of what the Lord meant when He states over and over again in the Bible, "The Just Shall Live by Faith." (Romans 1:17, Galatians 3:11, Hebrews 10:38) As we continue in this journey, the Lord is providing greater effectiveness in our efforts to bring spiritual and psychological healing to the increasing numbers of hurting people in our churches and our society.

References

Adams, Jay (1973). <u>The Christian Counselor's Manual</u>. Zondervan Publishing, Grand Rapids, Michigan.

Adams, Jay E. (1986). <u>The Biblical View of Self-esteem, Self-love, Self-image</u>. Harvest House Publishers, Eugene, Oregon.

Alsdurf, James & Alsdurf, Phyllis (1989). <u>Battered into Submission</u>. Intervarsity Press, Downers Grove, Illinois.

Avanzini, John F. (1988). <u>Faith Extenders</u>. HIS Publishing Company, Hurst, Texas.

Barklay, William (1976). <u>The Daily Study Bible Series, Vol. 7, the Acts of the Apostles</u>. The Westminister Press, Philadelphia, Pennsylvania.

Barna Research Group, Ltd. (1999). <u>The Barna Report, October 1999</u>. Barna Research Group Ltd., Ventura, California.

Blackaby, Henry T., and King, Claude V. (1990). <u>Experiencing God: Knowing and Doing the Will of God</u>. Lifeway Press, Nashville, Tennessee.

Broger, John C. (1994). <u>Self-confrontation</u>. Thomas Nelson Publishers, Nashville, Tennessee.

Bulkey, Ed (1997). "Can Counseling be Christian?" <u>Christian Counseling Today</u>, Vol. 5, No.1, Christian Counseling Resources Inc. Forrest, Virginia.

Clinton, Tim, and Sibcy, Gary (2002) <u>Attachments</u>. Integrity Publishers, Brentwood, Tennessee.

<u>Compton's Interactive Encyclopedia</u> (1996). Compton's New Media Inc., Carlsbad, California.

Court, John H. (1997). "Unraveling the Mystery of Hypnosis." Christian Counseling Today, Vol. 5, No.1, Christian Counseling Resources Inc. Forrest, Virginia.

Crabb, Larry (1977). <u>Effective Biblical Counseling</u>. Zondervan Publishing House, Grand Rapids, Michigan.

Dillon, David (1997)."The Enigma of EMDR." <u>Christian Counseling Today</u>, Vol. 5, No.1, Christian Counseling Resources Inc. Forrest, Virginia.

Douglas, Lloyd C. (1929). <u>The Magnificent Obsession</u>. Willett Publishing, Glencoe, Illinois.

Ellis, Albert. (1997). "Can Rational Counseling be Christian?" <u>Christian Counseling Today</u>, Vol. 5, No.1, Christian Counseling Resources Inc. Forrest, Virginia.

Filmore, Duncan (2003). "Audio Tapes of Sermon Series on Grace." Christian Life International, Camarillo, California.

Grant, B., et al (1994). <u>Epidemiologic Bulletin No. 35: Prevalence of DSM-IV alcohol abuse and dependence, United States 1992</u>. Alcohol Health & Research World 18 (3):243- 248.

Groolhuis, Douglas (1997). "The Hidden Dangers of Carl Yung." <u>Christian Counseling Today,</u> Vol. 5, No.1, Christian Counseling Resources Inc. Forrest, Virginia.

Hagin, Kenneth E. (1998). <u>Foundations for Faith</u>. Rhema Bible Church, Tulsa, Oklahoma.

Hagin, Kenneth E. (1996). <u>New Thresholds of Faith</u>. Rhema Bible Church, Tulsa, Oklahoma.

Hagin, Kenneth E. (1998). <u>Walking by Faith</u>. Rhema Bible Church, Tulsa, Oklahoma.

Harley, Willard F., Jr. (2001) <u>His Needs Her Needs</u>. Fleming H. Revell, Grand Rapids, Michigan.

Hart, Archibald, and Morris, Sharon Hart (2003). <u>Safe Haven Marriage</u>. W Publishing Company, Nashville, Tennessee.

Hart, Dr. Archibald D. (1994). <u>The Sexual Man</u>. Word Publishing, Dallas, Texas.

Hoorwitz, A. (1983). "Guidelines for treating father-daughter incest." <u>Social-Casework</u>, Nov. Vol 64(9) 515-524.

Hurnard, Hannah (1986). <u>Hind's Feet on High Places</u>. Tyndale House Publishers, Wheaton, Illinois

Kenyon, E. W. (1969). <u>The Blood Covenant</u>. Kenyon's Gospel Publishing Society. Lynwood, Washington.

Kreider, Rose M. and Fields, Jason M., "Number, Timing, and Duration of Marriages and Divorces: 1996", <u>U.S. Census Bureau Current Population Reports</u>, February 2002, p. 18.

Landau, Sidney I (1997). <u>The New International Webster's Concise Dictionary of the English Language</u>. Trident Press International, Naples, Florida.

Lindsey, Michael, McBride, Robert W., Platt, Constance M. (1996). <u>Change is the Third Path</u>. Gylantic Publishing Company, Littleton, Colorado.

McDowell, Josh (1972). <u>Evidence That Demands A Verdict Vol I</u>. Campus Crusade for Christ, Inc., U.S.A.

McDowell, Josh (1975). <u>Evidence That Demands A Verdict Vol II</u>. Campus Crusade for Christ, Inc., U.S.A.

McGee, Robert S., Springle, Pat, and Joiner, Susan (1990). <u>Overcoming Chemical Dependency</u>. RAPHA Publishing/Word, Inc., Houston and Dallas, Texas.

McGee, Robert S. (1990). <u>The Search for Significance</u>. Rapha Publishing, Houston, Texas.

Martin, Grant L. (1987). <u>Counseling for Family Violence and Abuse</u>. Word Publishing, Dallas, Texas.

Minirth, Frank, Meier, Paul, Fink, Siegfried, Byrd, Walter, and Hawkins, Don (1988). <u>Taking Control</u>. Baker House Publishing, Grand Rapids, Michigan.

Morris, Charles G. (1996). <u>Psychology: An Introduction</u>. Prentice Hall, Inc. Upper Saddle River, New Jersey.

Nee, Watchman (1972). <u>Spiritual Authority</u>. Christian Fellowship Publishers, Inc., New York.

Packer, J. I. (1973) <u>Knowing God</u>. InterVarsity Press. Downers Grove, Illinois.

Paymar, Michael (1993). <u>Violent No More</u>. Hunter House, Alameda, California.

Reiner, Troy D. (2005). <u>Principles for Life</u>. The Just Shall Live by Faith Series of Books. Pleasant Word Publishing, Enumclaw, Washington.

Reiner, Troy D. (2005). <u>Revelations That Set you Free</u>. <u>The Biblical Roadmap for Spiritual and Psychological Growth</u>. The Just Shall Live by Faith Series of Books. Pleasant Word Publishing, Enumclaw, Washington.

Reiner, Troy D. (2005). <u>Transformation! How Simple Bible Stories Provide In-depth Answers for Life's Most Difficult Problems</u>. The Just Shall Live by Faith Series of Books. Pleasant Word Publishing, Enumclaw, Washington.

Smalley, Gary (1988). <u>Hidden Keys of a Loving Lasting Marriage</u>. Zondervan Publishing, Grand Rapids, Michigan.

Smith, Ed M. (1996). <u>Beyond Tolerable Recovery</u>. Family Care Ministers, Campbellsville, Kentucky.

Smith, Hannah Whitall (1983). <u>A Christian's Secret of a Happy Life</u>. Whitaker House. New Kensington, Pennsylvania.

Smith, Malcom (Undated). <u>The Search for Self-worth</u> (An audio tape series). Malcom Smith Ministries, San Antonio, Texas.

Smith, William (1970). <u>Smith's Bible Dictionary</u>. Fleming H. Revell Company, Old Tappan, New Jersey.

Tan, Paul Lee (1979). <u>Encyclopedia of 7700 Illustrations</u>. Assurance Publishers, Rockville, Maryland.

Trench, Richard Chenevix (1961). <u>Notes on the Parables of our Lord</u>. Baker Book House, Grand Rapids, Michigan.

Vine, W. E. (1985). <u>An Expository Dictionary of Biblical Words</u>. Thomas Nelson Publishers, Nashville, Tennessee.

Wetzel, L., Ross, M. (1983). "Psychological and social ramifications of battering: Observations leading to a counseling methodology for victims of domestic violence." <u>Personnel and Guidance Journal,</u> Mar. Vol 61(7) 423-428.

Worthington, Everett L. (1996, Spring). "Marriage Counseling: The Road Ahead." <u>Christian Counseling Today,</u> pp. 9-10. Christian Counseling Resources Inc. Forrest, Virginia.

Wright, Norman H. (1996). <u>Marriage Counseling</u>. Regal Books, Ventura, California.

To order additional copies of books by Dr. Reiner:

Faith Therapy
The Ultimate Program for Salvation-based Counseling in the Church

Understand:
- How Salvation Works from a Psychological Viewpoint
- A New Modality of Salvation-based Counseling
- How to Win the Trial of Faith
- How to Assess and Grow Faith
- How Faith Overcomes Problems with Worth, Significance, Security and Love

Transformation!
How Simple Bible Stories Provide In-depth Answers for Life's Most Difficult Problems

Learn:
- A New Bible-based Comprehensive Method for Counseling
- In-depth Psychological Insights Based on Bible Stories
- A New Biblical Categorization of Psychological Problems
- A Biblical Understanding of Six Types of Codependency
- In-depth Counseling Models for 20 of Life's Most Difficult Problems

Revelations That Will Set You Free
The Biblical Roadmap for Spiritual and Psychological Growth

Perceive:
- The Biblical Roadmap for Spiritual and Psychological Growth
- How the Steps in 2nd Peter Chapter 1 Lead to Spiritual Maturity
- Assess the Process of Spiritual Growth
- The Revelation Necessary to Move On to the Next Level
- How to Counsel Other People to Assist Them in Their Spiritual Growth

Principles for Life
Using Biblical Principles to Bring Dynamic Psychological Healing

Know:
- The 13 Classical Methods of Biblical Change
- 44 Biblical Principles and Methods Leading to Wholeness
- An In-depth 9 Component Model of the Human Heart
- The "Train of Psychological Wholeness" Based on Proverbs Chapter 3
- An In-depth Method for Developing Counseling Plans from Biblical Principles

Have your credit card ready and call: 1-877-421-READ (7323)
or please visit our web site at www.pleasantword.com
Also available at: www.amazon.com and www.barnesandnoble.com

For DVD courses based on these books, certification as a Faith Therapist or a BA or MA
Degree in Christian Counseling from LOGOS Christian College and Graduate School:
Contact Word of Life Institute at 316-838-9200
or visit our web site at www.wolm.org
E-mail Dr. Reiner at treiner@wolm.org
or write to us at 3811 North Meridian Avenue
Wichita, Kansas 67204

Bosley Hair Restoration
800 569 7797

Printed in the United States
67436LVS00006B/91-94